WISDEN AT LORD'S

AN ILLUSTRATED ANTHOLOGY

WISDEN AT LORD'S

AN ILLUSTRATED ANTHOLOGY

EDITED BY GRAEME WRIGHT

WISDEN

1939.

M.C.C. v. WEST INDIES
MAY 13th, 15th, & 16th.

MIDDLESEX v. WEST INDIES
JUNE 3rd, 5th & 6th.

MINOR COUNTIES v. WEST INDIES
JUNE 14th, 15th & 16th.

ENGLAND v. WEST INDIES
JUNE 24th, 26th & 27th.

OXFORD v. CAMBRIDGE
JULY 1st, 3rd & 4th.

ETON v. HARROW
JULY 14th, & 15th.

The privilege of introducing the Ladies and Children (under 14) of a Member's household to the Ground, without payment, is withdrawn on the above-mentioned occasions.

R. S. RAIT KERR, Lieut.-Col.

Secretary, M.C.C.

WISDEN AT LORD'S
Edited by Graeme Wright

10 9 8 7 6 5 4 3 2 1

© John Wisden & Co Ltd and Marylebone Cricket Club, 2005
Published by John Wisden & Co Ltd and Marylebone Cricket Club, 2005

John Wisden & Co Ltd
13 Old Aylesfield, Golden Pot, Alton, Hampshire GU34 4BY

Marylebone Cricket Club
Lord's Ground, London NW8 8QN

ISBN 0-947766-93-6

Distributed by Macmillan Distribution Ltd

Typeset in scala and scala sans
Designed by Rob Kelland
Reprographics by Colour Systems
Printed and bound in China
Phoenix Offset Ltd / Hanway Press

Page 2: Lord's Cricket Ground, 1851, by Nicholas Wanostrocht (Felix)
illustrates how the ground looked when he and John Wisden played there.
Title page: John Wisden, 1852, by John Corbet Anderson.
Left: Lord's ground poster for the 1939 season.

Contents

FOREWORD BY TOM GRAVENEY **7**

WISDEN AT LORD'S **9**

AGES OF GRACE **15**

PRO–AM · THE GENTLEMEN AND PLAYERS **25**

TOP HATS AND BATS · ETON v HARROW **43**

CLUB AND GROUND · MCC MATCHES **53**

THE VARSITY MATCH · OXFORD v CAMBRIDGE **75**

UP FROM DOWN UNDER · AUSTRALIANS AT LORD'S **91**

SPRINGBOKS AND PROTEAS · SOUTH AFRICANS AT LORD'S **107**

OMNIUM–GATHERUM **115**

IN A CLASS OF THEIR OWN · OTHER SCHOOLS GAMES AT LORD'S **126**

SITTING TENANTS · MIDDLESEX AT LORD'S **131**

LORD'S IN WARTIME **150**

KIWIS, CALYPSOS AND SUBCONTINENTALS **157**

UP FOR THE CUP **175**

STAGE TO THE WORLD · WORLD CUP TOURNAMENTS **185**

INDEX **188**

PHOTOGRAPHIC ACKNOWLEDGMENTS **192**

Foreword

*"An innings by Graveney remains in the memory. Simply by closing our eyes
we can still see and delight in the free uplift of his bat, the straight lissome poise
and the rhythm of his swinging drives."*

[Wisden 1965]

**The Lord's Test, 1962:
Tom Graveney, last man out,
returns to the Pavilion with
153 against his name.
England No. 11 Len Coldwell
and the Pakistan fielders
lead the applause.
"His cover driving was
superb," Wisden reported,
"and he did not make
the slightest error."
A month earlier at Lord's,
Tom Graveney had scored
110 for MCC against the
tourists, his second fifty
coming in 35 minutes.**

CRICKETERS usually remember their first game at Lord's, and for those who don't, there's *Wisden*. I'm certainly not likely to forget my Lord's debut. It was for the Players against the Gentlemen in 1949, only my second year of county cricket and so a great honour. Denis Compton captained us – it was his benefit year – and we won by four wickets. If anyone wants to know my scores, there's always *Wisden*. There are some things you don't need to remember too clearly.

Even after Test matches came along in the 1880s, Gentlemen v Players at Lord's remained a major fixture in the English season. The best cricketers were on view and the game attracted good crowds. In that 1949 Players team, for example, only four of us hadn't played Test cricket at the time. However, Brian Close and Les Jackson made their Test debuts a week later against New Zealand, with Brian at eighteen becoming England's youngest Test cricketer. John Langridge would have toured India with MCC in 1939-40 but for the outbreak of war.

In the era of Gentlemen and Players, no one would have expected that a Player – a professional cricketer – would one day go on to become President of MCC. That I should be the first to do so is the highlight of my cricket life. As *Wisden* editor Hubert Preston wrote in the 1948 Almanack, paying tribute to Sir Stanley Jackson, the presidency of the Marylebone Club is the highest honour a cricketer can enjoy.

Hubert Preston once did the hat-trick at Lord's, playing for the Press against the Authors. A photo of the two teams appears in this book and contains some fascinating names. Then again, you wouldn't expect anything else in a book that links two of cricket's best-known names – Lord's and Wisden.

Cricket was first played on the present Lord's ground in 1814; *Wisden* was first published a half-century later, in 1864, and has been present at Lord's ever since. *Wisden at Lord's* gives us a snapshot of the great matches played on this wonderful ground in the past 140 years, as well as letting us enjoy some of Lord's and *Wisden's* lighter moments.

Tom Graveney

Tom Graveney • President, MCC

Wisden at Lord's

Wisden at Lord's

*"The vivid and concise reporting of Wisden taught a generation of youngsters
how to write their own language, far better than any formal English lesson,
without wasting words and space. Gibbon and Macaulay had plenty of time
to spread themselves, but S. H. Pardon and his successors
are among the masters of English prose."*

[Wisden 1961]

"Young Wisden", *The Times* dubbed him during those high-summer days of July 1850 when he and "Old Clarke" bowled the South and then the Gentlemen to innings defeats at Lord's. These days we think of him more as "The Little Wonder", the sobriquet that the famous nineteenth-century umpire Bob Thoms conferred on John Wisden on account of his height – five feet four and a half inches – and his success as both cricketer and businessman. But back in 1850, "Young Wisden" seemed an accurate and appropriate way of distinguishing him from his bowling partner, 51-year-old William Clarke.

Wisden himself was 23, already in his sixth season of first-class cricket, when on July 15, a day so hot in London that Smithfield reported slow trading in the meat market, he made himself unique. Playing for the North against the South, he bowled down all ten wickets in the South's second innings. Two years earlier, also at Lord's, Kent's Edmund Hinkly had become the first bowler to take all ten in the innings of a first-class match, with John Wisden among his victims as England were dismissed for 74. Wisden, incidentally, took twelve wickets in that match. But Hinkly was assisted by three catches and two stumpings. Wisden is the only man to hit the stumps ten times.

He had made his first-class debut in 1845, for Sussex against Kent in his native Brighton. That same year he represented the Players there against the Gentlemen, and at the end of June 1846 he played at Lord's for the first time, taking four and two wickets in a Sussex victory brought about when "MCC gave up the match at the close of the second day's play, they having but two wickets to go down and 227 runs to get". His victims included Alfred Mynn, the "Lion of Kent" – reckoned by some to be the spiritual ancestor of W. G. Grace – and 54-year-old William Lillywhite, "the Nonpareil".

One of Lillywhite's sons, John, subsequently played alongside John Wisden after the entrepreneurial Wisden broke away from William Clarke's All-England XI in 1852 and helped establish the United England XI in opposition. In 1855, Wisden went into partnership with John's younger brother, Fred, and opened a "cricket and cigar depot" in London's Leicester Square. The partnership lasted only three years – it seems Fred could be a quarrelsome fellow – but Wisden's connections with the Lillywhite family still had mileage. John Lillywhite's *Cricketer's Companion and Guide* (1865–1885) and brother James's *Cricketer's Annual* (1872–1900) provided the competition after John Wisden launched his little *Cricketer's Almanack* in 1864. However, just as Wisden the bowler had dismissed

Wisden Cricketers' Almanack was well represented when the gentlemen of the Press Club and the Authors' Club met at Lord's in 1898. Back (l-r): H. E. Fenn, Joseph Watson, S. L. Huges, E. H. T. Tottenham, George H. Duckworth, H. B. Smith, Morley Roberts, George Groves, Rev. Stephen Barras, Edgar Pardon (younger brother of *Wisden* editor Sydney Pardon), J. M. Barrie, John Davidson, Reginald Bennett, Herbert Jewell. Middle: Sydney J. Southerton, Hubert Preston, Dr Arthur Conan Doyle, C. Edwards, W. T. A. Beare, Miss Bennett, C. A. Tyssen, Miss Olive Pardon (Edgar's daughter), W. H. Winter, E. R. Ward, H. A. Holt. Front: Angus Evan Abbott, H. V. Jones (Press captain), G. C. Ives (Authors' captain), G. Bull, A. S. Openheiner. Sadly, by mid-summer Edgar Pardon had died at the age of 38. Southerton, younger son of James Southerton, the England, Surrey, Sussex and Hampshire slow bowler, went on to edit *Wisden*, as did Hubert Preston.

CRICKET.

A GRAND MATCH
WILL BE PLAYED IN
LORD'S GROUND,
MARYLEBONE,
On *MONDAY, JULY 31, 1848, & following Day*.

The Gentlemen against the Players.

Gentlemen.	PLAYERS.	Players.
Sir F. BATHURST		BOX
E. ELMHURST, Esq.		CLARK
N. FELIX, Esq.		DEAN
H. FELLOWES, Esq.		GUY
R. T. KING, Esq.		HILLYER
J. M. LEE, Esq.		LILLYWHITE
A. MYNN, Esq.		MARTINGALE
W. NICHOLSON, Esq.		PILCH
O. C. PELL, Esq.		W. PILCH
C. RIDDING, Esq.		PARR
G. YONGE, Esq.		WISDEN

MATCHES TO COME.

Wednesday, August 2nd, at Lord's—Harrow against Winchester
Thursday, August 3rd, at Lord's—Eton against Harrow
Friday, August 4th, at Lord's—Winchester against Eton

DARK'S newly-invented LEG GUARDS, also his TUBULAR and other INDIA-RUBBER GLOVES, SPIKED SOLES for CRICKET SHOES, & CRICKET BALLS, to be had of R. Dark, at the Tennis Court.

Cricket Bats and Stumps to be had of M. Dark, at the Manufactory on the Ground.

Admittance 6d.........Stabling on the Ground.........Ordinary at 3 o'clock.

Morgan, Printer, 38, Church Street, adjoining the Marylebone Theatre.

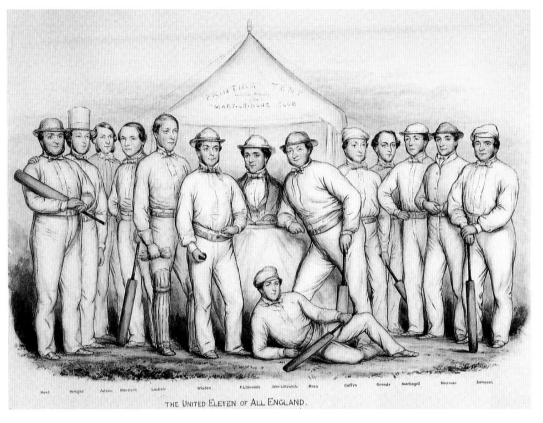

THE UNITED ELEVEN OF ALL ENGLAND.

John Corbet Anderson's lithograph depicts John Wisden and fellow United England XI players by the MCC printing tent, manned by Wisden's short-term business partner, Fred Lillywhite. The players are, from left to right, Thomas Hunt, Henry Wright, Tom Adams, William Mortlock, Thomas Lockyer, Wisden, John Lillywhite (on the ground), Jem Dean, William Caffyn, Jemmy Grundy, William Martingell, Thomas Sherman and Henry Sampson.

the father, so *Wisden* the Almanack saw off the rival Lillywhite publications.

None of which explains how John Wisden, Sussex born and bred, Sussex batsman and bowler, came to be playing for the North against the South in 1850. *Wisden* says he was "a given man", allowed to represent the North because he had business interests there, albeit only as far north as the Midlands. A year earlier he had become co-proprietor, with Nottinghamshire's George Parr, of a cricket ground at Leamington, where they set up Messrs Parr and Wisden's Cricket Club. At Lord's in 1850, George Parr's 17 was the North's top score until Wisden, sharing a ninth-wicket stand with MCC President

Lord Guernsey, hit up 22. Guernsey finished 27 not out and saw the North to 131.

What with the South having already been dismissed for 36 in their first innings, 131 proved a match-winning total – not something the cognoscenti were expecting, according to *The Times*. "If any man on Monday morning had chosen to have advanced a passing remark to the effect that it was 'possible', not

to say 'probable', that the South could be beaten in an innings by the North, he would have been regarded either as a madman or a fool by certain persons." William Clarke and Wisden, bowling unchanged, took six and three first-innings wickets respectively, with Clarke's underhand slows, flipped from the hip, perplexing the South's fancied batting line-up. This despite the fact that many had gained experience of his bowling when he was a ground bowler for MCC. Then again, they also knew Wisden's bowling of old and had no answer to him second time round. Jem Dean, the Rev. J. M. Lee, William Caffyn, Tom Box, Felix, James Chester, MCC Secretary Roger Kynaston, the mighty Mynn, John Lillywhite, Tom Sherman and Sir Frederick Bathurst: Wisden, from the Pavilion end, castled them all, "combining great pace," *Scores and Biographies* reveals, "with a fine break from the off".

Some say his break from the off turned in by a yard, and given the reputation of Lord's pitches back then – not forgetting the famous Lord's slope – it's probably no exaggeration. "All ridge and furrow," recollected Middlesex captain V. E. Walker. "You had to consider yourself lucky if you did not get two shooters in each over, and one on the head." After all, it was 1864 (obviously a good year) before MCC employed a groundsman; prior to that, Sir Pelham Warner relates in *Lord's 1787–1945*, "a few odd men on the ground prepared (!) the wickets. For many years the grass was 'kept down' by bringing sheep on to the ground a day or two before a match was due to begin."

So the South, to all-round surprise, were done and dusted in a day. Players, MCC members and other intending spectators found themselves with Tuesday off to swell the crowds that watched the funeral procession of the Duke of Cambridge, youngest son of George III and so Queen Victoria's uncle, as it made its ceremonial way from Hyde Park Corner to Kew. Then, a week later, Clarke and Wisden were at it again, bowling unchanged in both innings and taking twelve and eight wickets respectively as the Players beat the Gentlemen by an innings and 48 runs. Wisden also opened the Players' batting; his 24 was the third-highest score in their 148. "This affair," grumbled the *Times*' man at Lord's, "for match we cannot call it now... has proved about the most sorry experiment the 'gentlemen' have essayed for some years." Wisden's wickets in both innings included William Nicholson, who in 1866 put up £18,333 6s. 8d. so that MCC could purchase the freehold of Lord's.

Scores and Biographies describes Wisden's early bowling as "very fast indeed and ripping". Teddy Walker, who was in the Harrow XI when Wisden was professional bowler there between 1852 and 1855 – and in 1856 first played against him for the

The press

At Lord's the arrangements for press men are far from adequate and, I imagine, it is only the uniform courtesy which one experiences from everyone connected with the headquarters of cricket that has prevented strong representations being made to the MCC. The accommodation is far too rough and limited, and indeed quite unworthy of Lord's Cricket Ground, although the practice of granting newspaper men unlimited printed slips of the score during the day is a great convenience. [*C. Stewart Caine, 1893*]

. . .

In fulfilment of a promise made in the MCC annual report of 1906, the professionals' pavilion has been enlarged. This will provide permanent accommodation for the press, and will increase the room hitherto reserved for the bowlers and clerks. Balconies have also been added to the lower dressing-rooms of the Pavilion in order to meet a request made by prominent amateurs. These will be reserved exclusively for amateurs playing in a match. [*1908*]

. . .

Owing to complaints, the sale of daily and evening papers in the Pavilion will be discontinued. [*1912*]

Gentlemen – ranked him in pace somewhere between Nottinghamshire's William Attewell, certainly no more than medium-pace, and Surrey's W. H. Lockwood, at one time considered faster off the pitch than anyone in England. But on rough ground like Lord's, Wisden's unforgiving accuracy was the key to his success. He pitched the ball where it mattered, a legacy of the years spent bowling to Tom Box, the

legendary Sussex wicket-keeper and sometime Brighton publican, who took young John in after his father's death and employed him as a pot-boy. Box, as was the custom, stood right up to the stumps, concentrated on taking the off-side deliveries and "allowed the leg-balls to look after themselves". Wisden honed his method on the off-balls and perfected the "twists, screws, turns, rises and other 'dodges' to puzzle the batsman" that he describes in his only other known book, *Cricket and How to Play It*, published in 1866 and dedicated to "E. M. Grace, Esquire". Intriguingly, Wisden's collaborator on this book was "Captain Crawley", the nom de plume used by Victorian sports journalist George F. Pardon, two of whose sons would one day edit *Wisden Cricketers' Almanack*.

John Wisden played 68 first-class games at Lord's, including twelve between 1848 and 1859 for the Players in the showpiece match against the Gentlemen. Altogether he took 400 wickets there, claiming five in an innings 40 times and ten in a match 16 times. He also held 60 catches and scored 1,132 runs, with a highest score of 58 for the Players in 1858. His last match at Lord's was for Middlesex against MCC in his farewell season, 1863. The following year, as we've seen, he brought out the first of his Almanacks, another "little wonder".

That Wisden achieved his unique ten-wicket haul at Lord's enhances its distinction. For despite the ambitions of other grounds, and other countries' envy, Lord's remains the spiritual home of cricket. But for his being French, Marcel Proust would have loved it. Lord's can be the perfect Madeleine, awash with remembrances of times past. Yet at the same time it brings the promise of pleasures to come. It is more than an old man's ground. Pass through its gates and glimpse the green outfield through a gap in the stands; with or without the poet's run-stealers flickering to and fro, you have entered a different world. That other, everyday world is beyond the walls, haring up and down the Wellington Road or racing along St John's Wood Road. Even with Michael Hopkins' canopies on the Mound Stand, Jan Kaplicky and Amanda Levete's pod of a Media Centre, Nicholas Grimshaw's ocean liner of a Grand Stand – even with, someone must once have said, Verity's red-brick Pavilion – Lord's retains a timeless feeling; a magical feeling of time without change. Whether filled to capacity for a Test match or the hip-hop hype of a Twenty20 thrash, hosting rumbustious county supporters at a cup final or nigh deserted towards the fag-end of a Championship match, Lord's remains intimate, ancient and modern, central to the very story of cricket itself.

Its narrative has a cast list drawn from all walks of life. Royalty and railwaymen, aristocrats and socialites, establishmentarians and dissenters, brewers and distillers, cricketers whose mark was made in the West Country and the West Riding, in mill towns and mining villages, seasiders and City gents, entrepreneurs and entertainers, Hons and rebels, colonials, public school toffs on a path paved to high office and London lads who began a lifetime at Lord's by holding the horses of MCC members. There's S. F. Barnes on the occasion of the 1914 match to celebrate the centenary of the present ground, tall and severe, urging his fellow-professionals not to play unless MCC offered more money. No wonder Sir Neville Cardus wrote of Barnes in the 1968 *Wisden* that "a chill wind of antagonism blew from him on the sunniest day".

Maybe, given his unrelenting attitude, it comes as no surprise to learn that one of the great bowlers of the Golden Age, or any age, played only fourteen first-class games at Lord's: six of them for the Players

NOTE BY THE EDITOR
Cricket does not stand in need of alterations. When played in the proper spirit – every match on its own merits – the game is as good as ever it was. It must not be tampered with to please people who vainly think that it can have the concentrated excitement of an hour and a half's football.
[*Sydney Pardon, 1913*]

against the Gentlemen, two in the 1912 Tests against South Africa and Australia, and three for Wales when he was well into his fifties. But think again. Old Trafford was the only ground on which Sydney Barnes played more often in that eccentric first-class career of his, stretching over 36 years. Lord's might almost claim him as one of its own. His portrait was hung in the Long Room, and in 1949 he was one of the inaugural 26 England Test players elected honorary cricket members of MCC.

Establishments frequently exhibit this peculiar practice of gathering the nonconformists to their bosom, and the Marylebone Club has been no exception. Yet some have remained outside the embrace, notable among them another Sydney, S. H. Pardon, born in the year John Wisden and Fred Lillywhite opened their cricket and cigar depot and *Wisden's* longest-serving editor of 34 years until his death in 1925, aged 70. Sydney Herbert Pardon was as much an institution as Lord's and the Almanack he edited. If anyone were going to be an MCC member, you'd assume he would be. But at a time when MCC's autonomy went unchallenged in the world of cricket, Pardon's independence of the club allowed him the opportunity to make *Wisden* an alternative authority. He exercised that authority so responsibly that MCC officers and committeemen came to request and respect his counsel – even if it wasn't always to their taste. Here he is in his Editor's Notes to the 1901 *Wisden*.

"Although the matter does not greatly concern the public I cannot pass over without comment the treatment of the Press representatives at Lord's on the

Thomas Lord

A valuable and interesting addition to the picture gallery at Lord's is a portrait of the late Mr Thomas Lord, the original lessee of the ground, kindly presented to the Marylebone Club by his great-granddaughter, Miss Florence Lord. This has been placed in the large room of the Pavilion. [*1933*]

occasion of the Oxford and Cambridge, and Eton and Harrow matches. It was an ungracious and uncalled for act to shift them from the grand-stand to the roof of the ground bowlers' house in the corner of the ground. Happily the protest in the newspapers was so loud and unanimous that the MCC bowed before the storm, and at the Gentlemen and Players match the unhappy experiment was given up. I cannot see why the MCC should be so reluctant to build a proper press box, commanding an end-on view of the game, as a continuation of the new Mound stand. The plans

PRESS, PARDONS AND PRESTONS

When I entered the press box at Lord's some 40 years ago, Hubert Preston sat next to Sydney Pardon at the end of the front row, near the steps leading to the exit. It was a different press box then, far different from the large place of accountancy which today is metallic during the summers with typewriters. I doubt if Sydney Pardon would have allowed anybody to use a typewriter in his presence at Lord's or any other cricket ground.

. . .

I didn't dare go into the Lord's press box during my first season as a cricket writer for the *Manchester Guardian*. I was shy, provincially raw. I wrote my reports sitting on the Green Bank. I wrote them on press telegram forms, and at close of play handed them in at the telegraph office under the clock at the Nursery end. One afternoon Hubert Preston saw me as I sat on the Green Bank scribbling my message. "Why don't you come into the press box?" he said, in his own brisk, rapidly articulated way. He took me by the arm and led me up the steep iron steps. The tea interval wasn't over yet. Preston introduced me to Sydney Pardon, who then introduced me to the other members of the press box, some of them life members – Stewart Caine, Harry Carson, Frank Thorogood and others. Each made a courteous bow to me; it was like a levée. Pardon pointed to a seat in the back row. In time, he assured me, I would graduate to a front place among the elect.

[*Neville Cardus, 1961*]

. . .

Sydney Pardon was editor of Wisden *from 1890 to 1925, succeeding on the death of his brother, Charles Pardon; C. Stewart Caine followed from 1925 to 1933, and Sydney Southerton to 1935. Hubert Preston was editor from 1943 to 1951, and his son Norman until 1980. Between them, the Prestons enjoyed a family connection with the Almanack stretching from 1895 to 1980.*

Norman Preston (centre) was awarded the MBE in The Queen's Silver Jubilee and Birthday Honours of 1977 in recognition of 26 years as *Wisden* editor – an award he regarded as belonging as much to his beloved Almanack. Asked by The Queen what he did, he replied, "I am a sporting reporter, Your Majesty."

for such a box were, I understand, passed by a sub-committee nearly a twelvemonth ago, but afterwards rejected by the general Committee on the ground of expense. The MCC have spent thousands of pounds during the last few years to increase the accommodation for their members and the public and they might surely do for the newspapers what has been done at Manchester, Leeds and Nottingham... It is hardly the thing for the first cricket club in the world to thus lag behind the counties in so simple a matter."

Pelham Warner reports that MCC "set to work and built a press box at the north-west corner of the Pavilion, giving an end-on view of the game".

When it came to the game itself, and in particular to that recurring question of throwing, Pardon was proemially Swantonian. The Pardon influence is also appreciable throughout the whole of *Wisden*, and not only that of Sydney but of his two brothers: Charles Frederick, editor of *Wisden* for four editions until he

died, aged 40, in 1890; and Edgar Searles, whose twelve-year association with the Almanack ended with his death in 1898 at the age of 38. Under the Pardons, the florid style that embellished match reports in the 1870s and 1880s, while delightfully piquant, gave way to considered analysis of the play and players. Sydney Pardon and his colleagues at the Cricket Reporting Agency, which produced the Almanack for John Wisden & Co Ltd, knew their cricket intimately and reported it succinctly.

Cricket, we all know, has changed since Pardon's day, significantly so at Lord's. He watched most of his cricket there or at The Oval, confident that, Australians excepted, he would see the foremost players season after season. Today, the editor of *Wisden* can't necessarily stay in England if he wants to run a regular eye over the top cricketers. Lord's is no longer the nucleus it used to be.

Gentlemen v Players is history; the leading counties no longer visit Lord's each year to play MCC in first-class fixtures; Oxford v Cambridge and Eton v Harrow, once grand social occasions, have been downgraded to limited-overs games, played in front of a sprinkling of spectators; schools weeks, once so important that *Wisden* had a special correspondent there, have fallen victim to the policy of regimenting youth cricket within an age-group program. Middlesex no longer play all home games at Lord's. Counties used to meet in two major cup finals a season; not any more. Lord's is left with Test matches and one-day internationals to pull the punters in and pack what past *Wisdens* affectionately called "the old ground".

A healthy state of affairs? Time and the pages of *Wisden* will ultimately tell.

Ages of Grace

"Whatever may be in store for the game of cricket in the future, it seems safe to say that such a player will never be seen again. A rare combination of qualities went to the making of W. G. Grace."

[Wisden 1916]

1864 - 1876

IT WAS IN a MCC v South Wales Club match in the 1864 season that Mr W. G. Grace played for the first time at Lord's, and to prove how "coming events cast their shadows before them" in cricket, as in other affairs, Mr W. G. – then only a lad sixteen years old – played an innings of 50 runs so well that the captain of the SWC publicly presented him with a prize bat, and thus was inaugurated a batting career that for effective – if ugly – defence, astonishing hard play, wonderful power in placing the ball out of danger, and marvellous ability in accumulating large scores, hit from the very best bowling England can produce, never had an equal. [*1875*]

WG's 1,000 at Lord's

THE 85TH SEASON of the MCC was one of storms, showers, sunshine, good wickets, splendid batting, great scoring and one-sided matches. A thunder storm interrupted the progress of the opening match at Lord's; torrents of rain and hail stones of large size fell during the violent storm that stopped play in the MCC and G. v Cambridge University match on the old ground; frequent and heavy showers of rain made a mud pond of the wickets, and prevented the completion of that – so far – capitally contested match between the Gentlemen and Players of England; and the continuous heavy rainfall from morn to past mid-day that put cricket on one side for a whole day in Willsher's match, will not readily be forgotten by the very many friends of the Kent bowler who felt interested in the success of the cricket battle between the Benedicts and Bachelors of England. June was nippingly cold, and July was wet and windy, but there are two sides to all tales told, and if the greater portion of the three months up at Lord's in 1871 was unseasonably stormy and showery (and it was so), sunshine at other times beamed brilliantly on the famous old turf.

The ground had been carefully and unremittingly attended to throughout the recess, its excellent condition – all over – during the season being highly creditable to Jordan the ground-keeper. The general character of the wickets at Lord's in '71 won hearty praise from all classes of cricketers, and their truth and excellence deserved that praise, and that the batting on them was good, and the scoring great, is attested by the facts that in one match 915 runs were made for the loss of 29 wickets, and

Opposite: Famous
English Cricketers – 1880.
Standing (l-r): James Lillywhite jun.,
John Selby, Alfred Shaw,
George Ulyett, Lord Harris,
W. R. Gilbert, A. N. Hornby,
W. G. Grace, A. P. Lucas,
G. F. Grace, William Oscroft,
A. G. Steel, Richard Daft,
A. J. Webbe, Tom Emmett,
Ephraim Lockwood, Richard Pilling,
Fred Morley. Seated: Harry Jupp,
Ted Pooley, Billy Bates.

that at various times elevens played innings of 485, 338, 328, 323, 310, 308, 294 and 269 runs; and that during the season one batsman – Mr W. G. Grace – made 1,145 runs on the old turf.

Edward Mills Grace, of whom Sydney Pardon wrote in the 1900 *Wisden*: "I never look at [his] scores without wondering what would have been thought of him if he had not found in his own family a greater than himself."

The Grace brothers at Lord's
• June 25 and 26, 1868 •

Gloucestershire
E.M.Grace Esq., L.Abbott Esq., J.Halford Esq., W.G.Grace Esq., G.F.Grace Esq., W.Wall, T.G.Matthews Esq., F.Baker Esq., T.Brindley Esq., W.D.L McPherson Esq. and W.Kelley.
Scores: 135 (E. M. Grace 6, W. G. Grace 24, G. F. Grace 3, Matthews 27 not out; Farrands 4 wkts, Wootton 3 wkts) and 159 (E. M. Grace 65, W. G. Grace 13, G. F. Grace 2, Matthews 32; Farrands 4 wkts, Wootton 4 wkts).

MCC & Ground	1st innings		2nd innings	
W F.Higgins Esq.	lbw b E.M.Grace	6	b E.M.Grace	7
E.G.Sutton Esq.	c Wall b W.G.Grace	2	hit wkt b E.M.Grace	26
R.D.Balfour Esq.	b E.M.Grace	37	st Halford b E.M.Grace	16
W.Price	run out	4	c and b E.M.Grace	4
S.Biddulph	run out	4	run out	0
Lt-Col Bathurst	c G.F.Grace b W.G.Grace	1	b E.M.Grace	6
A.B.Coddington Esq.	c G.F.Grace b W.G.Grace	0	c Abbott b E.M.Grace	0
G.Wootton	b E.M.Grace	0	b W.G.Grace	15
W.H.Richards Esq.	b E.M.Grace	3	c W.G.Grace b E.M.Grace	3
A.W.Fitzgerald Esq.	c E.M.Grace b W.G.Grace	4	not out	3
F.Farrands	not out	4	b E.M.Grace	2
Extras	(byes 4)	4	(byes 2, l-b 7)	9
		69		**91**

Gloucestershire winning by 134 runs.
Umpires – Royston and Nixon.

WG's first hundred at Lord's

• June 29 and 30, 1868 •

Gentlemen	1st innings		2nd innings	
E.M.Grace Esq.	run out	1	not out	22
B.B.Cooper Esq.	b Willsher	28	not out	0
W.G.Grace Esq.	not out	134		
C.F.Buller Esq.	b Grundy	4	b Wootton	0
R.A.Mitchell Esq.	b Willsher	1		
H.A.Richardson Esq.	b Grundy	8		
W. F. Maitland Esq.	b Lillywhite	2		
V. E. Walker Esq.	c Pooley b Lillywhite	5		
C.A.Absolom Esq.	b Lillywhite	3	c Grundy b Lillywhite	8
J.Round Esq.	b Lillywhite	0		
R.Lipscomb Esq.	thrown out by Willsher	7		
Extras	(byes 5, l-b 3)	8		1
		201		**31**

Players	1st innings		2nd innings	
H.Jupp	c Absolom b W.G.Grace	4	run out	14
G.Summers	b Lipscombe	5	c and b Absolom	4
J.Ricketts	c Mitchell b W.G.Grace	1	b Lipscomb	13
James Lillywhite	c Maitland b W.G.Grace	0	b Absolom	0
W. Mortlock	b W.G.Grace	9	lbw b E.M.Grace	19
E. Pooley	b Lipscomb	21	c Buller b Lipscomb	4
F. Silcock	run out	0	b W.G.Grace	26
T. Mantle	c E.M.Grace b W.G.Grace	12	b W.G.Grace	4
G. Wootton	b W.G.Grace	8	c Richardson b W.G.Grace	18
J. Grundy	not out	29	c E.M.Grace b W.G.Grace	8
E. Willsher	c Round b Absolom	22	not out	3
Extras	(bye 1, l-b 3)	4	(leg-byes 2, w 1)	3
		115		**116**

The Gentlemen winning by eight wickets.
Umpires – Hearne and Royston.

---

*In addition to making his first hundred at Lord's,
the third first-class hundred of his career, W. G. Grace took
ten wickets in the match for 81 runs. He was nineteen at the time,
still several weeks from his twentieth birthday.*

England v Notts & Yorkshire

• July 8, 9, 1872 •

"MR GRACE FIRST, the rest nowhere." Such was the brief emphatic verdict pronounced by an old cricketer on the wonderful innings played by the great batsman in this match. This record requires a more extended notice of this extraordinary "bit of batting", and to the best of the compiler's ability it shall have one.

Mr W. Grace was first man in at a quarter past twelve; when 100 runs had been made, at five minutes to two, Mr Grace had made 51; when he had scored 72 he was nearly had at short leg by Emmett, and when his score was 141 the same man nearly had him at point. When the 200 runs were hoisted, Mr Grace's score was 124; when half the wickets were down for 225 he had made 135; when the eighth man was out, and the score at 264, Mr Grace had made 151 of those runs, and when the innings was up with the total 290 – 283 from the bat – Mr Grace had scored 170 not out, or 57 more than his ten colleagues had collectively contributed. The hits that made up this wonderful innings were 31 singles, 17 twos, 14 threes, 9 fours, 3 fives and 2 sixes, one a splendid straight drive to the northern wall from Emmett. The fives were all drives and great ones, and the nine fours included five drives; so those not present can readily realise what a splendid, magnificent driving display this 170 of the great batsman's was, and how lustily and long he was cheered by those that were present.

William Gilbert Grace, in his mid-20s, and his younger brother, George Frederick. All three Graces played in the first Test in England, against Australia at The Oval in 1880, but a fortnight later poor Fred was dead at 29.

The Americans at Lord's

CONSIDERABLE interest was excited in cricketing circles last summer by public announcements that representative teams of the two leading base ball clubs of America would, at the back end of our cricket season, visit England and, by playing their national game on our principal cricket grounds, endeavour to acclimatise that game in this country. The interest created by this announcement was increased by the statement that the Americans had also (but somewhat reluctantly) agreed to play a cricket match against an English club team on each ground they played their base ball match on. Of course Lord's was one of the grounds selected for these displays.

Athletic Club 9 v Boston Club 9

• August 3, 1874 •

THE BOSTON MEN were the base ball champions of America, and The Athletics (of Philadelphia) the ex-champions. The marking out the diamond-shaped base ground, and the subsequent play of the sides, was watched with marked interest by the audience, but they had not proceeded far with the match before many of the spectators were impressed with the idea that they were witnessing a modernised, manly – and unquestionably an improved – edition of that most enjoyable old game of their boyhood, rounders, the most patent differences being: a cricket-sized ball is used at base ball, instead of a ball of tennis size as at rounders; throwing the ball at the striker when running from base to base is allowed at rounders, but is (properly) barred at base ball; and instead of the ball being struck with a stick of broom-handle thickness held in one hand, as at rounders, it is at base ball struck by a formidably sized club, clutched and wielded by both

hands, a form of play that, to become efficient in, evidently requires lengthened practice and much skill. The play proceeded to the evident advantage of the Bostonians all through; and after a contest of two hours and ten minutes' duration, the Boston champions won by 24 to 7.

"An impatient batsman might make two spanking hits in succession off him," W. G. said of Alfred Shaw, "but he would not make a third."

Too forward by half

With a view to promote county cricket, and to establish a new and interesting series of matches at Lord's ground, the MCC Committee offered a challenge cup for competition. Regulations were drawn up and sent to the counties. The project was favourably received by some and declined by others. Five acceptances were received in the first instance, ties were drawn, and the prospect of an interesting season was afforded. For various reasons, two of the five accepting counties withdrew and finally, as the liberal views of the Committee did not meet with general support, or were otherwise misrepresented, the original idea was abandoned.

In justice to themselves, the Committee must repeat that the challenge cup matches were only projected with a view to promote county cricket. The fact that all expenses would be borne by the MCC, and that the matches would be played on a neutral ground, afforded a reasonable belief that such contests would be viewed with interest by cricketers in general. [1874]

MCC & Ground v Nottinghamshire

• June 14, 15, 1875 •

WIND AND WEATHER alone considered, this was the most unenjoyable match ever played out at Lord's, for throughout those two days the wind blew big and bitter blasts from the WSW, so cold that the air was more fitting for Ulsters and mid-winter than summer suits and midsummer, and so strong that – in addition to other casualties – the wind broke clean in half the trunk of a full-sized sturdy elm tree that stood at that end of the Regent's Park nearest to Lord's ground.

The batting was unequal and most certainly did not master the bowling, notwithstanding so many of the batting cracks of the period played. The bowling was very remarkable but, successful as some bowlers undoubtedly were, all were entirely put into shade by the brilliant ball work done by Alfred Shaw who, all told, bowled 95 overs (71 maidens) for 46 runs and nine wickets – averaging in the match less than half a run per over and a shade over five runs per wicket.

First innings: 54 overs, 35 maidens, 39 runs, two wickets.

Second innings: 41.2 overs, 36 maidens, 7 runs, seven wickets (six bowled).

Such marvellous bowling as in the second innings to such high-class batsmen has no equal in the history of the game. It brought out the full defensive powers of Mr W. Grace, Mr I. D. Walker, Mr Hadow, Mr Ridley and Mr Buller, none of these great hitters being able to get the ball away for runs, and during their stay at the wickets the attack from Alfred Shaw and their defence was indeed "splendid cricket" that will long be remembered with admiration by those who sat out that bitterly cold, boisterous but memorable Tuesday at Lord's.

Nevertheless, MCC won the match by 62 runs.

Gentlemen v Players of England

• July 3, 4, 5, 1876 •

WHEN the luncheon bell rang at 2.30, the Gentlemen's score was one wicket down, 174 runs scored: Mr W. G. Grace not out 110, Mr Webbe not out 14. They went at it again at twelve past three, and by 25 minutes to four they had made the 200 with only one wicket down, the delighted thousands present giving vent to their pleasure in a roar of cheers when those three figures were hoisted – cheers that were vigorously renewed again and again and still again when, shortly after, Mr W. G. Grace drove the first ball of an over by Emmett grandly to the on past the skeleton stand for six and – with a terrific smack – drove the third ball of the same over as far as it could go past the little chestnut trees for seven. Ah, that seven was a hit! The ring of it tingles in this compiler's ears whenever he recalls it to mind. Truly wonderful hitting was those 13 runs from two balls of one over. Emmett was then (very properly) rested.

Discussion upon the report being invited by the Chair, Mr Willoughby rose to make his annual onslaught on the accounts. The learned gentleman severely criticised the items of expenditure on the Embankment and the Tavern, expressing his belief that the members had not received much additional convenience. After various other strictures he drew attention to the match list, which he derided as "rubbishy": the members could play in better matches elsewhere. As to the professional players, it was also easy to explain their reluctance to play at Lord's, where they are worse treated and less liberally paid than on any other ground. He objected strongly to the introduction of the new game of lawn tennis at Lord's ground, and concluded with a few words of advice to the Secretary that, if he wished to persuade the members to take a more active part in the game, a little more politeness on his part would conduce to that desired object. [1876]

Secretary of MCC from 1863 to 1876, Bob Fitzgerald endeavoured to make Lord's the great centre of cricket, an ambition not always in tune with a Committee described as "deplorably lethargic and out of date". However, his overtures eventually led to Middlesex playing their home games at Lord's. In spite of Mr Willoughby's criticism, expressed above, others found Fitzgerald "sagacious, cheery and amusing", and above all an excellent Secretary.

1877 - 1899

Gloucestershire and Yorkshire v the Rest of England

• July 16, 17, 18, 1877 •

THE CATCH of the season, made by Mr I. D. Walker; a grand hit for six into Dark's garden by Mr W. G. Grace, 52 and 110 by the same batsman; a magnificent catch by Mr G. F. Grace; 105 and 33 not out by Mr A. N. Hornby; and weather so wretchedly wet as to preclude any cricket being played on the Monday are little matters that must mark this novel match as memorable in the chronicles of cricket played at headquarters in 1877.

On Tuesday, a dull, dark, dismal, cold day, Mr "W. G." was missed when he had made 27, and it was shortly after this that he made his six – a grand on-drive from Watson, the ball flying over the garden wall by the Armoury and pitching in the garden, about three yards from the wall, in St John's Wood Road. How the spectators did roar out their cheers at that hit, and well they might for it was indeed – both in timing and power – a splendid blow and one worthy the fame of the great batsman of the south.

The second innings of the counties was commenced on Wednesday by Mr W. Grace and Mr Gilbert; the latter made 2 and was then had at slip before Mr W. G. had scored, but who, it was remarked, "was bound to do something that day because it was his 29th birthday". And he did do something, for he drove one ball from Watson on to the top of the Pavilion for four; one from Morley he drove past the telegraph van for five, and when, at five o'clock, the score was at 200, Mr W. Grace had made 110. The "something" having been thus accomplished, cheers, loud and protracted, greeted the big batsman's return to the Pavilion, and those present at Lord's on that 18th of July will long remember with pleasure the splendid and characteristic form in which Mr W. Grace celebrated his 29th birthday.

Over Thirty v Under Thirty

• July 21, 22, 23, 1879 •

IT IS ADMITTED beyond all dispute that Mr W. G. Grace is the greatest cricketer "the world e'er saw". Whatever may be the prejudices of those whose memories carry them back to the heroes of the last generation, even they give way and yield the palm to the Gloucestershire captain. This being so, and considering the impetus which his reputation has given to the game, it was only natural that his admirers should wish to pay him a tribute more substantial than mere praise. Subscriptions were, therefore, invited in

the season of 1877 and the outcome of this was the presentation of a testimonial and a sum of money, to which were to be added the proceeds of the above match.

A disappointment, however, had befallen Shaw on account of the weather being so unfavourable on the occasion of his benefit match – North v South. With a generosity which met with hearty approval on all hands, Mr Grace asked that the match intended for himself should be devoted to Shaw. But, alas! the elements were even more perverse on the days intended for the Over Thirty v Under Thirty match than they had been on the occasion of North v South, and so far as Shaw was concerned little benefit was reaped from it. There is a rumour afloat, however, that another fixture will be given to the clever and deserving Nottinghamshire cricketer. Let us hope it may prove true.

Two exceedingly good teams had been selected, and large attendances were anticipated. The first day, Monday, proved a blank. So wet were the wickets, and moist the atmosphere generally, that not a ball was bowled. Even on Tuesday it was so bad that a beginning could not be made until a quarter past one. It was rather unfortunate that Mr W. G. Grace (who, with "the Doctor", went in first for Over Thirty) should have been clean bowled with the unenviable cypher affixed to his name on an occasion when he would probably liked to have shown to advantage. But such was his fate. He compensated in great measure for his poor batting by showing some excellent bowling. Over Thirty, as may be seen from the scores, won by seven wickets.

Under Thirty: R. G. Barlow, Hon. A. Lyttelton, F. Penn Esq., George Ulyett, G. F. Grace Esq., V. Royle Esq., Hon. Ivo Bligh, W. Bates, W. Barnes, G. G. Hearne jun. and F. Morley. *Scores*: 111 (Grace 35 not out; Shaw 4–34, W. G. Grace 3–55) and 80 (Barlow 26; Shaw 3–21, W. G. Grace 6–32).

Over Thirty: Dr W. G. Grace, Dr E. M. Grace, F. Townsend Esq., J. Selby, William Oscroft, Richard Daft, T. Emmett, F. Wyld, Alfred Shaw, E. Pooley and W. Mycroft. *Scores*: 138 (E. M. Grace 40, Townsend 43; Morley 4–57, Barlow 5–21) and 54–3 (E. M. Grace 33 not out).

MCC and Ground v Nottinghamshire

• May 28, 29, 1885 •

TO THE brilliant all-round cricket played by Dr W. G. Grace in this match the crushing defeat of the powerful Notts eleven by an innings and 59 runs was mainly due. Shrewsbury and Attewell were absent from the visiting team, but it was generally expected that the county would still be strong enough to more than hold their own against the moderate side opposed to them. The wicket was in fairly good condition, though it had not thoroughly recovered from the heavy rain of the previous Monday; it gave the bowlers some little assistance, and now and then the ball got up awkwardly. When stumps were drawn on the first day, the MCC had scored 173 for the loss of seven wickets in answer to Nottinghamshire's feeble innings of 96. There was a good deal of rain overnight, and the hot sun on Friday morning [the 29th] rendered the wicket slow and treacherous. The bowlers therefore had matters all their own way. Notts began their second innings at ten minutes to one, Dr Grace bowling from the Pavilion end, and in two hours the innings closed for 44. In scoring 63 and taking sixteen wickets at a cost of only 60 runs in such a match, Dr Grace achieved one of the greatest successes attached to his name.

Grace's figures were 43–26–40–7 and 35.1–25–20–9.

MCC and Ground v Sussex

• May 19, 20, 21, 1887 •

SUSSEX had a weak batting team in the annual match with the MCC but, apart from one or two players, the club side was a very good one, Mr Grace's services being again available. The

Presentation to Mr W. G. Grace

The presentation to which allusion has been made took place at the most appropriate spot which could have been selected – viz., in front of the Pavilion at Lord's. It consisted of a sum of money and a marble clock, bearing this inscription: "Presented to W. G. Grace, on July 22nd, 1879, on the occasion of the match Over Thirty v Under Thirty, played in his honour at Lord's", and two bronze ornaments representing Egyptian obelisks.

Lord Fitzhardinge, who had kindly undertaken to make the presentation, regretted his inability to control the weather, as he thought there were few such interesting occasions as that which had brought them together. Referring to the testimonial, his lordship said that the original idea had been to purchase a practice for Mr Grace; but he had talked the matter over with the Duke of Beaufort and they thought that Mr Grace was old enough and strong enough to take care of himself (laughter and cheers) and they would leave him to choose a practice for himself. The total amount, deducting expenses, which would be placed to Mr Grace's credit, including the value of the clock and the ornaments, was about £1,400. He could only say, on behalf of the people of Gloucestershire, that they wished him as much success in his profession as he had reaped in the cricket field (loud cheers).

opening day was very wet, cricket being practicable for only three hours and a quarter, and the second day was miserable, storms of hail and rain interrupting the game half a dozen times. The great batsman went in first and took out his bat for 81, his fine innings lasting two hours and a quarter.

Mr Grace made so large a proportion of the runs from the bat that his ten colleagues only got 37 between them, six batsmen being dismissed without scoring. Sussex's innings closed for 119, Mr Grace following up his success as a batsman by taking seven wickets for 53 runs. After luncheon the club did very badly and seven wickets were down for 83. Thanks to Mr Russel's good cricket the total in the end reached 125. With 135 to get to win, Sussex on the third afternoon won by four wickets, Quaife again batting in capital form and foreshadowing the brilliant cricket he showed later in the summer. The MCC lost a good deal through bad wicket-keeping, Mr C. W. Wright being sadly at fault. This gentleman, however, had only just resumed cricket after a long interval caused by an accident while steeplechasing, and could hardly be expected to excel.

MCC AND GROUND v YORKSHIRE

• May 23, 24, 1887 •

Mr W. G. Grace, who had intended to make one of the club team, was prevented at the last moment by a medical engagement.

MCC and Ground v Cambridge University

• June 25, 26, 27, 1894 •

THIS, the last of the Cambridge trials before the University match, was remarkable for exceptionally heavy scoring – no fewer than three of the ground records, so far as important matches are concerned, being broken. In the first instance, the aggregate number of runs – 1,332 – is the greatest ever obtained at Lord's; in the next, the MCC's second total of 595 is the highest ever made there; and in the third W. G. Grace's 196 is the most he has ever scored at the St John's Wood enclosure. As it happened, this brilliant display of the veteran champion's proved the highest individual innings in first-class cricket during the season. The visitors were beaten by the enormous majority of 374 runs.

MCC and Ground v Sussex

• May 9, 10, 11, 1895 •

THIS WAS a splendidly contested match from start to finish, and one in which the county, though the losing side by 19 runs, deserved as much credit as the winners. It was a batsman's triumph throughout, those who especially distinguished themselves being the veteran champion, W. G. Grace, who scored his first hundred of the season, and K. S. Ranjitsinhji, who, making his initial appearance for Sussex, made 77 not out and 150, his first three-figure innings in important cricket.

To Ranjitsinhji on a fast wicket, everything seems possible, and if the somewhat too-freely-used word genius can with any propriety be employed in connection with cricket, it surely applies to the young Indian's batting. [1897]

Gentlemen v Players

• July 18, 19, 20, 1898 •

WHEN THE fixtures for 1898 were being arranged, the Committee of the MCC had the happy inspiration to fix their Gentlemen and Players match for the 18th of July – Mr W. G. Grace's 50th birthday. More than that, they secured at the secretaries' meeting in December a perfectly clear date for the fixture and thus

made themselves certain of getting representative elevens. Their final selections, though extremely good, were not such as to quite disarm criticism, but the match more than fulfilled the most sanguine expectations and was quite the event of the season. Except for an hour's heavy rain on the morning of the second day, the weather was always dry, and the support accorded by the public was greater than at any previous Gentlemen and Players match at Lord's. The turnstiles showed that 17,423 people paid for admission on the Monday, 14,633 on the Tuesday, and 9,502 on the

Wednesday. Most important of all, the cricket was entirely worthy of the occasion. Feeling no doubt the honour of having been chosen, the cricketers on both sides played quite as keenly as if the match had been between England and Australia, and as a natural consequence a superb display was given. Mr Grace, though handicapped by lameness and a severe blow on the hand, did himself justice and, with Kortright's assistance, nearly succeeded in saving the match for the Gentlemen, it wanting only a few minutes to seven on the third day when the Players won by 137 runs.

Players: A. Shrewsbury, R. Abel, W. Gunn, W. Storer, J. Tunnicliffe, W. Brockwell, A. Hearne, A. A. Lilley, W. H. Lockwood, S. Haigh and J. T. Hearne. *Scores*: 335 (Gunn 139, Storer 59; Townsend 4–58, Woods 3–49) and 263 (Gunn 56, Storer 73; Woods 3–62, Mason 4–47).

Gentlemen: Mr W. G. Grace, Mr A. E. Stoddart, Mr F. S. Jackson, Mr C. L. Townsend, Mr A. C. MacLaren, Mr J. R. Mason, Mr J. A. Dixon, Mr S. M. J. Woods, Captain E. G. Wynyard, Mr G. MacGregor and Mr C. J. Kortright. *Scores*: 303 (Grace 43, MacLaren 50; J. T. Hearne 5–87, Lockwood 4–82) and 158 (Grace 31 not out, Kortright 46; J. T. Hearne 6–65, Lockwood 3–39).

Middlesex v Gloucestershire

• May 25, 26, 1899 •

THIS MATCH is likely to have an historical interest inasmuch as it was the last in which Mr W. G. Grace played for Gloucestershire before breaking finally with the county committee. The wicket had by no means recovered from the drenching rain at the beginning of the week and runs proved very hard to get. Gloucestershire practically lost the game at the start, being all out in an hour and ten minutes for 52 runs [Grace 11]. From this disastrous beginning they could not recover themselves. Grace finished up his county career with a very patient innings of 33, staying in an hour and twenty minutes on the difficult wicket. Middlesex, with only 70 wanted to win, and on a greatly improved pitch, won easily next morning by seven wickets.

MCC and Ground v London County

• May 18, 19, 20, 1903 •

WITH PLAY impracticable on either Monday or Tuesday owing to the heavy rain of the previous week having saturated the ground, there seemed little likelihood of a definite result being arrived at on the Wednesday, but by that time the surface had dried sufficiently to give the bowlers a tremendous advantage, and one more was added to the steadily growing list of matches commenced and ended in a single day. London County, for whom Grace and Murdoch made a fine start in each innings, were quite outplayed once the veterans were got rid of. All the honours of the game went to the club bowlers, of whom Hearne took eight wickets for 51 runs, while Trott in the second innings dismissed seven batsmen for 37 runs. The MCC won by nine wickets.

1900 ~ 1905

MCC and Ground v London County

• June 13, 14, 1901 •

BAD BATTING and extremely fine bowling marked the first stage of this match. Grace failed with the bat but surpassed himself with the ball, dismissing seven of the last eight MCC batsmen for 30 runs. With Grace, Fry, Wood, Vine and Goldie on the side, London County looked likely to gain a big advantage on going in against so poor a total as 94, but they found Mead and Trott equally as difficult as the club had found Grace and Vine and, in the end, there was a difference of only 15 runs in the scores. London County were set 184 to win and, with Fry, Goldie and W. Smith doing themselves full justice, won by four wickets. The best thing in the match was Grace's bowling; the veteran actually took thirteen wickets for 110 runs.

Above: W. G. with sons W. G. junior (left) and Charles Butler, both of whom played first-class cricket alongside their father for London County. W. G.'s last match at Lord's was for MCC and Ground against Dorsetshire in 1908, a month after his 60th birthday. Right: W. G.'s grandson, William Edgar Grace, around the turn of the century. *Wisden* editor Sydney Pardon would have said something about that elbow.

Pro-Am
The Gentlemen and Players

"We, MCC, are of the opinion that no Gentleman ought to make a profit by his service in the cricket field, and that for the future any cricketer taking more than his expenses in any match should not be qualified to play for the Gentlemen against the Players at Lord's."

[Wisden 1880]

The 1931 Gentlemen's side that drew with the Players at Lord's when rain ended play early on the third afternoon. Standing (l-r): Joe Hardstaff sen. (umpire), W. H. V. Levett, F. R. Brown, A. M. Crawley, D. G. Foster, Nawab of Pataudi, G. D. Kemp-Welch, H. I. Young (umpire). Seated: C. S. Marriott, R. E. S. Wyatt, D. R. Jardine, K. S. Duleepsinhji, R. W. V. Robins. Douglas Jardine's 49 was the highest score of a match blighted by the weather.

WE HAVE TAKEN great pains, and been at considerable expense, in collecting for the information of our readers, the matches which have been annually played between the Gentlemen and Players. We have begun with the first match in 1806, thinking it would prove an agreeable reading for our subscribers to see the doings of the past distinguished cricketers who in their day stood pre-eminent in the "Noble Game". We of course make no comments upon the matches, leaving the cricketer to form his own opinion with regard to the merits of the men, since a great many of our readers are at least equal, if not superior, to ourselves in arriving at a right judgment of the play. [1864]

By "some unaccountable oversight", the Lord's match of July 1851 was omitted. The scorecard appeared in the 1865 Almanack. Gentlemen v Players was first played on the original Lord's ground, in what is now Dorset Square.

• June 30, July 1, 1873 •

THIS WAS the first of three matches played last season wherein – by the valuable aid of Mr W. G. Grace – the batting superiority of the Gentlemen over the Players of England was so consistently and so markedly manifested, Mr W. G. Grace making 391 runs in three innings and the Gentlemen winning each of the three matches with an innings and lots of runs in hand.

On June 30 the weather was damp, the attendance scant (for such a match), the light bad, the ground soft, and the hitting mainly monopolised by the two Graces, who made 195 out of the 278 runs scored by the Gentlemen on that day. Mr W. G. Grace received the first ball bowled at 25 minutes past twelve; when rain stopped play for that day at eight minutes past five, he had made 151 not out of the 274 then credited to the Gentlemen for five wickets down. Mr G. F. Grace was one hour and a quarter scoring his 41 out of the 103 runs made during his stay.

On July 1 the weather and the attendance were of better form. Play was resumed at twelve minutes to

Arthur Neilson Hornby (left) played fifteen times for the Gentlemen at Lord's between 1869 and 1886. For many years he was captain of Lancashire and, with Dick Barlow, established the opening partnership immortalised by Francis Thompson in his poem, "At Lord's": "O my Hornby and my Barlow long ago!" Of slight build when a boy at Harrow he was nicknamed "Monkey", but the Lancashire players called him "The Boss". It's a moot point whether he was born to run. "First he runs you out of breath," Barlow complained, "then he runs you out." A double international, Hornby captained England at both cricket and rugby.

Gentlemen of England abroad, at Montreal in 1872: (l-r) Alfred Lubbock, tour leader R. A. Fitzgerald, Arthur Appleby, W. H. Hadow, C. J. Ottaway, W. G. Grace, W. M. Rose, A. N. Hornby, Hon. G. R. C. (soon to be Lord) Harris, F. P. U. Pickering, C. K. Francis and Edgar Lubbock. They won seven of their eight matches against XXIIs in Canada and the United States, having to leave the last unfinished on account of Boston's "gathering gloom". Grace was top-scorer with 540 runs at 49.09, while Rose's underarm slows accounted for 135 wickets.

twelve, and after nearly one hour's cricket Alfred Shaw very finely indeed "c and b" Mr Grace, who had made 163 runs out of the 300 then scored by the Gentlemen for six wickets. The wickets in this innings fell in the following form:

1	2	3	4	5	6	7	8	9 & 10
–	–	–	–	–	–	–	–	–
69	81	131	171	274	300	303	305	315

The Players commenced their first innings at twelve past one on the Tuesday; at six minutes to seven on the same day their second innings was played out and the Gentlemen had defeated them by an innings and 55 runs! Mr Buchanan's slows had ten of their wickets. Mr B's bowling averaged 5 runs per wicket in their first innings, and 20 per wicket in their second. McIntyre was top scorer in both of the Players' innings, but the best of their batting was William

Oscroft's 10 and 44. Finer leg hitting is rarely witnessed than that displayed by Oscroft in this match. One hit to square leg was a superb smack – the ball went clean from the bat hard against the Tennis Court wall and rebounded several yards up the ground – but all his fine hitting did not avert the most stinging and emphatic defeat the Players of England ever received from the Gentlemen.

Gentlemen: W. G. Grace Esq., G. H. Longman Esq., A. N. Hornby Esq., W. Yardley Esq., W. Law Esq., G. F. Grace Esq., A. W. Ridley Esq., C. K. Francis Esq., G. Strachan Esq., R. Bissett Esq. and D. Buchanan Esq.
Score: 315 (W. G. Grace 163; J. C. Shaw 6–107, A. Shaw 3–66).

Players: Bignall, H. Jupp, Richard Humphrey, William Oscroft, F. Wyld, R. Carpenter, Martin McIntyre, Fillery, Alfred Shaw, H. Phillips and J. C. Shaw.
Scores: 78 (McIntyre 27; Buchanan 6–33, G. F. Grace 4–41) and 182 (McIntyre 56; Buchanan 4–81, Francis 3–34).

• July 3, 4, 5, 1876 •

THIS MATCH was played in dull and dry but (for July) cool weather, and was so far attractive that 3,286 paid the sixpence admission on the first day and 3,386 on the second. The ring around the ground was one of the old cricket-enjoying, undemonstrative sort now so thoroughly at home at Lord's; and on the well-filled Pavilion seats and roof was seen many a famous participant in past G v P struggles for victory on the old battlefield. The new embankment seats were all crowded, and all that was wanting to make matters perfectly pleasant was that essential to the thorough enjoyment of the glorious old game – a little sunshine.

The wickets were evidently wonders for easy batting for those who first used the bat on them, and when it became known the Gentlemen had won choice, all prognosticated bad times for the Players – and a bad time they had that day. Not one of those famous bowlers could get the ball more than half-stump high until near the close of the day's play; by then the mischief had been done by those famous batsmen, whose batting on that third of July will long be remembered, especially by the eleven Players.

7 different bowlers were tried.
11 bowling changes were made.
227 overs and 3 balls were bowled.
Only 6 wickets had fallen; but
433 runs had been scored.

Tuesday morning the ball gained as great a victory over the bat, for Morley bowled 25 balls for 1 run and four wickets – three of the four clean bowled! The wickets in this innings, the largest yet made by the Gentlemen at Lord's, fell as under:

1	2	3	4	5	6	7 & 8	9	10
–	–	–	–	–	–	–	–	–
126	230	258	262	294	433	437	448	449

The Players' batting was commenced at twenty minutes past twelve on the second day, Daft and Lockwood starting it to the bowling of Mr W. G. Grace and Appleby. Lockwood was had at wicket for 6, Daft was easily caught out at point for 28 and, when 60 overs had been bowled for 86 runs, Jupp was bowled by a ball propelled by Mr Appleby's left hand with a force that broke one of the bails in two. Young Arthur Shrewsbury's first innings in these great matches was ended for 9 runs by a splendid bit of fielding by Mr W. Grace at point who, in one action, leapt up, caught the ball high up with his left hand, and swung it round on to the wicket.

The Players' first innings was ended at eighteen minutes past five for 219 runs, Emmett (at wickets 43 minutes) taking his bat out for 14. Their second innings was commenced at 38 past five by Emmett and Shrewsbury; from the first ball delivered, Emmett was caught out at wicket, and at 18 Shrewsbury was

Richard Daft and George Parr, "the Lion of the North". Daft played for the Gentlemen at The Oval in 1858, and after turning professional he appeared for the Players from 1860 to 1879.

bowled. The second day's cricket ending with the Players 79 for five wickets, all interest in the match was then gone, so on Wednesday morning nobody was surprised to hear only 181 had paid for admission to see the end of it. They resumed play at a quarter to twelve; at eight minutes to one, all was over, the innings being ended for 132 and the Gentlemen the winners by an innings and 98 runs. The Gentlemen not only made runs but saved runs splendidly, their rare batting form being backed up by equally fine fielding form, which stopped run-getting from many fine hits made by the Players.

Gentlemen: C. J. Ottaway Esq., W. G. Grace Esq., A. J. Webbe Esq., A. N. Hornby Esq., A. W. Ridley Esq., F. Penn Esq., G. F. Grace Esq., Lord Harris, W. H. Hadow Esq., Hon. A. Lyttelton and A. Appleby Esq. *Score*: 449 (W. G. Grace 169, Ridley 103, G. F. Grace 68 not out; Morley 6–73).

Players: Richard Daft, Ephraim Lockwood, H. Jupp, William Oscroft, Arthur Shrewsbury, Andrew Greenwood, E. Pooley, T. Emmett, Alfred Shaw, Allen Hill and Morley. *Scores*: 219 (Oscroft 58; Appleby 6–96, W. G. Grace 3–81) and 132 (Daft 39 not out; W. G. Grace 6–41, G. F. Grace 3–45).

• July 5, 6, 7, 1880 •

ONE WELL-KNOWN name was absent from the Players' eleven after finding a place there for six years in succession. That was Richard Daft. So far back as 1860 he formed one of the Players' team in their match v the Gentlemen, at Lord's, and altogether has appeared in thirteen of these matches at headquarters, scoring 39, 65, 4, 19, 7, 1, 8, 0, 0, 102, 43, 19, 28, 0, 28, 39 not out, 64, 18, 1, 0, 14 and 3, or an average of 23.91 per innings.

• July 9, 10, 1888 •

LIKE SO MANY great matches in 1888, Gentlemen and Players had to be played on a wicket which gave the ball a distinct advantage over the bat. For all that, the game was a thoroughly good one, and the finish proved the most sensational seen in this match on the St John's Wood ground since 1877. There was a curious contrast in the constitution of the two elevens: while the Players' team was made up of entirely familiar names, the amateur side included only four men – W. G. Grace, A. G. Steel, W. W. Read and J. Shuter – who had previously represented the Gentlemen at headquarters. Mr S. M. J. Woods, as the amateur bowler of the year, was of course bound to play, and no better change bowler could have been found than Mr C. A. Smith.

No escaping the class distinctions in Sir Robert Staple's depiction of the Lord's centrepiece in 1891. The Players, having batted on all three days between breaks in the weather, emerge from separate quarters tacked on to the Pavilion; the Gentlemen mingle with the members. The match was drawn.

The Players had only 78 runs to get to win, and with the wicket rather firmer and faster than on the previous day there was a general impression that they would make them. But when the luncheon interval was taken, the Players with half their wickets down wanted 33 runs to win. After luncheon came the cricket which will cause the match to be remembered. Seventy runs went up on the telegraph board with six wickets down; only 8 to win. As a last resource Steel handed the ball to Smith at 71 and this proved the turning-point of the game. With 1 added, Smith clean bowled Attewell and, as it happened, the Players did not get another run, the Gentlemen winning by

5 runs. Woods and Smith were the heroes of the moment, and no compliments could have exceeded their deserts.

———————

Charles Aubrey Smith (right) later made a name on the stage and became "a universal favourite on the films" [Wisden 1949]; he was knighted in 1944. His unusual run-up before delivering the ball earned him the nickname "Round the Corner" Smith. Sometimes he started from a deep mid-off position, at others from behind the umpire: W. G. Grace said, "It is rather startling when he suddenly appears at the bowling crease."

———————

As to the policy of the MCC in playing Mr Hedley, opinions were far from unanimous and, speaking for ourselves, we think it was an error of judgment. It is no secret that the Kent committee left off playing Mr Hedley because they could not profess to be satisfied with the fairness of his delivery, and assuredly a bowler who cannot satisfy the committee of his own county ought not to appear at Lord's for Gentlemen v Players.

To do Mr Hedley justice he tried his best to avoid bowling unfairly, and in the first innings succeeded, his delivery being practically above reproach. On the Tuesday afternoon, however, his action was different and, in our judgment, was several times unfair. [1891]

• July 9, 10, 1894 •

THE MCC in selecting their Gentlemen's eleven had none of the difficulties that beset the authorities at The Oval. Except that L. C. H. Palairet was on his honeymoon and Ernest Smith could not get away from his duties at Elstree School, they had an absolutely free choice.

The cricket on the second day was of a sensational and altogether unexpected character, F. S. Jackson and S. M. J. Woods bowling with such effect that, without a single change being necessary, the Players were got rid of for totals of 108 and 107. Since Wisden and Clarke in 1850, this feat of two men bowling unchanged through both innings of a Gentlemen and Players match had been performed on four other occasions – 1853, 1861, 1864 and 1879. Their performance was the more remarkable from the fact that, on the evidence of several of the beaten side, the condition of the ground afforded no sufficient excuse for the failure of the batting. There was nothing in the least astonishing in Woods' analysis, his six wickets costing him in all 124 runs; but Jackson did wonders, taking five wickets for 36 runs in the first innings and seven for 41 in the second. From lunch time to the end of the game he sent down fourteen overs, five of

The Gentlemen in 1894.
Back (l-r): James Douglas, J. R. Mason, G. J. Mordaunt, A. C. MacLaren.
Middle: S. M. J. Woods, H. T. Hewett, W. G. Grace, H. W. Bainbridge, F. S. Jackson.
Front: Gregor MacGregor, A. E. Stoddart.

The Players in 1894.
Back (l-r): William Chatterton, W. H. Lockwood, J. T. Hearne, Wilfred Flowers, William Hearn (umpire).
Middle: Ted Wainwright, Albert Ward, William Gunn, Fred Martin, Bill Brockwell.
Front: Johnny Briggs, Billy Storer.

Wisden at Lord's

F. S. Jackson – "Jacker", to his friends.

them maidens, for 24 runs and five wickets. It is safe to say that as a bowler the famous Cambridge and Yorkshire cricketer has never been seen to such advantage. [The previous day, Jackson top-scored for the Gentlemen with 63.]

The Gentlemen won just before four o'clock by an innings and 39 runs.

• July 16, 17, 18, 1900 •

THE GENTLEMEN v Players match at Lord's in 1900 was certainly the most remarkable game of the whole season and in every way worthy of comparison with the memorable match under

the same title on the same ground in 1898. It presented two points that were quite without precedent in the long series of Gentlemen v Players matches. R. E. Foster followed up his record innings in the University match by making two separate hundreds, a feat never before performed at Lord's or elsewhere for either Gentlemen or Players, and the Players, though set to make 501 in the last innings, won the game by two wickets. Never before in a match of such importance – and only once indeed in the whole history of first-class cricket – has a total of over 500 been obtained in the fourth innings. The one previous occasion – also at Lord's ground – was in 1896, when Cambridge were set to make 507 against the MCC and succeeded in accomplishing the task.

The performance of the Players was a magnificent one, but they could consider themselves lucky in having sufficient time left them in which to make such a huge score. On the second afternoon the Gentlemen already held what was on paper an overwhelming advantage, and Mr Woods, their captain, wishing to have the Players in before the close of the afternoon, instructed his side to play a hitting game and be out by a certain time. His instructions were loyally obeyed and, though the Gentlemen's score stood at 238 for three wickets when Foster left, the innings was all over for 339. From lunch time till the end of the innings, 279 runs were scored in two hours and twenty minutes.

No one was disposed to criticise Mr Woods at all severely, some people going so far as to say that if the Gentlemen could not win with a lead of 500 they did not deserve to win at all. This was all very well, but the fact remained that there was only one possible way by which the Gentlemen could lose the match, and that their captain adopted it. If he had not been so anxious for his side to be out before the end of the second afternoon, he could have made defeat absolutely impossible, and yet have left his side a whole day in which to win. Of course he could not regard it as at all within the range of probability that the Players would

make 500 runs in the last innings, but it is a wholesome rule to take nothing for granted at cricket, and to throw nothing away except under stress of absolute necessity. However, though the Gentlemen suffered a defeat to the risk of which they need not have been exposed, the public profited, the cricket on the last day being quite a marvel of sustained interest.

Gentlemen: 297 (Mr C. B. Fry 68, Mr R. E. Foster 102 not out; W. Rhodes 4–93) and 339 (Fry 72, Foster 136; A. E. Trott 6–142).

Players: 136 (R. Abel 30; Mr J. R. Mason 4–40) and 502–8 (Abel 98, T. Hayward 111, J. T. Brown, sen. 163; Mr C. J. Kortright 2–60, Mr G. L. Jessop 2–74).

Under the change to the Laws that came into effect in 1900, Woods could have declared any time after lunch on the second day. Prior to this, declarations were permitted only on the final day.

Sammy Woods – Anglo-Australian Gentleman and Test cricketer. Sent to England aged thirteen "to be trained as a proper gentleman," Peter Roebuck wrote, "he never really got the hang of it." Like "Monkey" Hornby, he captained England at rugby.

The Gentlemen of 1901, who lost to the Players by 221 runs. Back (l-r): W. M. Bradley, A. O. Jones, R. E. Foster, J. R. Mason.
Middle: D. L. A. Jephson, K. S. Ranjitsinhji, Gregor MacGregor, C. M. Wells, C. B. Fry. Front: G. L. Jessop, P. F. Warner.

Wisden at Lord's

• July 6, 7, 8, 1903 •

FOR TWO DAYS the Gentlemen were completely outplayed, following on 293 in arrear and entering upon the concluding day of the contest with one wicket down and 219 runs required to escape a single-innings defeat. Some truly grand batting by Fry and MacLaren, however, not only saved the amateurs from being beaten but left them with the honours of the match. These two famous cricketers came together at five minutes past one on the Wednesday with two wickets down for 191 and, on a pitch which had never been perfect, actually hit up 309 runs in rather less than three hours, MacLaren declaring shortly after five o'clock with the total increased to 500 and eight wickets still standing. In mis-hits which went out of reach and in balls which beat them without hitting the wicket, both Fry and MacLaren enjoyed a liberal share of luck, but considering the position of the game and the conditions which prevailed, the cricket they played was of a truly glorious description. In making 232 not out, Fry established a record for the Gentlemen v Players match at Lord's, the previous highest scores having been the 169 of W. G. Grace in 1876 and the 163 of J. T. Brown in 1900. Apart from Abel's 247 at The Oval in 1901, Fry's innings was, moreover, the biggest ever played in a Gentlemen v Players match on any ground. MacLaren's score of 168 not out came, of course, within one of the Lord's record. During the day 481 runs were scored, and only two wickets went down, the Players finishing at 55 for one.

• July 4, 5, 6, 1904 •

GENTLEMEN v Players at Lord's proved emphatically the match of the season. Played through from the first ball to the last in the keenest and most sportsmanlike way, it ended amid intense excitement late on the third afternoon in a victory for the Gentlemen by two

C. B. Fry – Gentleman,
scholar and all-round athlete.
C. J. Kortright "hurled the
ball down at a great pace".

wickets. The Gentlemen had not won at Lord's since 1899, and inasmuch as they were 156 runs behind on the first innings, their performance could fairly be described as wonderful. In picking the sides, the MCC had a free choice, but circumstances prevented them getting exactly the elevens they wanted. Accidents compelled Martyn and Brearley to decline the invitations sent them, and Hirst, doubtful about the leg which had troubled him in the previous season, thought it best to stand down. Moreover, Tyldesley, who had received a very severe blow in the ribs on the previous Friday, resigned his place on the morning of the match. His absence gave King, the Leicestershire batsman, an unexpected opportunity and he made the most of it, rivalling R. E. Foster's feat in 1900, hitherto unprecedented in Gentlemen and Players matches, of scoring two separate hundreds. The match proved a big attraction, 12,335 people paying for admission on the first day, 11,545 on the second, and 9,322 on the third. It was a matter for regret that, except on the last day, the wicket did not play well. From some cause, probably owing to a little damp remaining in the ground, the ball on Monday and Tuesday kicked up in a way that recalled to old habitués the cricket that used to be seen at Lord's in the sixties. Indeed on the Tuesday afternoon Hesketh Prichard's bowling was quite dangerous. Knight had the misfortune to get one of the bones in the back of his left hand broken, and it was a month before he could play any more cricket. If Lilley could have foreseen how the wicket would roll out on the last day, he would certainly have made the Gentlemen follow on, but his policy of letting his own side bat a second time seemed for the moment to put defeat out of the question.

Players: 327 (T. Hayward 88, J. H. King 104, W. Rhodes 50; Mr H. V. Hesketh Prichard 3–102, Mr B. J. T. Bosanquet 3–78) and 255 (King 109 not out; Hesketh Prichard 5–80).

Gentlemen: 171 (Hon. F. S. Jackson 58; L. C. Braund 6–50) and 412–8 (Mr H. K. Foster 52, K. S. Ranjitsinhji 121, Jackson 80, Mr A. O. Jones 56 not out; J. T. Hearne 3–97, E. Arnold 3–123).

A. C. MacLaren – batted in
the grand manner.
B. J. T. Bosanquet – googly
bowler and hammer thrower.

Mr Reginald Erskine Foster died at his home in London on the 13th of May, 1914. He was born at Malvern on April 16, 1878. Mr Foster's death from diabetes at the age of 36 came as a great shock to the cricket world, but was no surprise to his intimate friends. His health broke down in the summer of 1913

and a visit to South Africa did him no permanent good. He had not reached the age at which, by means of rigid dieting, diabetes can sometimes be kept in check. He was one of the pre-eminently great batsmen of his day, ranking with MacLaren, Fry, Jackson, Tom Hayward and Tyldesley among those who stood nearest to Ranjitsinhji.

• July 9, 10, 11, 1906 •

WITH NO Test games to overshadow it, the Gentlemen v Players match at Lord's had all its old attraction and drew crowds of people; the full attendance for the three days came to nearly 40,000. Proving in every way worthy of its traditions, the match produced some of the finest cricket of the season, the Gentlemen winning after a strenuous fight by 45 runs. Beyond everything else it will be remembered for the success of the fast bowlers, and especially for the great performance of Fielder, who in the first innings of the

Gentlemen took all ten wickets – a feat never performed before in a Gentlemen v Players match. Still, though he in a sense took the chief honours, Fielder was not so fast or deadly as N. A. Knox. The Surrey bowler, who was only just recovering from the effects of a strain, surpassed himself and, by taking twelve wickets, clearly won the game for his side. Bowling quite so fast as his has not been seen in the fixture since C. J. Kortright appeared for the Gentlemen in 1898. Keeping up his full pace in both innings, Knox was really intimidating and only three or four of the professional batsmen faced him with any confidence. Some of them were clearly unnerved by his terrific speed and the way in which even the good-length balls got up. In the whole game, only one wicket fell to bowling that was not fast, Lees, who met with great success in the Gentlemen's second innings, putting on a lot of extra pace for the occasion.

Up to a certain point in this innings the Gentlemen seemed likely to obtain a big score, Spooner and H. K. Foster making 156 together for the first wicket. However, three wickets were down for 211 and, after a tea interval, four more soon fell to Lees and Fielder in less than half an hour. Spooner played one of the finest innings of his life. He gave a chance at the wicket off Lees when he had made 29, but this was his only mistake during a stay of three hours. Batting better worth looking at than his was not seen at Lord's last season. Powerful on-driving and very skilful play on the leg side were the features of his cricket. Spooner had not previously made a hundred at Lord's since his 198 for Marlborough against Rugby in 1899.

Gentlemen: 167 (Mr B. J. T. Bosanquet 56; A. Fielder 10–90) and 321 (Mr R. H. Spooner 114, Mr H. K. Foster 67, Mr G. L. Jessop 73 not out; Fielder 4–131, W. Lees 6–92).

Players: 199 (T. Hayward 54; W. Brearley 4–63, N. A. Knox 5–73) and 244 (E. G. Hayes 55, Lees 51; Knox 7–110).

Neville Knox – sadly, his shins weren't up to fast bowling.

ARTHUR FIELDER

Very strong, Fielder undertook a rare amount of work without sign of fatigue. As a rule he bowled well outside the off stump and at times made the ball break back, but his best delivery was one which swung away. This made him very dependent upon the smartness of his slips.
[1950]

Schofield Haigh, George Herbert Hirst and Wilfred Rhodes, Yorkshire's finest, in 1905, the year they helped defeat the Gentlemen by 149 runs. Rhodes took eight wickets and, *Wisden* recorded, "had never before bowled half so well for the Players at Lord's. All through the last innings the bowling was maintained at a very high standard."

• July 8, 9, 10, 1907 •

THE MATCH had unfortunately to be left drawn at a most interesting point, drenching rain rendering cricket quite impossible on the third day. What the result would have been had play been practicable is quite an open question, the Gentlemen, with eight wickets to fall, wanting 216 more runs to win. Hayward on the opening day

surpassed himself. Going in first he carried his bat right through the innings, scoring 146 out of the 260 runs hit from the bat. His performance set up a new record, no one having ever before in the Gentlemen v Players match at Lord's gone through an innings for a not out score of over 100. One or two critics, excessively hard to please, found fault with Hayward for being too slow, but to most people his cricket seemed beyond reproach. The magnitude of what he did may be judged from the fact that no one else on the side, except Hirst, made more than 14 runs in the innings. His 146 not out therefore stood in quite a different category from a similar score obtained in a match of great run-getting. So perfect was his play that, during a stay of over four hours and a half, he did not give a chance of any kind. Indeed, from first to last he was completely master of the bowling. As usual with him when he is quite at his best, he rarely or never lifted the ball, all his drives going along the ground. He had three times before made 100 for the Players at Lord's; of the four innings we should unhesitatingly describe the last as the finest.

• July 14, 15, 16, 1913 •

JESSOP WAS NOT in the Gentlemen's team originally chosen, but after his wonderful form at The Oval it was essential that he should play, and at the last moment he was pressed into service, A. C. Johnston generously standing down to make room for him. So unprepared for cricket was he that he played his first innings in trousers and shoes that did not belong to him, and with a strange bat, but nevertheless he made 63 runs. Jessop received 58 balls and scored off 31 of them, hitting eight fours, two threes, four twos and seventeen singles. His innings, though not one of his best, was in the circumstances excellent. Bad weather interfered with the match, not a ball being bowled on the second day, but for all that the game was played out, the Players winning by seven wickets with only six minutes to spare.

Frank Henry Farrands, "a most excellent fast round-armed bowler" [*Scores and Biographies*] appeared occasionally for Nottinghamshire in 1871 and 1873 but, considering his skill, was seen all too seldom in matches of note. In 1870, at Lord's, he came into the Players' team at the last moment as a substitute and took ten wickets for 88 runs, but never again had an opportunity of appearing against the Gentlemen. In 1881 the match at Lord's between Over 30 and Under 30 was set apart as a benefit for him. He became a member of the groundstaff at Lord's in 1868 and remained there until 1908, becoming head of the staff. He was extremely well known as a capable umpire, especially at Lord's, and it was estimated that in 40 years he officiated in 2,000 matches. [1917]

• July 19, 20, 21, 1922 •

THOUGH in the end left drawn, the meeting of Gentlemen and Players at Lord's was in some respects the best match of the season. It was the opinion of many experts that on no other occasion did the cricket approach so nearly to the best pre-war standard. The keenly appreciative crowds saw some magnificent batting and fielding, though the bowling as a whole did not reach the same high level. Play had been impossible at Lord's on the day before the match, but the weather was so uncertain that the Players on winning the toss felt bound to take first innings. They stayed in nearly all day and, thanks to Hobbs, scored 330, a total that far exceeded their expectations. Hobbs played many splendid innings last summer but, having regard to the condition of the ground, the splendid fielding and the quality of Louden's bowling, his 140 was the best of the lot. He said himself he had to fight for every run, and he was tired indeed when at last, from a wild hit, he was caught from a skier at mid-on. The fielding of the Gentlemen was beyond praise, A. E. R. Gilligan, Carr, Chapman and Hubert Ashton bringing out rounds of applause by their dazzling brilliancy. Watching the display, no one could help contrasting it with the melancholy exhibition given by England on the same ground in 1921.

The second day's cricket was quite as delightful to watch as the first. The pitch had practically recovered and the Gentlemen, for the loss of seven wickets, scored 406. The cream of the cricket came during a wonderful partnership by Carr and Chapman, who put on 150 runs together in an hour and three-quarters. Chapman (left) found another first-rate partner in Mann, who helped to add 147 in less than two hours and might have gone on indefinitely if an unfortunate misunderstanding had not caused him to be run out. Bowled at last in playing forward, Chapman had the extreme satisfaction of following up his hundred in the University match with a great score of 160, equalling a record that had belonged exclusively to R. E. Foster. There was only one mistake in his innings, which for brilliancy on the off side could scarcely have been surpassed. He hit a six and fourteen fours. The fielding of the Players, though quite good in its way, seemed very ordinary compared with the dash and pace of the Gentlemen on the first day, but Hobbs did marvels at cover point. On the third day the Gentlemen were left with the practically impossible task of getting 235 in two hours. Naturally they played simply for a draw.

In style and execution, Martyn was one of the finest wicket-keepers ever seen in first-class cricket. Tall, and possessed of long arms and a beautiful pair of hands, he almost invariably stood close up to the fastest bowlers and, even so, made singularly few mistakes. He was in the Oxford eleven in 1899 and 1900, and then it was obvious that a great wicket-keeper had been discovered. In 1900 he enjoyed the distinction of playing for the Gentlemen at Lord's and, while he did great work for Somerset until 1906, his chief claims to remembrance rested on his appearances against the Players at Lord's. He was in the team in 1903, 1905 and 1906, and on this last occasion stood up to W. Brearley and N. A. Knox when those two famous fast bowlers were really terrifying in their pace. Martyn had no hand in the disposal of any of the Players, but he kept wicket magnificently, taking Knox's bowling on the first afternoon with the ease and certainty of a Blackham or a Pilling. [*1929*]

The Nawab of Pataudi, universally known as "Pat", was "a great fighter when a definite challenge was at hand" – as the Players learnt when he posted 165 against them in 1932. He achieved the rare distinction of playing Test cricket for England and India.

• July 18, 19, 20, 1923 •

THERE WERE FOUR other first-class fixtures on the same days but, as the counties let off any men required, the MCC in picking the teams had a perfectly free hand. The match will be remembered not so much for the fine cricket seen in it as for the astonishing blunders in the field by which, on the first day, the Players discounted their chance and left themselves nothing to hope for but a draw. One would not be dogmatic as to the exact number of catches missed, but they must have approached double figures, and to make things worse Smith, probably from over-anxiety, could do no sort of justice to himself as a wicket-keeper.

• July 16, 17, 18, 1930 •

LIKE SO MANY other matches during the summer of 1930, Gentlemen v Players was considerably interfered with by rain and resulted in a draw, the amateurs obtaining a small lead on the first innings and declaring in the second with four wickets down. Not until after lunch on Wednesday did the state of the ground allow of a start being made, and late on Thursday afternoon there came an interruption of 40 minutes, while Friday brought with it, in addition to one or two slight showers which mattered little, heavier rain that delayed the game for an hour. The contest was rendered memorable by the performance of Duleepsinhji who, in putting together two separate innings of a hundred, accomplished a feat which in Gentlemen v Players matches had stood to the credit of only R. E. Foster and J. H. King. Enjoying a narrow escape on Wednesday from being run out before he had scored, Duleepsinhji made no mistake in his 125, but in the course of his 103 not out in the second innings he might have been caught in the slips. This was the only real blemish in a great achievement on the part of the young Indian batsman. While he

obtained runs all round the wicket, showing remarkable facility and variety of stroke, the great feature of his play was admirably timed and powerful driving.

• July 13, 14, 15, 1932 •

EVEN if one or two alterations in the composition of the Gentlemen's eleven might possibly have been suggested, the Players were practically at full strength, so this match, in the quality of the teams contesting it, was quite in keeping with the great traditions of the fixture. The game, like those of 1900 and 1926 at Lord's, produced four separate three-figure innings, K. S. Duleepsinhji passing the hundred for the third time, the Nawab of Pataudi and Walter Hammond each attaining that distinction for the first time, and Hobbs, with six centuries previously to his credit in Gentlemen v Players matches at Lord's as well as at Scarborough and three in those at The Oval, putting together what was at once his fourth hundred of the season, the 189th of his career and his sixteenth in Gentlemen v Players. In completing his sixteenth three-figure innings in a Gentlemen v Players match, Hobbs beat the record of W. G. Grace for these great encounters. Defective light curtailed play slightly on the opening day and, while there came no serious interruption, the contest, when the Players' second innings closed shortly after half-past five on Friday, was abandoned as a draw.

• July 25, 26, 27, 1934 •

FOR THE FIRST TIME since 1914 the Players were beaten at Lord's. The Gentlemen owed their victory by seven wickets very largely to Wyatt. Giving the opposition first innings on a drying pitch, Wyatt used his four principal bowlers – Allen, Baxter, Brown and Holmes – with such skill that each came up fresh when called upon. Then,

A prince among Gentlemen, "Duleep" was affectionately known in cricket circles as "Mr Smith". When recurring ill health forced him to retire at 27, Wisden noted his being "of singular charm of character; extremely modest of his own wonderful ability; and with a love for the game which transcended his joy in all other pastimes."

The Hearnes

Thomas Hearne was late coming before the cricket public, little being known of him outside local circles till he was over 30. His reputation, however, was firmly established in 1859, and from that time till his retirement from the Middlesex eleven he played regularly in the best matches, proving himself a first-rate bat and by no means a bad bowler. He went to Australia with the first English eleven in 1861, but could not do himself justice in the colonies. His career as an active player terminated in 1876, in which year he had a very severe stroke of paralysis. He made a remarkable recovery, however, and for more than twenty years afterwards kept his post as chief of the groundstaff at Lord's. In personal character, no professional cricketer stood higher, and all through his life he enjoyed the respect of everyone who knew him. His eldest son, Thomas Hearne junior, is now the ground superintendent at Lord's and his second son, George F. Hearne, has for years been Pavilion clerk. [1901]

George Francis Hearne (right), a member of the famous cricket family, played in MCC matches for 32 years and altogether his service with MCC extended over 46 years. A useful bat and bowler, he once hit a hundred for Ealing and District v MCC at Lord's. As Pavilion clerk from 1873 to 1908, he was well known to all first-class cricketers and during that time was captain of the St John's Wood Ramblers (now Cross Arrows CC) for 36 consecutive seasons. [1932]

John Thomas Hearne held a prominent place among the very best bowlers from 1891 to 1914 and finished his career with a record of 3,060 wickets. Right-hand medium-pace, he took a fairly long run up to the wicket, and it would be difficult to recall a bowler with a more beautiful delivery, made as his left hand pointed down the pitch. Standing nearly five feet eleven inches, he

brought the ball over with a perfectly straight arm, and such was his command of length that a batsman might wait many overs for a ball from which he was certain to score. Even on the best wickets he got on quite an appreciable off-break and, varying his pace cleverly, he used at times to send down a fast ball which swung with his arm. On a bowler's wicket he could dismiss the strongest sides and on crumbling pitches he was simply unplayable. The leading bowler not only for Middlesex but for the MCC in the days when the club programme included quite a number of first-class matches, he was called upon for an amount of work which would have tired out most men in a very few years, but his splendid methods served so well that a career in first-class cricket, which opened in 1888, did not close until the 1914 war.

Jack Hearne came of famous cricket stock. A nephew

of old Tom Hearne and of George Hearne, both of whom played for Bucks and Middlesex, he was a cousin of G. G. Hearne, Frank Hearne and Alec Hearne, all distinguished professionals for Kent. His brother, Walter, also a good Kent bowler, broke down through knee trouble when he looked to have many years of success before him. [1945]

MIDDLESEX v SOMERSET
• June 4, 5, 6, 1900 •

J. T. Hearne's benefit proved a decided success, about 16,000 people being present on Whit Monday and fully 10,000 on the second day. Out of compliment to Hearne, Stoddart resumed his old place in the Middlesex eleven and by some wonderful batting secured a victory for his side by 209 runs. His 221 is the highest score he has ever made in a first-class match, but having regard to the quality of the bowling the innings could scarcely be compared to his previous best – 215 not out against Lancashire at Old Trafford in 1891. All the same he played splendidly. He was at the wickets nearly five hours and hit 36 fours.

MIDDLESEX v HAMPSHIRE
• May 10, 12, 13, 1913 •

Arranged to start on the Saturday before Whitsun, this match – awarded to Alec Hearne for his many years of service to the Marylebone Club – was a complete failure as a benefit. The proposed Saturday start proved impossible, and on Monday, when the attendance was the smallest seen at Lord's on a Whit Monday for many years, play was restricted to less than an hour and a half before lunch, while before half-past four on Tuesday the game had come to an end. Although the weather turned out pleasant on Saturday, heavy rain had fallen during the early morning, and this drenching, coming on top of previous downpours, resulted in no cricket being possible at Lord's for the sixth day in succession. Middlesex won by an innings and 36 runs.

The Hearnes

Thomas Arthur Hearne, the ground superintendent at Lord's since 1898, was a son of Tom Hearne, elder brother of G. F. and first cousin of G. G., Frank and Alec. He never was famous as a cricketer but possessed a very sound knowledge of the game. Before succeeding Pearce at Lord's, he was groundsman at Wellington College. [1911]

J. W. Hearne bids fair to keep up the reputation of a famous cricketing family. He is not yet twenty, but on occasions last season both his batting and bowling were remarkable. "Young Jack" has a thoroughly sound style of batting, being for so young a cricketer remarkably free from any serious defects of method. With so good a foundation to build on, it is only reasonable to suppose that, with increased strength and experience, he will do very well in the future. As a bowler he is of the leg-break type with an occasional googly thrown in. Not until the beginning of last June had he ever attempted this style in a match. In between the fall of the Somerset wickets at Bath, Hearne was bowling the ball down, and noticing that he could bowl both a leg-break and a googly I subsequently gave him a trial. He did not, as it happened, get a wicket, but he puzzled the batsmen, so that when in the next match, against Gloucestershire at Bristol, he bowled Board off his wrist with a ball which the Gloucestershire wicket-keeper thought was a leg-break, but which broke back sharply, I felt certain that we had got hold of a bowler of great possibilities. It was not until the Middlesex and Essex match at Lord's in August that he revealed his full capabilities. At lunch time on the first day, Essex had scored 97 for two wickets, and yet in three-quarters of an hour's play afterwards they were all out for 110, Hearne taking seven wickets for 3 runs. Hearne has the leg-break under absolute control, and his pace through the air is fast enough to prevent the batsmen jumping in to him, while he gets tremendous spin on the ball. He

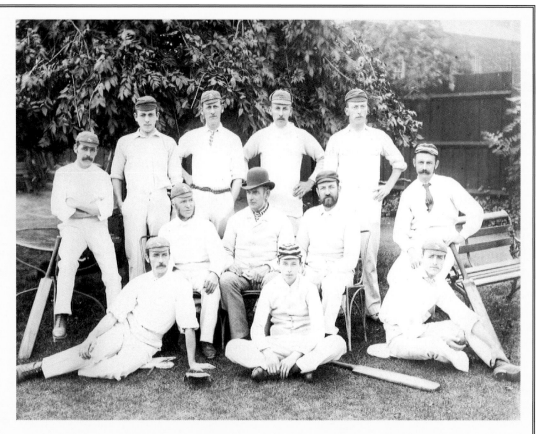

The Hearnes had no difficulty putting out a strong side in the 1880s. At the back are G. G. (half-sitting) and young J. T. with brothers Herbert and Walter; seated with George sen. and brother Thomas are T. A. and brother G. F., while G. G.'s brothers Frank and Alec flank young R. Hearne.

does not – wisely, I think – attempt to bowl the googly more than once or twice in every three overs. He gets a great many of his wickets by catches at slip, extra-slip and point, the batsmen playing forward at the good-length ball and the break causing the ball to go in their direction. [P. F. Warner, 1911]

MCC v MINOR COUNTIES
• May 21, 22, 1914 •

So completely were the Minor Counties outplayed in this match that the MCC actually scored 538 for six wickets in four hours and a quarter and, having declared, dismissed the Counties for 146 before the end of the first day. While all the home batsmen did well, everything else was overshadowed by the brilliance of J. W. Hearne's display. Assisted by Tarrant in an opening partnership of 237, Hearne scored 228 out of 377 in three hours ten minutes and, so far as could be seen, made only one mistake – when 188. It was most unfortunate for him that the match was not reckoned first-class.

when Hendren set the Gentlemen a task of getting 232 runs in two hours 50 minutes, Wyatt got his first century in this classic encounter at Lord's and made the winning hit – four all run for an on-drive from Sutcliffe. Until the Yorkshireman went on to bowl when extra time had been entered upon, the Players never relaxed their efforts to check the rate of scoring but not one of the bowlers could keep down the runs. They came in two hours and twenty minutes of actual play, and Wyatt, in making 104 of them, had a great reception in the Pavilion.

• July 15, 16, 17, 1936 •

DRAWN. The match will long be remembered for its stirring finish. G. O. Allen, who led the Gentlemen, declared his innings closed at five o'clock on the third day and set the Players 132 to get in roughly 75 minutes, including the extra half-hour. Extraordinary cricket followed. By six o'clock the Players had four men out for 33 runs. The breakdown was caused by Kenneth Farnes, the Essex fast bowler, who, taking a little longer run than usual and making the fullest use of his height, sent the ball down at a pace unequalled at headquarters since the days of C. J. Kortright. When Farnes bowled Gimblett, Hammond and Hardstaff, he sent a stump in each case catapulting head high to drop at the feet of Levett, who stood back more than a dozen yards. Allen, when Farnes tired, bowled with tremendous zeal, and he sent away Leyland's middle stump with a ball almost as fast as his colleague produced. Allen claimed the extra half-hour, an unusual thing in these matches, but Fishlock, the leading left-hander of the year, and Sinfield played out time, the Players finishing 68 behind with half their wickets in hand. J. W. A. Stephenson, Army and Essex, played a leading part in the match, for in the Players' first innings he bowled his medium-fast swinging deliveries with such deadly effect that, with nine wickets for 46, he accomplished his best performance in first-class cricket.

The Gentlemen of 1934. Back (l-r): W. H. V. Levett, E. R. T. Holmes, Alan Melville, F. R. Brown, J. H. Human, A. D. Baxter. Front: B. H. Valentine, C. F. Walters, R. E. S. Wyatt, G. O. B. Allen, M. J. Turnbull.

• July 13, 14, 15, 1938 •

GENTLEMEN won by 133 runs. For only the second time since 1914, the Gentlemen proved successful in the match with the Players at Lord's. A wonderful display of hitting by H. T. Bartlett and the bowling of K. Farnes, ably supported by that of Captain Stephenson and F. R. Brown, accounted for the professionals being outplayed. In captaining the Gentlemen after having led the Players at Lord's, W. R. Hammond enjoyed unique personal distinction.

The batting of Yardley and Bartlett stood out as a remarkable contrast after a poor start by the Gentlemen. The Cambridge captain of the current season scored more freely than did Hammond in a stand of 120, and by brilliant off-side strokes, with an occasional leg hit to vary his methods, he put eleven fours to his credit. Bartlett, Cambridge captain in 1936, found help in a sequence of useful partners and gave an amazing display of forcing cricket. Known as a very free left-handed hitter when at Dulwich College and the University, Bartlett, on first appearing for the

Gentlemen at Lord's, far surpassed anything he had done previously. He played the second-highest innings in this engagement to the 232 not out scored by C. B. Fry in 1903. Bartlett made 175 out of 256 while six wickets fell and took out his bat. Of four sixes which he hit, two were on drives far beyond the longest boundaries and one from Nichols, bowling at the Pavilion end, fell on the

highest part of the turret at the end of the Grand Stand. He followed with five fours in an over from the same fast bowler, and two fours and two sixes to the on in the next over from Peter Smith. This remarkable hitting finished the last-wicket stand with Farnes (10) which put on 82 in 45 minutes. During two hours and three-quarters Bartlett, besides his four sixes, hit 24 fours and when not attacking the bowling he showed sound defence.

Next day the Players were always struggling for runs. Hutton (52) stayed until just before lunch time and, though Woolley made many beautiful strokes, no effective resistance was offered to Farnes, who in a series of six spells took eight wickets for 43. This was probably the best fast bowling in this match since Arthur Fielder dismissed all the Gentlemen in 1906. Farnes always bowled at the stumps and fully earned his reward.

Above: Ken Farnes – Gentleman fast bowler who blew the Players away in 1936 and 1938.
Right: Leading the Players gave Len Hutton a stepping-stone to the England captaincy.

W. G. Grace
Birthday Celebration Match

• July 14, 15, 16, 1948 •

PLAYERS WON by seven wickets. A masterly innings by their captain, Hutton, carried the Players to victory after being set to get 233 to win in 145 minutes. The prospect of success looked small when accurate bowling restricted them to 70 runs in the first hour. A stand of 104 in the next hour between Hutton and Compton turned the scales, and Crapp helped Hutton in another big partnership which brought victory with five minutes to spare. Hutton, superb in strokeplay, did not offer a chance and hit eighteen fours in his unbeaten 132. In the first innings, Compton was nearly knocked out by a throw-in from short leg, and he received another painful blow, this time on the shoulder, from a fast ball.

• July 26, 27, 28, 1950 •

DRAWN. A match worthy of the traditions of its title became specially memorable because of two features. One was the gloriously thrilling finish. The Players accepted the challenge of a declaration by Brown which set them 253 to win in two and a half hours so spiritedly that with twenty minutes left, and seven wickets in hand, they required 36. From this point such a transformation occurred that, in seventeen minutes, six more batsmen were out for 25 runs, three the victims of a hat-trick by Knott. Amidst tense excitement Hollies, the last man, managed to keep the last five deliveries out of his wicket and away from the clutching hands of the ten fieldsmen crouched in a circle only a few yards from the bat.

A superb display by Brown, reminiscent of H. T. Bartlett's magnificent innings in the 1938 game, also placed the contest above the ordinary. On the opening day, after his side had been put in, Brown launched a remarkable attack on the bowling. So completely was he the master that he scored all but nine of the 131 runs made in the 110 minutes he batted. He hit sixteen fours and celebrated his century with a six into the Pavilion. As soon as the Gentlemen left the field upon Dollery's declaration on the second day, Brown was invited to captain the MCC side to Australia during the winter, and by the time his team began batting again he was sitting in committee discussing the first cricketers to be picked for the tour.

• July 13, 14, 15, 1960 •

DRAWN. In a remarkable finish the scores were level when Dexter, from long-on, threw down the middle stump as Allen and Moss were going for the second run which would have given the Players victory off the last ball of the match. Dexter's throw travelled fully 35 yards. The last over had arrived with the Players needing 13 and two wickets left.

• July 18, 19, 20, 1962 •

DRAWN. With the MCC side to visit Australia due to be chosen ten days later, this match was in some respects a Test Trial. As far as the press and the public were concerned, the appointment of Dexter as captain of the MCC was settled only during the second day of this game after Sheppard had apparently strengthened his claim for

It is the eve-of-departure dinner in the Tavern. H. S. Altham and Ted Dexter talk tactics; Lord Nugent looks ahead to his forthcoming presidency of MCC; the Duke of Norfolk and Colin Cowdrey contemplate life in Australia under Ted.

the leadership by hitting an excellent century. Sheppard's class was clear to everyone, and next day the popular newspapers acclaimed him as the MCC captain-elect, only for the official announcement to come later the same day that Dexter had been invited and had accepted. Originally, Cowdrey was nominated as the Gentlemen's captain, but he went down with kidney trouble so that Dexter, second choice when the game began, was the man of the moment when it finished.

With the Advisory County Cricket Committee's decision in November 1962 to do away with amateur and professional status, this became the last Gents-Players match at Lord's.

John Murray

Gillette Cup Man of the Match in 1965.

He believes that standards of cricket have declined overall, and connects this with the lessening of discipline in cricket and outside. I think that by "discipline" he sometimes means hardship and knowing one's place. When he first came on to the groundstaff at Lord's in 1950, at the age of fifteen, his place was clear, and very low in the hierarchy. He never resented the fact that he had to sweep the stands, that he had only one session a week reserved for net practice, or that he was not allowed in the Pavilion unless he was playing in the game. But the ambition was clearer and stronger; he could see exactly what he wanted to achieve and what he wanted to get away from. Today, he thinks, it is perhaps too easy for young cricketers, and too many of them think they know too much.

At the same time J. T. was always aware of the limited rights a cricketer had in the face of arbitrary or whimsical decisions by administrators, and of his limited say in the running of the game. He was one of those responsible for the launching of the Cricketers' Association, and was for many years its treasurer. [*Mike Brearley, 1976*]

MIDDLESEX v SURREY
• May 31, June 2, 3, 1975 •

Drawn. Murray completed a memorable week when he equalled Strudwick's record of 1,493 victims (stumpings and catches) in a career with a catch off Owen-Thomas, having taken himself to the fringe of the record with two spectacular diving catches. Surrey looked assured only when Younis Ahmed and Roope were adding 66 for the fourth wicket, Lamb returning his best figures of six for 49. Middlesex also had their troubles on the difficult pitch, seventeen wickets falling on the first day. The second day provided only 76 minutes of cricket, and Edrich (90 not out) saw Surrey through several crises on the last day.

I imagine, though I have never heard him talk about the subject, that John Murray must have been disappointed not to have been appointed captain of Middlesex. He was vice-captain for five years, under both Titmus and Parfitt, so that he did, of course, captain the side when they were away. He always did the job with flair and character; he liked to attack. He was also fairly conventional in his ideas about tactics and field-settings. He had very strong views about the right way to play the game, which included looking to get on top whether batting or fielding, total honesty, and unquestioning acceptance of a decision.

Wisden at Lord's

Top Hats and Bats
Eton v Harrow

"Eighty-eight matches have been played, of which Eton have won 35, Harrow 35, and 18 have been drawn. This is the generally published record, but Harrow men object very strongly to the first game in 1805 being treated as a regular contest between the two schools, contending that it is no more correct to count that than the fixture in 1857, for boys under twenty, which has been rejected."

[Wisden 1914]

Charles Inglis Thornton

THE FEAT which gained him great celebrity was his hit over the Pavilion at Lord's in Eton v Harrow in 1868. I was in with him at the time and thought we must make a big score, but the next ball – a dead shooter, of which there were plenty that day – took his wicket. [*Lord Harris, 1930*]

• July 8, 9, 1870 •

THEIR ROYAL HIGHNESSES the Duchess of Cambridge and the Prince and Princess of Teck, with a host of the nobility, honoured this match with their presence at Lord's. The Grand Stand was thronged, a large majority of its occupants being ladies. The Pavilion seats and roof were crowded with members and their friends. "The Ring" was deeper and more densely packed, and the outer ring of carriages more extensive than at any preceding match. Such an assemblage of rank, fashion and numbers had never before been seen even at Lord's. It was computed that quite 30,000 visitors attended the ground on those memorable two days. Down by Mr Dark's house, up by the NE corner, and fronting the whole row of well-known dwarf chestnut trees, the accidental but graceful grouping of ladies elegantly attired added a picturesque

Opposite: No denying that the carriages are "fairly freighted", to echo an 1870 *Wisden* description, in the painting of Eton v Harrow, c. 1889, by Albert Ludovici jun.
Left: Albert Chevallier Tayler's painting of the 1886 match contains the old Lord's "A" enclosure and, next to it, the Pavilion over which Etonian "Buns" Thornton (inset) hit his famous six in 1868.

brilliancy to the old ground not seen at other matches.

Two sights unusual on cricket grounds, and curious by contrast, were witnessed at this match: the first occurred on the Friday, when on the "boys" retiring to luncheon the whole playing area of the ground was covered by a gay company promenading; the other on the Saturday when, on rain commencing falling at noon, the youthful cricketers were suddenly surrounded by a dense ring of some thousands of opened umbrellas. Weather, attendances and exciting finish considered, there surely never was played a more successful Eton v Harrow match than this.

Eton won by 21 runs – the best contested match played since 1843. Thousands of excited Eton and Harrow men gathered in front of the Pavilion; and amid shouting, cheering and all that kind of thing, the captains and prominent players were carried, jolted, tossed about from Pavilion to wickets and back again.

Carriage Trade

• July 12, 13, 1895 •

Col Francis William Rhodes, CB, DSO, died of blackwater fever at Groot Schuur, Cape Colony, on September 21, 1905. An elder brother of the late Mr Cecil Rhodes, he was educated at Eton and Sandhurst, and in 1869 and 1870 appeared against both Harrow and Winchester. His greatest success in the public school matches was gained in the Harrow match of 1870, when his scores of 31 and 18 had a great deal to do with his side's success. Among his contemporaries at Eton were the late C. J. Ottaway, S. E. Butler, G. H. Longman, A. S. Tabor, Lord Clifton, the Hon. (now Lord) Harris and A. W. Ridley. In 1895 he played a leading part in the Jameson Raid, for which, with four others, he was sentenced to death by Judge Gregorowski. He was buried at Dalham Church, near Newmarket.

THE QUESTION of the admission of carriages at the Eton and Harrow match is becoming a difficult one. Last year many members were refused carriage tickets owing to want of space; and if the number of applications for carriage tickets goes on increasing, the admission of carriages may have to be stopped altogether. It having come to the knowledge of the MCC Committee last season that carriage tickets were in several cases disposed of to persons who were not members of the club, the Committee desire to remind members that carriage tickets are not transferable, and that it is most unjust that strangers should have carriage tickets when many members cannot obtain them. [1879]

BY REASON of the exciting incidents which marked its closing stage, the match of 1895 may rank among the most remarkable games played in recent years between Eton and Harrow. It was agreed on the second morning to play on if necessary till half-past seven; and when at half-past five Pilkington, the Eton captain, declared his second innings closed at 283 for nine wickets, leaving Harrow to score 218 in an hour and 40 minutes, a very quiet and uneventful finish seemed in prospect. As it turned out, the Harrow boys succeeded in drawing the match with their last pair at the wickets, and in all probability another five or ten minutes would have brought about their defeat. The people who stayed at Lord's up to the close of one of the longest day's cricket we have ever sat through had a very exciting time of it.

The surprise of the match was the bowling of fifteen-year-old Dowson, a son of the Mr E. M. Dowson so well known years ago in connection with the old Surrey eleven. The little cricketer had only gone up to Harrow from Elstree after the season of 1894, and we have seldom seen anyone so young and small in the match. As to the quality of his left-handed slow bowling, however,

there could not be two opinions. With the easy natural action of a first-rate professional, he kept his length perfectly during long spells of work, made the ball do a good deal, and took five wickets for 90 and three for 105.

Given, owing to his stature, the nickname of "Toddles", Edward Maurice Dowson was called this by his friends for the rest of his life. He stood no more than five feet and bowled extremely slow. Coming into the match at such an early age, he played no fewer than five times against Eton (1895–1899) and was captain in the last two years. In 1898, when Harrow won by nine wickets, he scored 47 and took nine wickets. Going up to Cambridge, he took part in all four Varsity matches from 1900 to 1903 and led the side to victory in his last year. He proved a valuable all-rounder, especially in 1902 when he took five wickets in each innings and scored 40 and 29; in his last three years at Cambridge he exceeded a four-figure aggregate. Mr Dowson, had he played regularly in the Surrey team, would unquestionably have taken a high place among amateurs, but the cricket field saw little of him after he came down from Cambridge. [1934]

Public attendances 1871 - 1880

	Friday	Saturday	Total	
1871	13,494	11,132	24,626	1s. admission
1872	16,450	11,005	27,455	" "
1873	15,868	11,214	27,082	" "
1874	9,039	6,325	15,364	2s. 6d. admission
1875	3,540 (wet)	9,982	13,522	" "
1876	7,452	5,787	13,239	" "
1877	8,089	5,327 (wet)	13,416	" "
1878	7,176	5,593	12,769	" "
1879	7,411	4,841 (wet)	12,252	" "
1880	7,621	7,426	15,047	" "

• July 9, 10, 1897 •

FOR THE FOURTH time in succession, and for the eleventh time since 1874, the Eton and Harrow match had to be left drawn. The fact of the game having been again unfinished led to a great deal of discussion. A number of Old Etonians signed a petition asking that a third day might be allotted to the match, and the subject gave rise to quite a lengthy controversy in the columns of *The Times*. The Rev. J. E. C. Welldon, the Head-Master at Harrow, favoured the change and was supported by the MCC Committee and several well-known cricketers, notably Mr I. D. Walker. The decision remained with Dr Warre, the Head-Master at Eton, who, after the close of the cricket season, said that he did not feel justified in departing from the existing arrangements. In his article on public school cricket in the present issue of this Almanack, Mr W. J. Ford makes light of the number of drawn matches between Eton and Harrow, but he has perhaps not taken sufficiently into account the fact that there were no unfinished games before 1860. Since then the proportion of draws has certainly been very large. We cannot believe that scholastic work at Eton would suffer through a third day being given up to the match and, though there is no present hope of reform, we trust that Dr Warre will reconsider his decision.

On the Saturday of the Eton and Harrow match, July 9, 1898, an event of peculiar interest occurred in the Pavilion at Lord's, a presentation being made to Mr R. A. H. Mitchell by the captains of the Eton eleven from 1865 to 1897 upon the occasion of his retiring from the position of principal adviser and "coach" of Eton cricket. Lord Harris on behalf of the subscribers drew attention to the fact that all the past captains during this period were living, with one exception, namely, Mr E. O. H. Wilkinson, who was captain in 1872, and who was killed in the Zulu war, "like a good cricketer and a good Englishman giving his life for his side". The others had gladly come forward to give proof of their appreciation of Mr Mitchell's services to Eton cricket, and their personal affection for himself.

Capt. Francis Octavius Grenfell, VC (9th Lancers), born on September 4, 1880, fell in action on May 24. In 1899 he was a member of the Eton XI under W. Findlay's captaincy, scoring 327 runs with an average of 40.87: his highest innings was 136 not out v I Zingari. That year it was said of him: "In batting he has the highest average, and has made the only century for the school; he bats in a taking style and scores quickly; he watches the ball well, and makes good strokes all round the wicket." He took part in the South African War in 1901-02, receiving the Queen's Medal with five clasps, and he was the first officer in the Army to gain the VC in the present war. The action for which he was awarded the latter was described in the *London Gazette* in these terms: "For gallantry in action against unbroken infantry at Andregnies, Belgium, on 24th August 1914, and for gallant conduct in assisting to save the guns of the 119th Battery Royal Field Artillery, near Doubon, the same day." Twice he had returned to England badly wounded.

• July 14, 15, 1899 •

LIMITED, unfortunately, as before to two days, the Eton and Harrow match for the fifth time in six years ended in a draw. The sensation of the match came when Eton started their second innings. Longman and Grenfell went in and Longman, when he had made only 5, was missed at slip. For this blunder Harrow had to pay a tremendously high price, the two batsmen staying together for two hours and a quarter, and in that time scoring 167 runs. Longman was the first to leave, his innings of 81, apart from the chance, being superb. He played in most attractive style and scored all round the wicket. As most readers of *Wisden* will be aware, he is a son of Mr G. H. Longman – so famous at Eton and Cambridge as a batsman in the first half of the '70s. Grenfell, who was out at 184, was not quite so good to look at, but played equally sound cricket. Curiously enough he made exactly the same score.

Writing in the 1906 *Wisden* of "Dear old Mike! as he was familiarly called", R. D. Walker described R. A. H. Mitchell as "a first-rate judge of the game, and an excellent and judicious captain". Under Mitchell's captaincy, Oxford beat Cambridge from 1863 to 1865.

• July 8, 9, 1904 •

FOR THE SECOND year in succession Eton beat Harrow in a single innings, but they had to work much harder and longer for their victory than in 1903, little more than half an hour remaining for play when, on the Saturday evening, the end was reached. Eton won by an innings and 12 runs, as against an innings and 154 in the previous year, but their superiority was almost as marked as before, the difference being that Harrow made a much better struggle to avoid defeat. The match will always remain a memorable one, inasmuch as D. C. Boles, of Eton, by scoring 183, beat a record which had stood for 63 years. The highest score previously obtained in the matches between the two schools was 152 for Eton in 1841 by the still-living Emilius Bayley. One heard after the match that though Boles was thought likely, by reason of his straight bat and great advantages of height and reach, to do well in the match, he did not have a reputation such as was enjoyed at Eton in the past by R. A. H. Mitchell, Alfred Lubbock, the late C. J. Ottaway, Alfred Lyttelton, W. F. Forbes or C. T. Studd. Still, whatever his merits, he played an extraordinarily fine innings. Assuredly no one in a school match has ever shown greater self-control or a more remarkable power of adapting his play to the varying conditions of the game. Up to a certain point, while things were going badly for his side, he was caution itself, being actually at the wickets an hour and three-quarters for his first 20 runs. No one – unfamiliar with his style – watching him during that time, could have suspected the tremendous hitting power he afterwards displayed. After reaching his hundred, he made his third fifty in 35 minutes, driving in wonderful form; just at the end he scored 35 runs from two consecutive overs. His hits included 27 fours.

Golden days at Lord's as Edwardian society turns out in splendour in 1905. "The Schools' match ended in a draw," *Wisden* recorded, "but even if a definite result had been arrived at, the finish could not have been more exciting, Eton just avoiding defeat after it had seemed any odds they would be beaten." Their last pair, N. C. Tufnell and Hon. P. A. Methuen, held out for 33 minutes in fading light to deny Harrow victory.

• July 12, 13, 1907 •

THE ETON and Harrow match of 1907 was one of the most memorable contests between the two schools, M. C. Bird, the Harrow captain, accomplishing the great feat, never before performed for either side, of making two separate hundreds – 100 not out and 131. The bowling he had to face was, it must be confessed, very moderate in quality, but as to the excellence of his batting there could not be two opinions. As was truly said in one of the reports, no batsman had stood out by himself to quite the same extent in the match since Walter Forbes scored his 113 in 1876. Tall and powerfully built, he, like Forbes, seemed to be a man playing among boys. He scored his 100 not out in an hour and three-quarters, and for his 131 he was at the wickets two hours and a quarter. Forcing the pace so as to be able to declare, he made his last 31 runs in a quarter of an hour. Essentially a forward player in style, he was greatly helped by a splendid wicket. At no time was the bowling strong enough to tax his defence.

This 1880s illustration, "A Close Run", depicts not only smart Eton fielding, with good backing-up, but also, in the background, the old Pavilion at Lord's.

Fowler's Match

• July 8, 9, 1910 •

ETON AND HARROW have been meeting on the cricket field for over 100 years, but they have never played a match quite so remarkable as that of 1910. Indeed in the whole history of cricket there has been nothing more sensational. After following their innings Eton were only 4 ahead with nine wickets down, and yet in the end they won the game by 9 runs. The struggle will be known for all time as Fowler's Match. Never has a school cricketer risen to the occasion in more astonishing fashion. When Harrow went in with only 55 to get, Fowler took command of the game, secured eight wickets – five of them bowled down – and brought off what might fairly be described as a 40 to 1 chance.

Until the second afternoon was far advanced, the match proved one-sided to a degree. On the first day Harrow, going in on a soft but by no means difficult pitch, ran up a total of 232, and when bad light caused stumps to be drawn, five of Eton's best wickets had fallen for 40 runs. On Saturday morning, Eton's first innings was soon finished off for 67 and a follow-on against a balance of 165 was involved. At first things went so badly that half the wickets were down for 65, no one being able to get the ball away on the slow pitch. The first change in the game came with the partner-ship between Fowler and Wigan, 42 runs being added for the sixth wicket in 50 minutes. When Wigan left, Boswell joined Fowler , three-quarters of an hour's play producing 57 runs.

Still, despite Fowler's heroic efforts – his 64 was the highest innings in the match – the position was reached of Eton being only 4 runs ahead with a wicket to fall. Then began the cricket which will for ever make the match memorable. Kaye joined Manners, and so finely and fearlessly did Manners hit that in less than 25 minutes the total was carried from 169 to 219. A remarkable catch in the slips at last brought the innings to an end, Hopley just reaching the ball and turning it to Jameson, who held it a few inches from the ground.

In the case of any ordinary match the ground

Lord's Ground.

ETON v. HARROW.

FRIDAY & SATURDAY, JULY 8, 9, 1910. (Two-Day Match.)

HARROW.

		First Innings.		Second Innings.	
1	T. O. Jameson	c Lubbock, b Fowler ...	5	b Fowler	2
2	T. B. Wilson	b Kaye	53	b Fowler	0
3	G. W. V. Hopley	b Fowler	35	b Fowler	8
4	T. L. G. Turnbull	l b w, b Fowler	2	c Boswell, b Fowler	0
5	G. F. Earle .... (Capt.)	c Wigan, b Steel	20	c Wigan, b Fowler	13
6	W. T. Monckton	c Lubbock, b Stock	20	b Fowler	0
7	J. M. Hillyard	st Lubbock, b Fowler ...	62	c Kaye, b Fowler	0
8	C. H. B. Blount	c Holland, b Steel	4	c and b Steel	5
9	A. C. Straker	c Holland, b Steel	2	b Fowler	1
10	O. B. Graham	c and b Steel	6	not out	7
11	Hon. R. H. L. G. Alexander	not out	2	c Holland, b Steel	8
		B 18, l-b 2, w , n-b l	21	B l, l-b , w , n-b	1
		Total	**232**	**Total**	**45**

FALL OF THE WICKETS.

1-15	2-84	3-88	4-121	5-133	6-166	7-191	8-201	9-216	10-232
1-0	2-8	3-8	4-21	5-21	6-21	7-26	8-29	9-32	10-45

ANALYSIS OF BOWLING.

Name.	1st Innings.						2nd Innings.					
	O.	M.	R.	W.	Wd.	N-b	O.	M.	R.	W.	Wd.	N-b
Fowler	37.3	9	90	4	...	...	10	2	23	8	...	...
Steel	31	11	69	4	...	...	6.4	1	12	2	...	...
Kaye	12	5	23	1	...	l	3	0	9	0	...	...
Stock	7	2	12	1	...	...	...	...	...	...	...	...
Boswell	8	4	17	0	...	...	...	...	...	...	...	...

ETON.

		First Innings.		Second Innings.	
1	R. H. Lubbock	l b w, b Earle	9	c Straker, b Hillyard ...	9
2	C. W. Tufnell	b Hillyard	5	l b w, b Alexander	7
3	W. T. Birchenough	c Hopley, b Graham	5	c Turnbull, b Jameson...	22
4	W. T. Holland	c Hopley, b Hillyard ...	2	st Monckton, b Alexander	5
5	R. St. L. Fowler ...... (Capt.)	c Graham, b Jameson ...	21	c Earle, b Hillyard	64
6	A. I. Steel	b Graham	0	c Hopley, b Hillyard ...	6
7	D. G. Wigan	c Turnbull, b Jameson...	4	b Graham	16
8	A. B. Stock	l b w, b Alexander	2	l b w, b Earle	0
9	Hon. J. N. Manners	c Graham, b Alexander	4	not out	40
10	K. Lister Kaye	c Straker, b Alexander	0	c Jameson, b Earle	13
11	W. G. K. Boswell	not out	0	b Earle	32
		B 10, l-b , w l, n-b	11	B 2, l-b , w 3, n-b	5
		Total	**67**	**Total**	**219**

FALL OF THE WICKETS.

1-16	2-16	3-26	4-34	5-36	6-57	7-62	8-64	9-66	10-67
1-12	2-19	3-41	4-47	5-65	6-107	7-164	8-166	9-169	10-219

ANALYSIS OF BOWLING.

Name.	1st Innings.						2nd Innings.					
	O.	M.	R.	W.	Wd.	N-b	O.	M.	R.	W.	Wd.	N-b
Earle	12	9	4	1	...	...	17.3	3	57	3	l	...
Hillyard	19	9	38	2	l	...	23	7	65	3	l	...
Graham	9	7	3	2	...	l	18	12	33	1	...	...
Jameson	4	1	4	2	...	...	9	1	26	1	...	...
Alexander	4.1	1	7	3	...	...	14	4	33	2	l	...
Wilson	...	...	...	...	...	...	2	2	0	0	...	...

Umpires—Moss and Whiteside.   Scorers—G. G. Hearne and Newman.

ETON WON BY 9 RUNS.

would have been half empty before the Eton innings closed, but an Eton and Harrow crowd is a law to itself and when Harrow went in with 55 to get, about 10,000 people watched the cricket. Whatever their feelings, they must have been glad they stayed as they may never see such a finish again. Probably Harrow made a mistake in having the heavy roller put on. At any rate Fowler was able to bowl his off-break with deadly effect. He bowled Wilson in the first over; at 8 he bowled Hopley; and at the same total Turnbull was caught in the long field. Earle seemed likely to win the match for Harrow but a catch at slip sent him back at 21. Without the addition of a run, Monckton was bowled and Hillyard well caught low down at short mid-on. As the result of half an hour's cricket, six wickets were down for 21, Fowler having taken them all.

Blount was caught and bowled at 26 by Steel, who had just gone on for Kaye, and then Jameson, who had been batting for nearly 40 minutes without getting a run, was so badly hurt that for a few minutes the game had to be delayed. A yorker bowled Straker at 29 and, after Graham had hit a three, Jameson was bowled by Fowler. It was not to be expected that Graham and Alexander would get the 23 runs still required, but they made a desperate effort, carrying the score to 45, or only 10 to win. Then a catch low down in the slips got rid of Alexander and a wonderful match was over. The scene of enthusiasm at the finish was quite indescribable. Steel with his leg-breaks gave Fowler excellent support, and the Eton fielding all round was magnificent.

Harrow: T. O. Jameson, T. B. Wilson, G. W. V. Hopley, T. L. G. Turnbull, G. F. Earle, W. T. Monckton, J. M. Hillyard, C. H. B. Blount, A. C. Straker, O. B. Graham and Hon. R. H. L. G. Alexander.

Eton: R. H. Lubbock, C. W. Tufnell, W. T. Birchenough, W. T. Holland, R. St L. Fowler, A. I. Steel, D. G. Wigan, A. B. Stock, Hon. J. N. Manners, K. Lister Kaye and W. G. K. Boswell.

Capt. Robert St Leger Fowler, MC, died at Rahinston, Enfield, County Meath, on June 13, 1925, aged 34. Owing to his profession, he was not very well known to the general cricket public, but he was the hero of a match which may, without exaggeration, be described as the most extraordinary ever played.

"Samuel Johnson late, like you, / Found his fame, his Boswell too,
'Manners maketh man,' God wot! / Manners maketh 'forty not'.
Put them in? Why, man alive, / Put them in for forty-five!"
These lines were penned by W. D. Eggar, a science master at Eton, to celebrate their 1910 victory. John Manners' father, Lord Manners, is said to have left Lord's at lunch time on Saturday in despair at the thought of a Harrow victory. Later that afternoon, when his butler tried to tell him what Eton had since accomplished, the 9th Earl reputedly told him to "Go away", convinced that the news could only be bad.

MCC v Public Schools

• August 1, 2, 1910 •

OUTPLAYED on Bank Holiday despite a fine innings by E. C. K. Clarke of Westminster, the Schools made a brilliant attempt to snatch victory on the second day and, in the end, lost by only two wickets. MCC, put in to make 125 on a difficult wicket, had had eight men out for 72. Fowler of Eton dismissed six batsmen for 49 runs and did the "hat-trick".

future present, and Past

ETON V HARROW.

• July 8, 9, 1921 •

IT WAS IN 1908 that Harrow last beat Eton at Lord's, and since the drawn game of the following year defeat has always been their portion. Their friends hoped last summer that they would manage to break the spell, and their general form at home was so good as to suggest that this might not be beyond their power. As things turned out, however, the atmosphere of Lord's and the recollection of many disasters proved too much for them. They practically lost the match when, on batting first, they were out in a little over an hour and a half for a wretched score of 64. It was urged in excuse for their deplorable failure that the wicket had been too recently watered, but this was indignantly denied by the ground-keeper. One

Many years later, as a result of frequent visits to the Warner home, I got to know Lady Warner extremely well – and the better I knew her the more I admired her. She was a fine judge of cricket, and did not W. H. Patterson once say, "If you cannot have Warner on the Selection Committee you should ask his wife." She was present at the famous Eton and Harrow match of 1910 – Fowler's Match – and with Eton apparently well beaten she turned to a friend and said, "I shall not send my boy to Eton as they cannot play cricket", and then left Lord's for her home in Kent as the end seemed so near. When she reached Caring she found a telegram awaiting her: "Better send him Eton won by 9 runs."
[A. W. T. Langford, 1964]

"Plum" has roquet on his mind; Lady Warner makes
sure that the proprieties are observed.

must therefore attribute the collapse to nervousness, and to the demoralising effect of the pace at which G. O. Allen bowled at the start of the innings. In the later stages of the game Harrow proved that their

batting had not been over-rated, making a total of 295, but nothing could make up for the lamentable beginning. Eton, by scoring 238, secured a very substantial lead on the first innings and won by seven wickets.

• July 12, 13, 1929 •

IN THE 100th match between Eton and Harrow there occurred a return to the draw which had been the result six times consecutively before Eton won by 28 runs in 1928. Failure to reach a definite issue did not denote lack of keenness in the endeavour of each side to prevail, or entail a dull ending. Runs indeed always came fast until Harrow were compelled to exercise caution to avoid defeat. The two days yielded an aggregate of 1,037 runs, 31 wickets falling and the game being prolonged until 25 minutes past seven in order that Eton, if possible, might force home their superiority. Nearly 22,000 people were present on Friday and the company on Saturday was estimated at 25,000, the scene each afternoon, in the glorious weather, being charming to a degree.

• July 14, 15, 1939 •

HARROW WON by eight wickets. Those who were present at the headquarters of cricket on Saturday, July 15, 1939, will never forget the delirious excitement aroused by Harrow's first victory since 1908 over their great rivals. As Lithgow, the Harrow captain, finished the match with three successive drives to the Pavilion boundary, the crowd invaded the field and carried both Lithgow and Crutchley in triumph to the Pavilion. Then for twenty minutes an ordered assembly, numbering about 8,000, cheered the heroes. The victorious team, with Hendren, their popular coach, appeared on the balcony; the Harrow school song was sung and there followed a free fight for top hats. Not for twenty years had the meeting of Eton and Harrow ended with such

Class divisions: Harrovians Peter Wagner (left) and Thomas "Timmy" Dyson come under the scrutiny of local lads George Salmon, Jack Catlin and George Young as they wait outside the Grace Gates for Dyson's parents. But a family tragedy haunts Bert Hardy's famous social commentary of toffs and urchins. The following year, 1938, Dyson travelled to India to join his parents for the summer holidays, caught diphtheria on the ship out and died shortly after arriving. His father, Lt-Colonel George Dyson, MC, himself an Old Harrovian, died in Korea in 1942 while a prisoner-of-war of the Japanese.

a frenzied scene. Before the 1920 match, the Eton captain, W. W. Hill-Wood, in consequence of the fighting that followed the conclusion of the first game after the 1914–18 war, issued a notice that any repetition of such misconduct would lead to the Eton and Harrow match being taken away from Lord's. That warning had the desired effect and the behaviour had been exemplary until this 1939 meeting.

• July 9, 10, 1954 •

HARROW WON by nine wickets. Superior in all departments, they owed much to Neame, the captain, who batted excellently in the first innings and, by astute off-spin bowling, practically assured his side of success. He enjoyed a match analysis of eleven wickets for 77 runs. Bloomfield, fast-medium, helped to destroy the confidence of the Eton batsmen. He took three wickets in

one over and only Pugh, who stayed for nearly three and a quarter hours, and Hill-Wood batted surely.

Boisterous scenes, degenerating into rowdyism, followed the match, and water was poured from the Harrow dressing-room balcony on to Eton supporters trying to tear down the colours of the victors. A clergyman had his hat knocked off and kicked about. The happenings recalled similar occurrences in the 1939 and 1919 matches.

• July 12, 13, 1975 •

HARROW WON by an innings and 151 runs to record their easiest victory over Eton in the 140 years' history of the fixture. It was a personal triumph for their captain, Fosh. He recorded the third-highest score in Eton-Harrow matches by hitting 161 not out, and emphasised his all-round ability by taking the first three wickets when Eton followed on 207 runs behind. Fosh batted only two hours 25 minutes and hit four sixes and 24 fours. A left-hander, he showed excellent footwork in getting into position to play his variety of aggressive strokes. Eton were never happy facing the fiery pace of Pigott, who took eight for 59 in the match.

• July 3, 1982 •

DRAWN. The oldest fixture at Lord's was played there for the first time as a one-day match. Eton, in scoring 216 for three declared and then taking the first five Harrow wickets for 45 runs, held the upper hand for most of the day. But in the final hour Field and fifteen-year-old Nirmalalingham, from Sri Lanka, stoutly defended to save the match with an undefeated partnership of 63. After Eton had been put in to bat, Fleming (52) and Gibbs took full advantage of the easy-paced pitch in an opening partnership of 72.

• July 5, 1986 •

DRAWN. The overnight rain that delayed the start until three o'clock returned in the late afternoon after Eton, who won the toss, had dismissed Harrow for 37, their lowest total since 1827. Eton were unable to commence their innings and the match was abandoned, leaving members and others to recall another famous collapse by Harrow, "Fowler's Match" in 1910 when their score was 45.

Eton had stellar support in 1969. Queen Elizabeth the Queen Mother and actress Elizabeth Taylor were among the party Peter Cazalet invited to Lord's when his son, Victor, captained the eleven. Cazalet (extreme left) had been training horses for Her Majesty for twenty years. With them are Lord Gage, Victor's younger brother Anthony and their sister, Sheran Hornby. The match was drawn, after Victor Cazalet's cultured 49 and subsequent declaration set Harrow to score 208 in two and a half hours.

• June 24, 1992 •

DRAWN. The oldest surviving fixture in the Lord's calendar was threatened with extinction, because its traditional Saturday was unavailable. A compromise shifted it to Wednesday, coincidentally the 80th birthday of Etonian and broadcaster Brian Johnston, who made Lord's the venue of his celebrations. His old school put Harrow in, and within nine overs had reduced them to 13 for three; they recovered to set a target of 210 in what became 44 overs. It was a tall order for an inexperienced Eton side, none of whom had appeared at Lord's before. Hawkins claimed five wickets for the second year running, but too little time was left and Walsh steered Eton to the close with three wickets in hand.

• May 25, 2000 •

HARROW WON by 19 runs. Harrow won the traditional fixture for the first time since 1975, when it was still played over two days. This was its first year as a simple limited-overs match, to circumvent over-cautious declarations. The change had been thwarted by a washout the previous season. Another wet morning delayed the start until 2 p.m. and reduced each innings from 55 to 40 overs. Nick Compton, whose grandfather Denis had made the first of his many appearances at Lord's 70 years earlier, was soon at the crease. He added 68 in eighteen overs with Dunbar before both fell to Aubrey-Fletcher's spin. Eton, needing 144, seemed well on course for victory when their captain, Ferreira, steered them to 98 for two. But Compton and Willetts snatched three wickets for no runs in seven balls, triggering a fatal collapse of eight for 26 in six overs.

Club and Ground
MCC Matches

"Changes are frequent in these days, but it is doubtful if any place has changed more completely than Lord's Cricket Ground in the last 30 years, or any institution grown more in administration than the MCC which owns it."

[Wisden 1930]

v Nottinghamshire

• July 5, 6, 7, 1869 •

THIS WAS the only match at Lord's in 1869 that took three days to play it out. The weather was dry and warm, the wickets and cricket good, and 746 runs were scored in the match.

Tuesday was "Daft's day". He went in at 25 minutes past twelve, the Notts second innings at 33 for three wickets, and he stayed in until eight minutes to seven, when the innings was over for 295 runs and Daft had made 103 not out; so as many as 262 runs were made for the shire whilst he was in. For cool, scientific, cautious and successful defence, this innings of Daft's was a marvel; slow it certainly was, but then it was sure. Whilst he was defending, Alfred Shaw and Wild were hitting freely and well. There can be no doubt but to the steady, effective defence of Daft and the free hitting of Wild and A. Shaw, the success of Notts in this truly great match is due.

Wednesday was Mr W. Grace's day. Mr Grace went to the wickets, first man in, at five minutes past twelve; he was sixth out at ten minutes past four, his

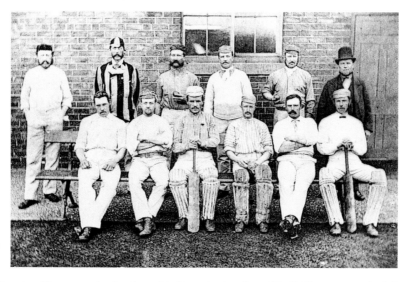

121 having been hit from the bowling of J. C. Shaw, Wootton, Alfred Shaw, Tinley and others. After Mr Grace left, the end quickly came as J. C. Shaw in two overs and two balls obtained the last three wickets without a run having been obtained from those ten balls. Nottinghamshire won by 102 runs.

Nottinghamshire: 129 (W. Oscroft 19; T. Hearne 5–27) and 295 (Richard Daft 103 not out, Wild 54, Alfred Shaw 62).

MCC and Ground: 112 (W. G. Grace Esq. 48; J. C. Shaw 6–48) and 210 (Grace 121; J. C. Shaw 5–99).

Jack Platts (front row, third from right) was a professional bowler engaged by MCC when he delivered the fatal ball that struck Nottinghamshire's George Summers. Derbyshire team-mate William Mycroft (left, front) was also a Lord's professional.

v Nottinghamshire

• June 13, 14, 15, 1870 •

A LAMENTABLE CELEBRITY will ever attach to this match, through the fatal accident to Summers, whose death resulted from a ball bowled by Platts in the second innings of Notts. The wickets were excellent, and the sad mishap universally regretted. Summers' last innings was a good one. At 12.48 on the first day he went in one wicket down with the score 29; at dinner call he had made 35 (the score 137); and at 3.30 his wicket fell to a shooter from the same hand that subsequently bowled the fatal ball. The score was 158 when Summers was out for 41 – a fact that tells how steadily and carefully he batted. This his final innings comprised eleven singles, eights twos, three threes and one five – that five (a fine forward cut to the Tavern) being the last hit the poor fellow ever made, as he was then bowled by Platts. The first ball bowled to him in the second innings was the fatal one.

George Summers died four days later, on June 19, at Nottingham, becoming the first player killed as the result of an injury received in a first-class match.

Yorkshire's Derby Days

• May 22, 23, 1871 •

YORKSHIREMEN are as good judges and genuine admirers of cricketers and cricket as of racehorses and horse-racing, and this match being set to be played on Monday and Tuesday in the Derby week, it was not surprising to find Lord's ground on those days numerously attended by men from the great shire to witness their eleven fight the good fight against the very strong eleven of MCC. But fortune was adverse to Yorkshiremen in that memorable week, for at Lord's they lost the valuable bowling aid of Freeman, they lost choice of innings, and they lost the match; and at Epsom the Yorkshire horse, Bothwell, lost the Derby.

• May 29, 30, 1876 •

THE WEATHER was bright, balmy and hot; the wickets were good; the cricket was first-class and unsensational; the ground was well attended, and the match so ably and evenly contested that, when the stumps and the game were drawn at 7.30 on the Tuesday evening, no man – not even a "Cricket Critic" – could give a positive opinion as to which side had the best of it. It was regrettable such a match could not be finished, but there was no help for it, for the third day was that day of days, "The Derby Day", and so perforce the match was drawn and

---

Queensberry rules, ko

His Bosie did for Oscar Wilde

1866: Marylebone Club v Royal Artillery
Marquis of Queensberry b Smith   18 – b Smith 0

1866: MCC & Ground v Gentlemen of Yorkshire
Marquis of Queensberry c Verelst b Sale 9 – b Sale   5

Oscar Wilde, Lord Alfred Douglas and the Marquis of Queensberry – leading players in a Victorian *cause célèbre*.

---

the Yorkshiremen were enabled to witness Kisber canter in first past the Epsom winning post.

v The Metropolitan Police

THIS ONE-DAY MATCH, played at Lord's on August 3, 1871, is here noticed to put on record the summary manner in which The Police *moved off* the three MCC pro's – West, Price and Farrands. West was bowled for 1 run by PC Shaw, who with the following ball bowled Price for 0; subsequently PC Byde bowled Farrands for 0, so the three were out for 1 run. PC Byde "run them in" so successfully that he bowled as under:

Overs: 11.3, *Mdns*: 8, *Runs*: 7, *Wkts*: 5 – all bowled.

John Platts, the well-known Derbyshire cricketer – one of the best all-round players possessed by the county in its early days – died on August 6, 1898. He was in his 50th year. A tragic interest attached to the start of Platts' career as a cricketer, as it was a ball bowled by him in the MCC and Notts match at Lord's in 1870 that caused the death of George Summers. At that time a very fast bowler, Platts afterwards lessened his pace and the catastrophe made such a painful impression upon him that it is said he never in subsequent years could play with any pleasure at Lord's ground. After dropping out of active work in the cricket field, he became one of the regular county umpires.

v Surrey

• May 14, 1872 •

INCESSANT RAIN from dawn to dusk on the 13th (the day set to commence the match) necessitated a postponement until the following day, when on dead, deceitful-playing wickets, and in a queer light for batting, Mr W. Grace and John Smith commenced (!) MCC's marvellous little innings of 16 runs, wherein seven of the wickets (including the crack's) went down in 25 minutes to Southerton and Marten before a run was scored. Captain Becher then made a two from the first ball of Marten's fifth over, but in Southerton's sixth over (another maiden) a clever catch by Pooley got rid of Biddulph for the eighth 0. When Captain Becher had made his – and the club's – score 8, a truly splendid left-hand caught and bowled – low down – by Marten settled him. Rylott and Howitt doubled the score before Marten bowled Howitt (his sixth wicket) and so, in exactly 45 minutes, were the MCC eleven out for an innings of 16 runs.

Mr Henry Perkins, so well known to all classes of cricketers as Secretary of the Marylebone Club, died on the 6th of May, 1916. He was in his 84th year and had survived nearly all the contemporaries of his early days in the cricket field. He went from Bury St Edmund's Grammar School to Cambridge, and played once against Oxford at Lord's, scoring 5 and 27 in 1854. Mr Perkins never rose to fame as a player, but he was a hard-hitting bat, a fearless fieldsman and, following the fashion of his time, he bowled lobs. He did not become a personage in the cricket world till he succeeded Mr Fitzgerald at Lord's. He became Secretary of the MCC in October 1876 and ruled – an easy-going autocrat – till the end of 1897. Even after the time for retirement had come he was constantly at the old ground – he was one of the MCC auditors to the day of his death – and it always struck me that in those later years he liked particularly to talk to men who had known him in his days of power. No one could meet him without being struck by his personality and strength of character. He had a wonderful memory for cricket, and to the end it remained unimpaired. He had his foibles – all his friends knew them – but scores of famous cricketers to whom the Pavilion at Lord's was a holy place will retain pleasant and kindly thoughts of Henry Perkins. [*Sydney H. Pardon, 1917*]

At ten minutes past one the Surrey innings was commenced; at 2.30 it was concluded for 49 runs. At five minutes past three, the second innings of MCC was commenced. John Smith made 19, the top score in the match, but at 5.30 the innings was over for 71 runs. At a quarter to six Jupp and R. Humphrey commenced Surrey's second innings and at twenty minutes to seven the county had won by five wickets. If Captain Becher had not missed R. Humphrey when he had scored only 3 runs, and Mr Howell when he had scored but 2, the probability was the match would have been a very close affair.

v The Royal Artillery

• June 6, 7, 1872 •

UNPLEASANT WEATHER attended this match at Lord's on June 6, when it was as cold as January, and as wet as an old-fashion St Swithin's day, so no one will be surprised to know that the splendid band – upwards of 70 strong – of the RA charmingly played a selection of choice music to an admiring and sympathetic audience of twenty visitors and one reporter. On the 7th the weather was brighter up to 5 p.m.

v Middlesex

• July 7, 8, 1873 •

FINE WEATHER favoured this match, which was concluded on the evening of the second day, the club defeating the county by 84 runs. Mr I. D. Walker was the great scorer of the match, making 40 in each Middlesex innings, and in the second he made his now-famous square-leg hit for six from A. Shaw's bowling, the ball being sent flying through the open window of the billiard room. This hit was well timed, clean and of immense power, and was unquestionably "the hit of the season" at Lord's. But perhaps the finest cricket in the match was played by Mr Hornby, whose 52 included two clinking off-drives up the ground for five each, and whose fielding was simply magnificent and one of the most enjoyable cricket treats of the 1873 season at Lord's. Mr Hornby's left-hand catch at mid-off, that wound up Mr Walker's second 40, was one of the most wonderful bits of judgment, pluck and nerve seen throughout the season. Mr Walker drove the ball hard – very hard – and Mr Hornby leapt up and, with his left hand extended as high as possible, stopped and clutched the ball which, if let alone, would have gone away for five at least.

Twelve of MCC and Ground v Sixteen Amateurs who had never played at Lord's

• May 28, 1874 •

THIS MATCH was one of the novelties of the MCC season. It failed to create the faintest interest in cricketing circles, brought to light no wonder in the "amateur" line, and was not proceeded with after one day's cricket that left the score in the following form:

Sixteen Amateurs: 79 and 45–12; **MCC and Ground XII**: 133.

v The North of England

• June 1, 2, 1874 •

ALFRED SHAW'S bowling obtained all the ten wickets in the North's first innings of this revived contest. In any match this is a great bowling feat to bring off, but in a first-class affair like this, wherein the ten include such wickets as Mr A. N. Hornby's, Oscroft's, Lockwood's and Greenwood's, it is a remarkable bit of bowling deserving special notice in all records of the game. Four of the ten wickets were bowled; two were caught out at slip, one at long-on, one at point and the other two were captured at wicket. The identical ball wherewith Shaw obtained the ten wickets was handsomely and appropriately mounted at the expense of MCC and presented to Alfred as a memento of the club's appreciation of his successful bowling. Shaw is properly proud of the present, which will be carefully preserved by him as a family heirloom and as an incentive to the Alfred Shaws of the future to "go and do likewise".

MCC and G v The North was first played in 1840, when the Northmen were victorious by two wickets. This time they won by 45 runs.

v The Royal Artillery

• June 3, 4, 1875 •

TWO QUIET DAYS at Lord's were enjoyed by the few visitors who witnessed the cricket in this match – the oldest now played by MCC. Barring a few (then) welcome summer showers, the weather was bright and hot, and the happy absence of crowd, cads, card-criers and other unpleasantries necessarily suffered at a great match, increased the enjoyment, which would have been thorough had better out-cricket been played by both teams. The RA batting brought to notice a promising colt in Bandsman Boys, quite a lad, who played and hit in good form and – albeit this was the first time he kept wicket – he stood up to his sticks like a man. Boys went out to the slows with great daring and much success in scoring 44 and 21. The two last RAs scored 13 runs each in their first innings, and in so doing each made a noteworthy hit, as in one over Mr Leach hit a ball up the ground that bounded through the open window of the printing shop, and in the succeeding over Mr Mayne hit a ball down the ground that bounded through the open doorway of the Riflemen's Armoury.

MCC won by an innings and 7 runs.

BANDSMAN BOYS PLAYS AN ENCORE
Royal Artillery v Household Brigade

• May 9, 10, 1878 •

THE BIGGEST and best bit of batting by the gunners was Bandsman Boys' 52, an innings that included a truly fine on-drive for five and an innings that won him the applause of the whole HB eleven and of the umpires.

Guarding the Armoury door after the ball has bounded.

v England

• May 14, 15, 1877 •

THE REVIVAL of this match, first played in 1792, created some interest among the London cricketing public; but wretched wet weather on the first day discounted all that, broke up the wickets, and knocked the second day's play into cocked hats, one eleven being out for 36 runs, the other for 26, a 10 being the only double-figure score made in their second innings by those 22 men – some of them the finest bats in England.

The MCC team was an especially strong batting team; but on the soft wickets they could do but little. Although five of them made double figures in their first innings, Mr Russel's 24 was the highest score and the lot were out for 114, Watson's slows having seven wickets (three bowled) for 39 runs. Then, at 5.30, England batted until play ceased for the day. Barlow (in with the score at 14) was not out 32 – a real good bit of batting, played under great difficulties, his

fine forward play smothering danger balls, delighting all who admire science v slogging.

On the Tuesday it rained hard up to ten o'clock, making the wickets as pasty as an uncooked pudding crust. After ten a clear sky, a bright sun, and a keen, health-blowing air formed an enjoyable contrast to Monday's gloom and wet; but the top of the ground dried rapidly, the cut-up wickets played the more falsely the more they were played on. Barlow was out at 88, his 37 being a really finely played innings. The lot were out for 100.

Then came the two memorable short-time innings. In 70 minutes MCC were all out for 36, Mr Ridley's 7 being top score. This was a queer innings, but a queerer remained to be played, for in another 70 minutes the England men were all out for 26, their highest score being 10 by Mr Gilbert, who was 62 minutes at wickets making these 10 runs. When only 12 runs had been scored, six wickets had fallen, William Mycroft having then bowled eight overs for 4 runs and six wickets. Mycroft had been helped by some clinking good fielding, but he bowled well and MCC and G won the match by 24 runs.

MCC and Ground: A. N. Hornby Esq., W. G. Grace Esq., F. Penn Esq., A. W. Ridley Esq., C. E. Green Esq., J. S. Russel Esq., T. S. Pearson Esq., F. Wyld, C. F. Buller Esq., F. Morley and W. Mycroft.

England: G. F. Grace Esq., W. Gilbert Esq., R. G. Barlow, Arthur Shrewsbury, Ephraim Lockwood, William Oscroft, William Barnes, R. Fillery, A. Watson, George Pinder and John Tye.

v Fifteen Canadians

• June 10, 1880 •

IF 50 CANADIANS of the calibre of this fifteen had been brought into the field it is possible, even probable, that MCC would still have been victorious, so miserable was the display made by the visitors. H. Lemmon, who scored 14 not out, and G. F. Hall, 13, were the only two who managed to reach double figures, while no less than six of the Canadians figured with "a pair of them". The hat-trick was twice accomplished in this match – by Morley in the first innings and by Shaw in the second. There was absolutely nothing either in the batting, bowling or fielding of the visitors calling for praise.

MCC and Ground: 192; **Fifteen Canadians**: (14 batted) 33 and 36.

MCC v Canadians • July 31, August 2, 1954
Canadians won by 13 runs. The first game played at Lord's by an official Canadian side coincided with the last match there of the former England captain, G. O. Allen. From first to last the cricket provided rich entertainment which culminated in considerable excitement. MCC, needing 225 to win in two hours and a quarter, went for the runs but lost their last wicket with five minutes remaining.

. . .

Middlesex v Canadians • September 1, 2, 1954
Canadians won by 3 runs. They wound up the tour with a colourful match in which they gained a narrow victory with only a few minutes to spare. Percival, 73 in the first innings, and Trestrail, 100 with sixteen fours in the second, shone most with the bat for the Canadians, and Christen showed himself a fast bowler of distinct merit with match figures of nine for 151. Middlesex contributed to entertaining cricket by spirited hitting.

A man of means

  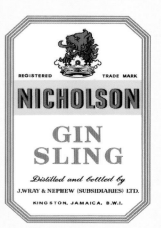

Mothers' ruin, Lord's salvation. Managing director William Nicholson kept "the old ground" safe from the developers.

Mr William Nicholson, DL, JP, of Basing Park, Hants, a trustee of Lord's Cricket Ground, and one of the oldest members of the MCC, died at 2 South Audley Street, London, on July 25, 1909. He was in the Harrow eleven for three seasons, commencing in 1841, and captain in his last. He became a member of the MCC in 1845, and appeared for the Gentlemen against the Players from 1846 to 1858.

Great as Mr Nicholson's skill as a player undoubtedly was, it is probable that he will always be best remembered for the unstinted support he was ever ready to accord the game. When the fate of Lord's was almost in the balance, before the sudden increase of wealth from Eton and Harrow and University matches, Mr Nicholson stood in the gap, and after all England had been drawn for subscriptions to save the ground – for few escaped Mr Roger Kynaston and his red book – he advanced the money as mortgage on a security which the outside public would not take. Little was said about it, as men who do such things do not talk about them, but there is little doubt he saved Lord's from the builders. The celebrated Mr William Ward did a similar thing many years before. He drew a cheque for £5,000, and gave it to Lord for the lease, and as it happened this turned out a good investment, as indeed did Mr Nicholson's mortgage also, though he ran the risk for the love of cricket, and the sum advanced was a large one – a very long way into five figures. This action on his part should cause his name always to be gratefully remembered, not only by members of the Marylebone Club but by all English cricketers in whatever part of the world they may be domiciled. His generosity enabled the old club to purchase the freehold of Lord's; but for him the ground might have been built over and the MCC, the recognised head of the game, have been rendered homeless. In 1879 Mr Nicholson was elected to the presidency of the club. His portrait can be seen in the large picture published in 1908 entitled "Eton v Harrow".

v 22 Colts of England and a Captain

• May 9, 10, 11, 1881 •

THE MCC TEAM for this annual match, though strong in bowling, was comparatively weak in the batting department and this circumstance, coupled with the fact that the bowling of the Colts was remarkably good, will account for the small score of 64 as a total for the club's first innings. By the time the stumps were drawn on the second day, the Colts had scored 101 out of 128 required to win, and had still sixteen wickets to fall, and it certainly looked any odds on the club being beaten easily. But on the morrow a sample of sensational bowling by Morley and Shaw pulled the match out of the fire and the MCC's eleven were the victors by 5 runs. So marvellously successful was the bowling of Morley and Shaw, but particularly of Morley, that sixteen wickets fell for 21 runs, four going with the total at 101, five at 120 and four at 121.

MCC and Ground: 64 (W. Barnes 18; J. H. Richards, *Surrey*, 3–9, J. Woott, *Kent*, 3–28, W. Attewell, *Notts*, 3–11) and 203 (W. Hearn 56, A. Shaw 49 not out; E. Burdett, *Leics*, 3–14, S. Talboy, *Warw*, 3–16).

Colts of England: 140 (F. Butler, *Notts*, 47; Shaw 10–54, F. Morley 5–33, Barnes 5–34) and 122 (Butler 34; Shaw 6–54, Morley 13–37).

v Kent

• May 25, 26, 1882 •

ON THE SECOND morning, bright sunshine on the wet wicket caused it to play very falsely, and after the club men were out for a score of 92, or 11 behind, an extraordinary collapse of the Kent batting ensued. Not one of the side reached double figures, and twice in that very brief innings of 33 two batsmen were out with consecutive balls. Rylott and Woof took all the Kent

wickets in both innings. Each bowler was credited with ten, and though Woof's trundling in the second innings (six for 14) was the most successful bit of bowling in the match, Rylott's, on the whole, came out a trifle the best.

	Overs	Mdns	Runs	Wkts
Rylott	48.3	27	48	10
Woof	47.3	22	57	10

MCC won by nine wickets.

A PARTNERSHIP PRODUCING 454 RUNS!

MCC and Ground v Leicestershire

• June 1, 2, 1882 •

THE WHOLE of the interest in this match centred in the extraordinary batting performances of Barnes and Midwinter, whose long partnership left all previous records of the kind far behind. The longest stand ever before made was that by Messrs G. F. Grace and I. D. Walker, for the Gentlemen of the South v the Gentlemen of the North at Beeston, Nottinghamshire in 1870, who scored 288 while they were together (Mr Grace 189, Mr Walker 179). Barnes went in with the score at 1 for the first wicket; he was joined by Midwinter at 19 for two wickets at about ten minutes past four. When play ceased for the day at seven o'clock they were still together, the total being 283, Barnes 146 not out, Midwinter 120 not out. Up to that time they had scored at the rate of nearly 100 runs per hour. Midwinter had not given a single chance and his score included a splendid square-leg hit for six, the

MIDWINTER

ball bounding from the roof of the Grand Stand clean out of the ground. Barnes narrowly escaped stumping when he had scored about 20, gave a somewhat hard chance to point when he had made 110, and another to the bowler when his score stood at 126; he hit a big on-drive for six past the new dining pavilion.

The game was continued at 11.40 on the Friday and at the luncheon interval Barnes and Midwinter were still in, the former having made 264 and the latter 186. On resuming, a very few minutes' play sufficed to bring the longest stand on record to an end, Barnes being caught at mid-off for 266. Only one more run was added before Midwinter was caught at extra cover point. The pair were at the wickets within a few minutes of five and a half hours, scoring at the rate of more than 80 runs per hour and raising the score from 19 for two to 473 for three.

Barnes' previous best score was 143 for Nottinghamshire v Gloucestershire at Cheltenham in 1880, and his 266 is the second-highest score at Lord's, Mr Ward's 278 in 1820 being the biggest innings on the old ground. When little more than a boy, Midwinter played an innings of 256 at Bendigo, Sandhurst, Victoria, but his 187 is the highest score he has made in England. He gave one chance when he had made 130, and Barnes also had another life on the Friday.

George Pickering Harrison, known familiarly as "Shoey", an abbreviation of his trade as shoemaker, was a typical Yorkshireman of the old school. He came to the front when first given a trial in 1883, and his career ended almost as suddenly in 1892 from the effects of injury. A right-handed fast bowler, he appeared for Colts of the North at Lord's and clean bowled nine Colts of the South – five of them in six balls – at the low cost of 14 runs. When accepting the invitation, he had asked Mr Henry Perkins, the MCC Secretary, to meet him at King's Cross as he had never been to London. [1941]

v Gentlemen of Philadelphia

• June 16, 17, 1884 •

THE GENTLEMEN of Philadelphia naturally looked forward to this match with the keenest interest. All were anxious to be seen at their best at the headquarters of cricket, and all felt that with Charles Newhall, their principal fast bowler, unable to help them, the chances of success against the first-class team selected to oppose them were but small. In choosing their eleven the Marylebone Club had not lightly estimated the capabilities of the visitors. It is possible that the knowledge that they were entering on the most important engagement of the tour at a

disadvantage may have militated against their success, but to whatever cause their failure may be ascribed, the fact remains that on this occasion the Americans were seen to less advantage in all departments of the game than on any other during their stay on this side of the Atlantic. Their fielding, though excellent at times, was often slovenly and slow; the ball was frequently off the wicket on the leg side; and the pitch was, in the case of most of the bowlers, considerably too short. Their first score of 174 was a fair performance, all things considered, but the dismissal of the whole side on a good wicket for 61 runs in the second innings was a long way their poorest exhibition in this country, and one for which it is impossible to find a satisfactory excuse.

The 1884 Philadelphians won eight, lost five and drew five of their matches against teams restricted to Gentlemen.
Back (l-r): John B. Thayer jun., William Brockie jun., Edward W. Clark jun., Charles A. Newhall, Howard MacNutt, J. Allison Scott, William C. Lowry. Front: William C. Morgan jun., Robert S. Newhall (captain), Francis E. Brewster, Hazen Brown, Sutherland Law, David P. Stoever, T. Robins jun. (scorer and scribe).

The Gentlemen of the MCC won by an innings and 171 runs. This was the most crushing reverse the Gentlemen of Philadelphia sustained during their sojourn in the old country, and the only occasion on which they were defeated in a single innings.

v Cambridge University

• June 23, 24, 1884 •

THE VICTORY of the MCC was the triumph of one man, and the splendid all-round cricket played by Wilfred Flowers, the Nottingham professional, will be found to have few parallels in the history of the game. The University secured first innings, but mainly through the extraordinarily successful bowling of Flowers, who sent down 51 overs for 20 runs and six wickets, the whole side were dismissed for 74. Up to the time Flowers commenced his very brilliant innings at 4.30, only 115 runs had been scored in three and a half hours, and thirteen wickets had fallen. But owing to the remarkable freedom with which Flowers hit all the bowling, no fewer than 179 runs were put on in the space of two and a half hours for the loss of six wickets. Flowers actually scored 122 while his various partners made 35. He was out with the MCC total at 201 and his magnificent innings – made without a chance until he had scored his hundred – consisted of eighteen fours, mostly hard drives, five threes, eight twos and nineteen singles. Cambridge went in for the second time 155 runs to the bad, and Flowers wound up his splendid work by taking eight of the eleven wickets at a cost of 60 runs. Twelve a side batted, though only eleven fielded.

Secretary R. A. Fitzgerald nicknamed the MCC professionals "the Professors". William Gunn, Walter Price, William Attewell, Billy Barnes, Wilfred Flowers and Mordecai Sherwin, Notts men all, swap bat and ball for board and gown.

v Yorkshire – A Record

• June 1, 2, 1885 •

A PERFORMANCE which has never been equalled in a first-class match was accomplished by Gunn (left) and Barnes (right) on the second day. Except for the remarkable bowling of Attewell, who sent down 42 overs (31 maidens) for 16 runs and five wickets, the opening day's cricket was uneventful. The MCC, whose team included six members of the Notts eleven, began the batting at noon and were all out at four o'clock for 148. Yorkshire were all dismissed before 6.30, a follow-on being saved by a single run. Next day Gunn and Barnes became partners at about a quarter to one, with the score at 72 for three wickets, and when they were separated at seven minutes after six the total stood at 402. Thus while they were together they actually put on 330 runs. Deducting the interval for luncheon, Gunn and Barnes were batting together on Tuesday for as nearly as possible four hours and 40 minutes, and during that time seven bowlers were tried against them. Gunn hit two sixes in his innings of 203 – one of them a tremendous on-drive over the Grand Stand and out of the ground – one five, twenty fours, eight threes, 24 twos and 34 singles, and

---

HIGHEST INNINGS EVER SCORED ON LORD'S GROUND

v Norfolk

• July 24, 25, 1885 •

N ORFOLK had first innings, the brothers L. K. and C. J. E. Jarvis commencing the batting. Both played carefully at starting, only 10 runs being made in the first twenty minutes; but after this the rate of scoring increased and they treated all the bowlers pretty much alike. Their partnership of 241 lasted two hours and 45 minutes, and the bowling was fifteen times changed. When stumps were drawn for the day, the score stood at 527 for four. This historical innings was brought to a close at ten minutes to two next day when Rudd, the last man, was stumped. The MCC commenced batting directly after luncheon and from the start runs were put on very rapidly. When the match, limited to two days, was abandoned as a draw, 992 runs had been scored for the loss of sixteen wickets, giving an average of exactly 62 runs per wicket.

Norfolk

L. K. Jarvis Esq.	c Hearn b Price	181
C. J. E. Jarvis Esq.	c Hearn b Smith	130
Hansell	c Hay b C. Wilson	136
Rev. C. L. Kennaway	c Wheeler b Mycroft	39
C. H. Morton Esq.	c Wheeler b Mycroft	16
H. Birkbeck Esq.	not out	89
Rev. A. P. Wickham	c Mycroft b Fothergill	0
J. "Blunt" Esq.	b Fothergill	2
F. E. Patteson Esq.	st Wheeler b C. Wilson	31
A. M. Jee Esq.	c Smith b Mycroft	14
Rudd	st Wheeler b C. Wilson	19
Extras	(b 26, l-b 12)	38
		695

MCC bowling	Overs	Mdns	Runs	Wkts
W. Mycroft	91	41	154	3
A. J. Fothergill	57	20	117	2
S. J. Wilson Esq.	3	0	7	0
C. Wilson Esq.	60.3	20	129	3
"C. Smith" Esq.	39	3	56	1
G. Hay	34	7	87	0
F. Price	14	2	49	1
J. Turner Esq.	6	1	27	0
J. Wheeler	8	1	31	0

MCC and Ground: 297–6 (C. R. Seymour Esq. 75, Turner 86; Morton 3–62, C. J. E. Jarvis 3–97).

Barnes' score of 140 was made up of eleven fours, nine threes, fifteen twos and 39 singles. As may be readily supposed, this extraordinary hitting was not unaccompanied by good fortune. Wednesday being Derby Day, the match was limited to two days and was left drawn.

v Sussex

• May 20, 21, 1886 •

A GAIN WERE THE MCC unlucky in their weather as on the opening day rain prevented any play between ten minutes past one and three o'clock. On the second day, however,

the state of the ground was even worse and the match came to a surprisingly rapid conclusion. The remainder of the Sussex second innings lasted only 50 minutes, the side being all out for the paltry total of 48. Wootton, in the two innings, took twelve wickets at the cost of only 62 runs. Although the club was left with but 104 runs to get, the task proved far too great, and the batting broke down completely before the bowling of the brothers Hide, who, in the course of an hour and a half, got rid of the whole ten wickets for 44, not a single batsman reaching double figures. Jesse Hide again had a wonderful analysis and in the two innings he obtained twelve wickets for 60 runs. His brother, Arthur, in the whole match, took six wickets for 15 runs.

MCC and Ground v England

• June 13, 14, 15, 1887 •

IT WAS in every way fitting that the MCC should celebrate its centenary on a large scale, and it is not easy to say what better fixture could have been selected for the opening of the week than the Club and Ground against England. The one disadvantage was the fact that the club includes in its ranks so many of the prominent gentlemen of the day that the only amateurs for whom places could be found in the England eleven were Mr W. W. Read and Mr Stoddart. Even at this time Mr Stoddart was up for election to the club, and a few weeks later he could not have been chosen. Both sides were very strong but, as events proved, the MCC Committee would have done much better to have left out one of the batsmen from their side and played either Attewell or Wootton. The want of another good bowler was sadly felt before the game came to an end.

One professional, the other amateur, their destinies linked by more than their golden hours together in June 1887. Arthur Shrewsbury (left) and Andrew Stoddart both took teams to Australia and captained England in Tests. Each died by his own hand.

Winning the toss, the MCC went in first in magnificent weather and, as the wicket was in capital condition, there seemed every prospect of some high scoring. Lohmann, however, bowling from the Pavilion end, found a spot to help him and the early play was disastrous. Lohmann took six wickets for 62 runs – a very fine performance. Shrewsbury and Mr Stoddart commenced England's innings at 25 minutes to five, and when seven o'clock came they were still together, the amateur being not out 111, Shrewsbury not out 70, and the total 196 for no wicket. Both batsmen played magnificently but Mr Stoddart had one great piece of good fortune. When he had scored 13, and the total was 32, he drove a ball back to Mr Grace, who half-stopped it and, having taken all the

force out of the hit, put it up to mid-off. Under ordinary circumstances Mr Webbe would have had a certain catch but, with a strong sun shining full in his eyes, he lost sight of the ball, which hit his face and fell to the ground.

On the second morning the two batsmen resumed their innings and were not separated until the score had reached 266, only 17 runs short of the great score made by Messrs W. G. Grace and Cooper for the first wicket at Kennington Oval in 1869. Mr Stoddart was first out, having scored in three hours and 40 minutes, 151 – the highest innings he has ever played in a first-class match. With such an extraordinary start, the other England batsmen had a very easy task and it was not until ten minutes to six that the innings

closed, the total being 514 – the largest score ever made at Lord's in a match of first-rate importance. Mr Hornby did not manage his bowlers with so much judgment as might have been expected.

Wanting no fewer than 339 runs to save a single-innings defeat, the MCC had 50 minutes' batting before the drawing of stumps and lost Mr Webbe's wicket for 58 runs. On the Wednesday, play was resumed at twenty minutes to twelve, and just after two o'clock the MCC were all out for 222, England winning the match by an innings and 117 runs. Some capital batting was shown by Barnes and Flowers, who hit the score from 116 to 190.

MCC and Ground: Mr W. G. Grace, Mr A. N. Hornby, W. Barnes, Mr A. J. Webbe, W. Gunn, G. G. Hearne, Mr J. G. Walker, Hon. M. B. Hawke, W. Flowers, J. T. Rawlin and M. Sherwin. *Scores*: 175 (Gunn 61; Lohmann 6–62) and 222 (Grace 45, Barnes 53, Flowers 43; Briggs 4–77, Bates 5–46).

England: A. Shrewsbury, Mr A. E. Stoddart, R. G. Barlow, M. Read, Mr W. W. Read, W. Bates, G. Ulyett, L. Hall, J. Briggs, G. Lohmann and R. Pilling. *Score*: 514 (Shrewsbury 152, Stoddart 151, W. W. Read 74, Ulyett 46; Barnes 6–126).

Mr John Somerville Russel was born at Edinburgh in 1849 and his boyhood was spent in his native city, his early education being received at the Royal High School. In July 1870 he made his first appearance at Lord's, assisting The North of Ireland against MCC, though what qualification he possessed to figure on the side of the former is hard to understand. He was an excellent batsman when at his best. His style was not attractive, but his on-drives were hard and all along the ground, and his late cuts sharp and well-timed. [1903]

v Lancashire

• July 18, 19, 1887 •

THERE WAS some sensational cricket on the Tuesday, the match, which at lunch time looked likely to run well into the third day, being all over at a quarter to six. Mr Grace had played very fine cricket and was not out 72 at lunch, the total being 116 for one wicket. A remarkable collapse afterwards was mainly due to the bowling of Watson, who sent down nineteen overs and three balls, fifteen maidens, for 10 runs and six wickets, all bowled. In as nearly as possible an hour, the nine outstanding wickets were taken for the addition of 26 runs. Lancashire were set only 82 runs to win, but the ground had broken up a good deal and the task proved very difficult. Indeed, had the MCC wicket-keeper [Wheeler] been fully efficient, it is quite likely that the county would have suffered defeat. Instead, they managed to secure a victory by two wickets.

This was 42-year-old John Wheeler's last first-class match; he remained on the Lord's groundstaff for another 21 years.

v Wiltshire

• August 1888 •

THIS MATCH was remarkable inasmuch as it produced the highest total, 735, ever obtained on Lord's ground. The next best was 695 by Norfolk against MCC in 1885. On the opening day the club scored 514 with only two men out.

MCC: 735 (Mr J. S. Russel 54 retired hurt, Mr E. Sainsbury 180, Mr D. D. Pontifex 54, Mr F. G. J. Ford 91, Mr H. Brougham 117, W. Flowers 88, extras 71).

Wiltshire: 130 (Mr F. C. Batson 38; Ford 5 wkts, Flowers 5 wkts) and 60–2.

Doubly Painful

MR HARRY Thompson Arnall-Thompson, whilst playing Shacklock's bowling in the Leicestershire v MCC and Ground match at Lord's in 1889, had a painful and curious experience. The ball flew off the edge of his bat on to his eyebrow and rebounded to the bowler. Arnall-Thompson was momentarily stunned, and as the blood flowed freely suggested he should retire and finish his innings later. It was then gently broken to him that he was out, caught and bowled. [1917]

v Sussex

• May 12, 13, 1890 •

THE RAIN in the latter portion of the previous week and during the early part of Monday had so thoroughly saturated the ground that it seemed extremely likely the commencement of this fixture would have to be postponed. However, on Monday afternoon the weather cleared up and, though it was found impossible to start until twenty minutes to four, so much progress was made that the MCC completed an innings of 57 and Sussex were all dismissed for 41. Jesse Hide created something like a sensation by taking four MCC wickets – those of Flowers, Mr Ford, Mr Wright and Mr Russel – in one [four-ball] over. On Tuesday the wicket proved as difficult as before, and the bowlers again had matters their own way. Hide and Mr C. A. Smith dismissed the MCC in the second innings for 36 and then Attewell and Martin got rid of six Sussex men before the county could make the 53 required to win. The whole match occupied barely four hours; only two men made double figures and thirteen batsmen failed to score at all. Hide and Attewell each took nine wickets at around 4 apiece, but Mr Smith, who obtained seven wickets for 16 runs, did absolutely the best performance in the match.

v Sussex

• May 2, 1894 •

THE SEASON at Lord's opened in rather sensational fashion, the Marylebone Club's match with Sussex being commenced and finished in a single day. In order to secure a good attendance at the annual dinner of the MCC, it was decided to follow the precedent of 1893 and begin the game on Wednesday, and that the public were anxious to see the cricket was evidenced by the large company that assembled despite the cold and cheerless weather prevailing. Unfortunately the game was played on a soft, treacherous wicket, which favoured the bowlers, and only one batsman met with anything like success. The ball beat the bat completely throughout, as may be judged from the fact that the cricket did not begin until five minutes past twelve and yet was all over by twenty minutes past five, by which time the MCC had won in a single innings with 2 runs to spare.

Sussex: 42 (Mr W. Newham 14; J. T. Hearne 3–27, F. Martin 7–12) and 59 (R. Lowe 14 not out; Martin 4–17, W. Mead 6–39).

MCC and Ground: 103 (Mr A. E. Stoddart 44; F. Parris 6–44, F. W. Tate 4–48).

v Cambridge University

• June 25, 26, 27, 1896 •

AN ASTONISHING and altogether unparalleled triumph was gained by the University eleven, Cambridge actually obtaining the 507 runs set them to win, with three wickets to spare. As all previous attempts to make 400 under similar circumstances had failed, the Cambridge men are to be heartily congratulated upon what must rank as one of the most remarkable performances on record. On Saturday, Druce and Wilson, who had come together the previous evening at 38 for two, raised the total to 280 and this stand made the victory possible. The rest of the innings was noteworthy for the brilliancy exhibited by Marriott and Bray, who became partners when 118 runs were required and hit them off in 75 minutes. In the three days, 1,235 runs were scored for 36 wickets.

MCC and Ground: 134 (H. Carpenter 37; Mr H. Gray 5–62, Mr E. B. Shine 4–48) and 483 (Carpenter 161, Mr F. A. Phillips 74, Mr R. W. Nicholls 59; Mr H. H. Marriott 4–60).

Cambridge University: 111 (Mr W.G. Grace, jun. 26; F. Martin 4–32, A. E. Trott 6–59) and 507–7 (Mr N. F. Druce 146, Mr C. E. M. Wilson 82, Marriott 146 not out; Martin 3–109).

v Sussex

• May 13, 14, 15, 1897 •

WHEN RANJITSINHJI eclipsed all his previous performances in first-class cricket by scoring a superb innings of 260 for Sussex against the MCC, a victory for the club seemed almost out of the question, and yet, thanks to their careless fielding in the final stage, the county eleven were actually beaten by 46 runs after the MCC had followed on 152 in arrear. It was a match of great scoring throughout, though of course Ranjitsinhji's innings overshadowed everything else. While his leg-placing was as remarkable as ever, his driving was far more powerful than usual, and the fact that he hit a six, 36 fours, fourteen threes and seventeen twos, and kept up an average of about 60 an hour from his own bat, sufficiently indicates the general character of his cricket.

Sussex: 418 (K. S. Ranjitsinhji 260, Mr W. L. Murdoch 51; J. T. Hearne 4–104, G. Davidson 3–65) and 137 (E. H. Killick 48; Davidson 5–37).

MCC and Ground: 266 (Mr M. R. Jardine 52; C. Bland 6–105) and 335 (W. Chatterton 79; Bland 3–113, F. Parris 3–39).

"We may never see his like again," *Wisden* editor Sydney Southerton wrote of Ranji (left), "for he burst on the cricket horizon at the start of what has been described as its most brilliant era, when there existed scope for introducing new ideas and methods." *Wisden* welcomed Wilfred Rhodes by proclaiming that "a first-rate slow bowler is a pearl of price not often found".

v Yorkshire

• May 12, 13, 14, 1898 •

ALTHOUGH THE MCC were stronger at all points than when they met and defeated Lancashire, they suffered a reverse at the hands of Yorkshire. The match will be long remembered as that in which Wilfred Rhodes, of Kirkheaton, made his first appearance in important cricket. Like the previous fixtures at Lord's, the game suffered from bad weather, and the bowlers, more or less, always held the upper hand. Heavy rain during the night destroyed any chance the MCC might have had of pulling the match out of the fire on the third day, Jackson and Rhodes, in three-quarters of an hour, taking the last six wickets for an additional 24 runs and giving Yorkshire the victory by 99 runs. Rhodes, with the conditions favourable to bowlers, came out of his initial trial in first-class cricket with every credit. With twelve wickets, J. T. Hearne once more accomplished a fine performance.

Yorkshire: 118 (J. T. Brown 46, W. Rhodes 4; J. T. Hearne 8–48) and 185 (E. Wainwright 63, Rhodes 16; J. T. Hearne 4–56, A. E. Trott 6–96).

MCC and Ground: 135 (W. Storer 36; Rhodes 2–39, Wainwright 4–43) and 69 (Mr W. G. Grace 17; Rhodes 4–24, Mr F. S. Jackson 6–45).

v Yorkshire

• May 14, 15, 16, 1900 •

THIS ENGAGEMENT will be best remembered by its result – the solitary defeat sustained by the Yorkshiremen throughout the season. The MCC were very strongly represented and their first innings of 346 gave them a lead of 159. Warner preferred to go in a second time instead of making Yorkshire follow on, and that his policy was the right one was proved by the fact of the club playing a second innings of over 300 and setting the county no fewer than 472 to win. The credit of the triumph was due in the first place to Carpenter, Warner and C. O. H. Sewell (playing under the assumed name of C. L. Lewes), and in the second to J. T. Hearne, the last-named only just failing to take all ten wickets in the county's first innings.

MCC and Ground: 346 (H. Carpenter 125, Mr P. F. Warner 83; W. Rhodes 6–76) and 312 (Mr C. O. H. Sewell 87, Warner 69; Rhodes 3–85, J. T. Brown jun. 3–55).

Yorkshire: 187 (J. T. Brown sen. 67; J. T. Hearne 9–71) and 289 (D. Denton 71; H. Young 6–77).

Orthodox sweeper

Sir Francis Eden Lacey will be remembered chiefly for his work as Secretary of the Marylebone Club. Appointed in 1898 on the retirement of Henry Perkins, he held office for 28 years. A barrister by profession, Mr Lacey used keen perception and business instincts in changing for the good all the easy-going methods obtaining for many years before he accepted the position. Drastic methods were necessary and were forthcoming in no uncertain manner. Under the new regime a strictly business tone prevailed during all matches and any slackness on the part of the employees disappeared. The new broom swept a little too clean perhaps, but in the end the Marylebone Club benefited enormously in having as their executive officer a man so able, so masterful and so painstaking. [1947]

v Oxford University

• June 30, July 1, 1902 •

RESTRICTED AS USUAL to two days, and affected by the Oxonians resting four of their best players in view of the forthcoming game with Cambridge, there was not much interest in this fixture. The one great feature of the first day was Lord Hawke's 107, the first hundred he had ever made at Lord's. He went in with Grace and carried his bat out after a display occupying three hours and a half.

v Oxford University

• June 29, 30, 1903 •

OPPOSED to a fairly strong side of the MCC, the Oxford team, with Evans away and Bomford keeping wicket instead of Findlay, gave a poor account of themselves in the last of their trial matches, and only the fact that, as usual, the fixture was limited to two days saved them from a severe reverse. Extras played an important part in the match, no fewer than 92 byes being given away: 50 by Oxford and 42 by MCC.

v Yorkshire

• May 7, 8, 9, 1906 •

SOME CHARACTERISTIC hitting by Gilbert Jessop, who made 63 out of 94 in 50 minutes, and capital performances by Hardstaff and Wynyard placed the MCC in a happy position during the opening stage when Yorkshire lost five wickets for 100 runs at the end of the day, and on Tuesday, despite Hirst's splendid cricket, the county were left in a minority of 86 on the first innings, and the club batsmen, of whom Jessop again carried off

chief honours, rendered a good account of themselves by making 242 at their second attempt. The famous hitter on this occasion contributed 55 out of 71 in half an hour and, as on the Monday, Hardstaff and Wynyard were responsible for the next largest scores. Set a heavy task – they required 329 – Yorkshire were beaten by 40 runs.

v Cambridge University

• June 30, July 1, 2, 1913 •

PUTTING an extremely moderate eleven in the field against Cambridge, the MCC, who were very short of professional bowling, suffered a decisive defeat by an innings and 152 runs. The University, who scored 189 for three wickets before the end of the first day, increased those figures to 609 for eight wickets before they declared at four o'clock on Tuesday. This score, it may be mentioned, is the highest ever obtained at Lord's, being two in excess of the 607 scored by the MCC against Cambridge in 1902. The feature of the MCC second innings was an admirable 65 by E. M. Dowson, whose reappearance in important cricket, after a long interval, was very welcome.

MCC: 249 (G. Brown 72; Mr E. L. Kidd 4–81) and 208 (Mr E. M. Dowson 65; Mr G. B. Davies 5–25).

Cambridge University: 609–8 dec. (Mr R. B. Lagden 125, Kidd 150, Mr S. H. Saville 77, Hon. F. S. G. Calthorpe 87; Mr G. G. Napier 3–117, Mr P. W. Cobbold 3–92).

v Yorkshire

• May 13, 14, 1914 •

FOLLOWING the example of Kent, Yorkshire also beat the MCC in an innings and with even greater ease, for they had 119 runs to spare at the finish. The first day's play resulted in an innings each being completed, but the MCC fared so deplorably against Booth and Drake that they scored only 39 and had to follow on the next morning against a lead of 253. [J. C. Hubble was top-scorer with 8, and again in the second innings with 62.] Booth had a veritable triumph with the ball, his eleven wickets in the match costing him only 42 runs. Drake ably seconded his colleague, taking eight for 59.

Mr William Findlay was Secretary of MCC from 1926 to 1936, and President in 1951-52. A wicket-keeper and batsman of considerable ability, he captained Eton in 1899 and, going to Oxford, gained his blue in 1901 and the two following years. From 1902 he played irregularly for Lancashire till 1906, helping to win the County Championship in 1904. He began important secretarial duties in 1907, when succeeding C. W. Alcock as Secretary of Surrey. Going to Lord's as assistant to F. E. (later Sir Francis) Lacey in 1919, he became Secretary of MCC in 1926, for which his genial, diplomatic manner and never-failing courtesy suited him admirably. During his term of office at Lord's the new Grand

Lancastrians
William Findlay and
Walter Brearley.

Stand, with the famous "Father Time" weather-vane, was erected. In 1937 he made one of his biggest contributions to cricket legislature when heading a commission appointed by MCC to explore the question of the difficulties of counties taking part in the County Championship and which is always referred to as "The Findlay Commission". [1954]

MCC South African Team
v The Rest of England

• June 22, 23, 24, 1914 •

TO CELEBRATE the centenary of the present Lord's ground, the MCC arranged a special week's cricket. The first match, between the team that won the rubber in South Africa and the Rest of England, was the best that could have been chosen, but there was nothing specially appropriate in the fixture at the end of the week between the Navy and the Army. Unfortunately the big match proved a disappointment. The South African team was sadly handicapped by the loss of Barnes (right), who though present was prevented from playing by a badly strained leg, and to make things worse the side had bad luck with regard to the ground, bowling all through the first day on a perfect wicket and batting after rain had damaged the pitch. Still, bad cricket had something to do with the result, the batsmen who had

done such brilliant things at the Cape being altogether at fault against Hitch's fine bowling. The match, without proving a great attraction, was well patronised and on the second day The King honoured the ground with his presence, being accompanied by The Prince of Wales and Prince Albert. The captains of the two elevens, J. W. H. T. Douglas and C. B. Fry, were presented to him in full view of the crowd. The Rest of England won by an innings and 189 runs.

The Rest of England: 467 (E. Humphreys 111, Mr S. G. Smith 78, Mr C. B. Fry 70, Mr A. P. Day 79; F. E. Woolley 3–93).

MCC South African Team: 94 (C. P. Mead 21; W. Hitch 7–42) and 184 (W. Rhodes 52; Hitch 5–51, Smith 4–39).

In 1914, when he took over 100 wickets, George Geary was picked for his first representative match, the centenary at Lord's, the Rest of England against MCC's South African team. This should have given him his one chance of seeing the great Sydney Barnes bowl, but, when he arrived in the dressing-room, he found Barnes urging the others not to play unless they received more money. Wisden says Barnes was prevented from playing by a strain. [1982]

Spooner, Mr A. W. Ridley, Canon Edward Lyttelton, Sir T. C. O'Brien, Mr G. MacGregor, Mr J. R. Mason, Mr John Shuter, Mr A. J. Webbe, Mr H. K. Foster and the members of the two elevens taking part in the match. Lord Hawke proposed the toast of the evening, "Lord's Cricket Ground and the MCC", and in doing so made a feeling reference to the recent death of Mr A. G. Steel. Mr C. E. Green proposed "The County Cricket Clubs". To this toast Lord Harris and Mr W. G. Grace replied, W. G. when he rose to speak being given an overwhelming reception. The Hon. F. S. Jackson proposed "The Two Centenary Teams", with Mr C. B. Fry responding. The dinner was in every way a memorable gathering.

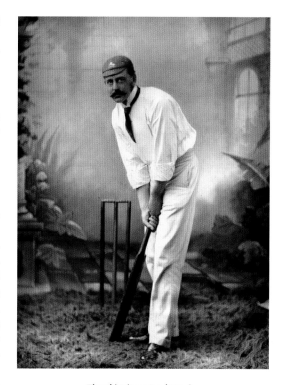

The ubiquitous Lord Harris.

The Centenary Dinner

IN HONOUR of the centenary the MCC gave a dinner on the second evening of the match at the Hotel Cecil. Lord Hawke (above) presided, having on his right hand Prince Albert of Schleswig-Holstein. Never, perhaps, have so many famous cricketers, young and old, been gathered together. To mention only the best known names, the company included Mr W. G. Grace, Lord Harris, The Hon. F. S. Jackson, Mr A. C. MacLaren, Mr A. P. Lucas, Mr R. H.

v Philadelphia Pilgrims

· August 11, 12, 1921 ·

THIS WAS THE CHIEF fixture of the Philadelphians' holiday trip to England. It was, of course, a pleasant game, but the MCC were too strong, winning by an innings and 31 runs. In compliment to the Philadelphians, Lord Harris turned out for the club. It was 53 years since he played his first match at Lord's – for Eton v Harrow in 1868.

v Oxford University

· June 21, 23, 24, 1930 ·

TWO REMARKABLE spells of bowling by Peebles and some brilliant batting by A. M. Crawley were the dominating factors in Oxford's victory by seven wickets. Ineffective at the Nursery wicket in Marylebone's first innings, Peebles, with the score at 167 for five wickets, changed over to the Pavilion end and from there, in six overs and a ball, dismissed five batsmen, only 13 runs meanwhile being obtained off him. Even more remarkable was his performance in the second innings. On this occasion, following upon the tea

100 years at Lord's

Another retirement at Lord's was that of R. T. (Dick) Gaby, the club superintendent, after serving MCC for 44 years. The family association began in 1873 and will not yet be broken as his brother, Joe, who has been at Lord's 51 years, continues. Their father, also Dick, was lawn tennis professional there, and later chief dressing-room attendant before he finally took charge of one of the scoreboards. He retired in 1936 after 66 years with MCC. Also on the groundstaff were two other brothers, Charles and George, but both were killed while on active service in the First World War. MCC commemorated the Gabys' century with a reception at which Mr Aidan Crawley, President, presented a silver salver to each of the Gaby brothers bearing the MCC monogram and inscribed: In appreciation of the Gaby family – 1873–1973. [1974]

Mr James Cannon, for 65 years with MCC at Lord's, started as a ball-boy for the tennis courts when twelve and held the horses for members when they visited the ground. Gradually he climbed the ladder, becoming boot-boy in the cricket dressing-rooms, and then went into the office where for many years he was chief clerk. A small, popular figure, "Jimmy" Cannon was given the title "King of Lord's" by Sir Pelham Warner. A keen gardener, he was recognised by hundreds of people by his straw hat and buttonhole of sweet-peas, rose or carnation. On his retirement in 1944 he was elected an honorary member of MCC. [1950]

Dick Gaby (left), father of R. T. ("Young Dick") and G. M. ("Joe"), with James Cannon. According to William Findlay, "Cannon never failed to put his finger on any point which might by chance have been overlooked in preparation for a Test match." His retirement, Sir Pelham Warner noted, "did not pass unnoticed even in such far-distant places as Bagdad, Basra and Calcutta".

interval taken with the score at 228 for five wickets, he went on – again at the Pavilion end – and in two overs took four wickets, all clean bowled, for a single run.

v Cambridge University

• July 1, 3, 4, 1933 •

ALL THINGS CONSIDERED, Cambridge put up a very good show and at one time looked to have an excellent chance of winning, but, handicapped by the absence of Farnes after the first day, they suffered defeat by seven wickets. When the club went in to get 208 to win, three wickets fell for 49. Then the Nawab of Pataudi and Hendren hit off the remaining runs in a brilliant unfinished partnership that realised 164 in an hour and three-quarters. The Indian revealed his best form, getting his runs with effortless ease. A misunderstanding between the scorer and the umpires resulted in the game continuing after the winning hit had been made, Pataudi adding 5 runs to his score.

v Surrey

• May, 2, 3, 4, 1934 •

E. R. T. HOLMES, the new Surrey captain, had the satisfaction of leading his side to victory in the opening match of the season at Lord's, by an innings and 173 runs. He took a big share in this success by a remarkable piece of bowling on the first afternoon. Going on a second time at 127, he sent down three overs and four balls and obtained the last six club wickets at a cost of only 7 runs. He deceived batsmen by his pace off lifeless turf. Very different cricket was seen when Surrey went in. Hobbs batted in his own masterly style for an hour and a half, and on the second morning the moderate club bowling was mastered. Altogether Surrey batted five hours 50 minutes for their 558 runs.

v Yorkshire

• May 1, 3, 4, 1937 •

MCC WON by 25 runs with twenty minutes to spare. It was their first victory over the county for 30 years. Yorkshire, in making such a close finish after being set to get 406 to win, were largely indebted to Hutton, who stayed in for all but the last fifteen minutes of an innings that lasted over five hours. When he left, his side were within 49 runs of victory but the one remaining wicket fell quickly. Hutton's defence was superb, and some of his off-driving was beautifully done. Compton, Wyatt, Robins and Edrich all batted well for MCC, and throughout the game the cricket was full of enterprise and never lacked interest.

The MCC's 150th Anniversary

TO COMMEMORATE the 150th anniversary of the Marylebone Cricket Club, a week's representative cricket was arranged at headquarters. The counties readily agreed to the release of some of their best players so that the event could be celebrated in a fitting way. Although the weather was most unfavourable on the opening day, and the difficulties of travelling during the bus strike must have kept many people away, the number of persons paying for admission during the six days [May 22–28, 1937] was 27,383. There were 13,444 people at the North v South game, which began on Saturday, and 13,939 at the match between the MCC Australian XI and the Rest of England. Gover's ten wickets for 12 runs apiece for the Rest represented the best bowling during the week of high-class and thoroughly interesting cricket.

A dinner in celebration of the anniversary was held at the Savoy Hotel, London, on July 15, at which over four hundred were present.

v Yorkshire

• April 30, May 2, 3, 1938 •

DRAWN. A strange incident, probably without parallel, caused lively discussion at headquarters on the opening day of the season. The announcements board bore a notice that MCC would bat, but this was contradicted and an official statement explained that "The delay in starting the match was due to a disagreement regarding the validity of the first toss won by the MCC. As a result the captains agreed to toss again, on which occasion Yorkshire won." The first toss was made in the dressing-room, the second in front of the Pavilion.

v Surrey

• May 2, 3, 1951 •

SURREY WON by an innings and 8 runs. Bowlers made the most of a rain-affected pitch, Laker, with off-breaks, taking in the match ten wickets for 34. MCC made no recovery from losing four wickets for 12, and only a stand of 33 between Robertson and Insole prevented Alec Bedser

MCC men in war and peace

Good cricketer though he was, Ronny Aird will always be chiefly remembered for his work at Lord's, which covered first to last 60 years. Appointed assistant-secretary in 1926 when William Findlay was promoted to Secretary, he continued to serve under Colonel Rait Kerr and himself succeeded as Secretary in 1952. He retired in 1962, but was President in 1968-69 and a trustee from 1971 to 1983, when he became a life vice-president, remaining active on the Committee almost to the end. Lord Cornwallis, who as an ex-President and a trustee was in a position to know, said of him in 1950, "No one realises how much that man has done for Lord's."

Colonel Rait Kerr and Ronny Aird.

He was a man of wide and varied talents and interests, so varied that few of his friends can have been aware of them all, just as few knew the details of his war record. They knew, of course, that he had been a major in the Royal Tank Regiment, that he had won the Military Cross in the desert and been wounded. They did not know that he had been in almost a record number of tanks that were totally destroyed or that twice he had been the only survivor; that he had been wounded twice, once severely, and that on both these occasions his one thought had been to get back to active service as soon as possible. Few of his friends can have known the full story, but none will be surprised when he hears it. [1987]

. . .

It was never Aird's way to seek the limelight. He was not responsible for any startling reforms or innovations. But as one of the papers said after his death, "Lord's was never a happier place than during his secretaryship." There was an aura of happiness and it was a joy just to be there, whatever the occasion: all the staff in the Pavilion, the tennis court or elsewhere greeted one as an old friend. The atmosphere was typical of Aird himself and his greatness lay rather in what he was than in what he did. One could not imagine him ever being involved in rows or unpleasantness. He was imperturbable.

Colonel Rowan Scrope Rait Kerr, CBE, was Secretary of MCC from 1936 to 1952. In 1947, he re-drafted the Laws of Cricket, upon which subject he was an authority, and three years later he published a guide to the Laws. At the time of his death in 1961, aged 69, he was chairman of the MCC special committee enquiring into the future of the first-class game. Rait Kerr served in the Royal Engineers in the First World War, being awarded the DSO and the MC, and in the Second World War was chairman of the War Office Selection Board. [1962]

and Laker bringing about a complete rout. Surrey held a strong position when passing 50 with one man out, but they collapsed against the flighted off-breaks of Knott, who finished with seven for 69. Before the first day ended, Surrey got down four MCC wickets for 32; Laker and Surridge finished the game in 55 minutes next morning.

v Essex

• May 9, 10, 11, 1951 •

DRAWN. After the loss of the first day through rain, Essex sent in MCC and, helped by indifferent batting, dismissed them for 75 before lunch. In turn the county fared badly against the off-breaks of Laker who, though hit for two sixes by R. Smith, returned remarkable figures of 25–11–36–7.

v Surrey

• May 4, 5, 6, 1955 •

SURREY WON by seven wickets. The experimental smaller ball was again employed, but as in the previous game, against Yorkshire, bowlers thought it made little difference to their effectiveness. The spin bowlers, particularly Laker and Lock, took their opportunities on damp turf and both owed a good deal to smart catching. On the last day Wardle pulled a ball from Bedser over the Tavern scorebox and out into the road, but Laker took the four remaining MCC wickets for 8 runs out of 27, and Surrey, racing the rain, hit off the 54 runs wanted in an hour. Laker had match figures of eleven for 67.

During the 1955 season a smaller ball was tried in 25 non-competitive first-class matches. Most bowlers showed no enthusiasm for it, and the experiment was shelved.

v Cambridge University

• June 24, 25, 26, 1964 •

MCC WON by seven wickets after sending their opponents in to bat. Bailey, the captain, batted steadily for MCC, and stands of 114 between him and Mushtaq (56) and 58 with D'Oliveira (twelve fours in 54), followed by hard-hitting from Murray, led to a declaration 30 runs ahead at 308 for six. The University seemed destined for early defeat when losing seven men for 120, but Kerslake joined Griffith in an unfinished partnership of 88. So MCC needed 179 to win, and D'Oliveira (62 not out) and Hill (four sixes, five fours, 63 not out) carried them to success by adding 103 in 45 minutes without being parted.

Mushtaq Mohammad and Basil D'Oliveira were qualifying for Northamptonshire and Worcestershire respectively, and unable to play in first-team county competitions.

v Yorkshire

• April 26, 28, 29, 1969 •

MCC WON by seven wickets. Not many batsmen have out-hit Milburn. But the South African Greig did so on the last day of a match which sent cricket at Lord's off to a fine start. With four sixes, one off Cope clearing the Tavern scoreboard into the street, and eight fours, he reached his unbeaten 82 in 80 minutes. Milburn helped him to add 95 in 49 minutes as the Yorkshire bowlers were thumped to all parts of the ground, but he took an hour and three-quarters over his 82 (two sixes, six fours). The partnership enabled MCC to win comfortably after being set to get 188 in two and three-quarter hours.

Mike Brearley in 1978 – the fashion is the future.
Basil D'Oliveira struts his stuff in 1964.
Jim Laker – many happy returns in the '50s.
Barry Richards on the wing with Hampshire.

v Hampshire

• April 24, 25, 26, 1974 •

DRAWN. There could be no better way of opening a season at Lord's than Richards in full flight. The South African obliged in the supreme manner, punishing the MCC bowlers to most parts of the ground while scoring 189 out of Hampshire's 249 for six in three and a half hours. He hit Edmonds into the Grand Stand for two sixes and sprinkled 32 fours as well, many of them driven majestically off the back foot through the covers. Jesty, who like his illustrious partner spent the winter playing Currie Cup cricket, helped in the most productive partnership of 134 in an hour and a quarter, but of those, 107 came from Richards.

v Middlesex

• April 19, 20, 21, 1978 •

DRAWN. Following a first day that was bitterly cold but nevertheless full of incident, rain intervened and there was no further play. A half-century by Brearley, anxious to show as early as possible that the left arm broken in Pakistan during the winter was well on the mend, gave the game a notable start. He and Smith, who had grown a substantial beard since his last appearance, put on 67, after which a young member of Brearley's touring party, Botham, took over the show with the first hat-trick of the season on its very first day. All the victims – Radley, Barlow and Featherstone – were bowled, the last two by yorkers, the second of which was played on. The Somerset medium-pacer finished with five for 43 as reward for some incisive bowling.

v Nottinghamshire

• May 1, 3, 4, 1982 •

DRAWN. Bad weather marred the start of the season at headquarters. Todd had the unenviable distinction of making a "king pair", Newman dismissing him with the first ball in each of Nottinghamshire's innings.

Changes at Lord's

There has been something of a struggle for power at Lord's, the significance of which may become more apparent with time. It came to a head in the autumn of 1982, when Mr G. O. Allen, for the last half-century the game's most influential and dedicated administrator, resigned as one of MCC's representatives on the Cricket Council, the governing

body of English cricket. He did so in protest at the way, through a realignment of voting rights, the TCCB had been assured of what he feels amounts to control of the Council. A few weeks earlier, Mr Allen had celebrated his 80th birthday at a candlelit dinner, given in his honour, in the Long Room at Lord's. The only other dinner of its kind, at any rate in living memory, was to Sir Pelham Warner in 1953.

Commenting on his resignation, Mr Allen said that he believed the Cricket Council should be fully representative of all levels of cricket. While accepting that the TCCB now provides most of the money for official

coaching schemes, as well as for the more recreational branches of English cricket, Mr Allen expressed strong opposition to a national game being virtually controlled by a body that is mainly concerned with its professional side. An analogy might be if the Football Association were to come under the ordinance of the Football League. Mr Allen is afraid that the Council's new constitution, which follows the recommendation of a working party, will make it no more than a rubber stamp for the TCCB.

How will the TCCB exercise its potential control? That is crucial. If, besides running its own show, namely English Test and county cricket, the TCCB is now to have, should it wish, the final word in matters affecting the 25,000 clubs and 150,000 players who form the heart and soul of cricket in these islands, Mr Allen may have been right to sound a warning. He and MCC stand for cricket with a capital "C"; the TCCB, as it has to be, is more commercialistic.

In Australia, where the marketing people have been given a large say in who does what, and where and how, the character of the game has been quite drastically changed. With sponsorship taking an even firmer hold, it is not impossible to imagine something similar happening in England. I hardly think it will – but it could. Beware the small, executive sub-committee of businessmen, to whom the charm of cricket is little more than a technicality: that was the burden of Mr Allen's message. [Notes by the Editor, 1983]

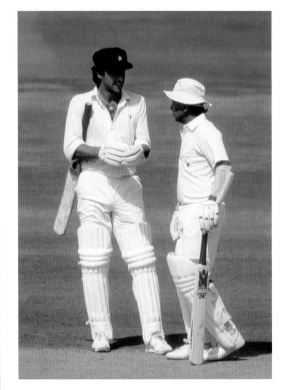

v Rest of the World

• August 20, 21, 22, 24, 25, 1987 •

DRAWN. Rain washed out the last day's play, with the Rest of the World, 13 for one overnight, needing another 340 to win. It was a sad finish to a match which provided many marvellous moments while, off the field, friendships were renewed and nostalgia was indulged in as cricketers, young and old, came together to celebrate the 200th anniversary of MCC. Yet it may have been appropriate that neither side won. In their performances and their sportsmanship, the finest players in the world had recognised that cricket should be the winner. Because of the spirit in which the match was played, MCC increased from £25,000 to

Left: Indo-Pakistan summit on neutral ground.
Imran Khan advises Sunil Gavaskar to keep his cool.
Right: Gavaskar's heir, Sachin Tendulkar, turned out to be
as much master-blaster as "Little Master".

£30,000 the prizemoney to be shared by the teams in the event of a draw.

Gatting won the toss for MCC with a Spade Guinea, minted in 1787, the year of the first game at Thomas Lord's original ground. And when Greenidge clipped Imran's first ball for four, it signalled the batting feast to follow. Broad missed out, but this brought in Gooch, playing because Martin Crowe had withdrawn. Gooch had had an unhappy summer; now he was to rediscover his form and his confidence. He and Gatting had added 103 for the fourth wicket when he went down the wicket and drove Harper straight. In an instant Harper fielded the ball and, while Gooch was still moving forward with the momentum of his stroke, threw down the stumps, the action of taking and throwing being as one. Even Gooch was drawn to smile in admiration, and well he could afford to. His 117, from 210 balls with eighteen fours, had taken him from a shadow into sunlight. In recent seasons he had swayed at the crease like an oak in the wind: here, he was upright and still, waiting for the ball and punching it with the authority of his best years. Gatting, hitting his fourth hundred in a month – two of them in Tests – was in wonderful form, especially powerful off the back foot and deft with orthodox and unorthodox sweeps. He scored 90 of the 136 runs that came on the second morning and there were 26 fours in his 179.

The Rest's innings began with a no-ball from Marshall. His first legitimate delivery, fast and low, struck Gavaskar on the pad and he was fortunate to get away with a leg-bye instead of a leg-before. Next ball, Haynes was dropped by Gatting at third slip. Hadlee to Gavaskar was a duel between two masters, the bowler probing for an opening, the batsman,

correct and studious in defence, awaiting the chance to counter-attack. Gavaskar won the bout. When 75 he had a lucky escape when the ball rolled from his pads to rest against the stumps; and next day, contemplating a suicidal second run to bring him his first hundred at Lord's, he was firmly sent back by Imran Khan. The smiles on their faces were large; here was a moment to savour. And when Gavaskar turned Shastri backward of square, the hug of congratulation from the bowler was spontaneous. Imran was an ideal foil for the "Little Master" as they put on 180 in two hours 40 minutes. He hit Emburey straight for six, reached 50 with two lovely off-side fours from Hadlee, and carted Emburey high into the President's box above the Tavern concourse.

Border's declaration that evening gave Greenidge the opportunity to score the hundred he had desired

on the first day. He was careful over it, needing 223 balls, but Gooch, Gower and Hadlee kept the score moving nicely and MCC made their 318 in 88 overs, having to keep a tight rein on the innings at the end to stop it from bolting. By then, however, the sky was threatening rain, and soon all that had passed would be merely memories. But what memories.

MCC: C. G. Greenidge, B. C. Broad, G. A. Gooch, D. I. Gower, M. W. Gatting, C. E. B. Rice, R. J. Hadlee, R. J. Shastri, J. E. Emburey, M. D. Marshall and B. N. French. *Scores*: 455–5 dec. (Greenidge 52, Gooch 117, Gatting 179, Rice 59 not out) and 318–6 dec. (Greenidge 122, Gooch 70).

Rest of the World: S. M. Gavaskar, D. L. Haynes, D. B. Vengsarkar, Javed Miandad, A. R. Border, P. J. L. Dujon, Imran Khan, Kapil Dev, R. A. Harper, C. A. Walsh and Abdul Qadir. *Scores*: 421–7 dec. (Gavaskar 188, Imran Khan 82; Marshall 3–53, Shastri 3–130) and 13–1.

v Rest of the World XI

· July 18, 1998 ·

REST OF THE WORLD XI won by six wickets. Two strong teams were assembled for this match, played on the 150th anniversary of W. G. Grace's birth, in aid of the Diana, Princess of Wales Memorial Fund, which benefited by some £520,000. Many of the participants were flown in from overseas, while the South African tourists released Donald and McMillan. The innings of the day was played by Tendulkar, the World XI captain, who made a memorable 125 from only 114 balls. Batting with studied nonchalance, he stroked fifteen fours and four sixes, being especially severe on Aamir Sohail's occasional left-armers. Tendulkar was almost matched by de Silva, who contributed a twinkling 82 to their stand of 177. Their strokeplay overshadowed Chanderpaul's earlier unbeaten 127, from 144 balls. There seemed to be a gentleman's agreement not to dive in the field, and the fast bowlers operated a little below full throttle, but it was an enjoyable match, free from the tension of most modern-day internationals.

Oxbridge blues again. Sandy Singleton has a moment with Miss Potter in 1935, the second of his four years in the Oxford side; Lord Harris, three times a Dark Blue in the 1870s, arrives at Lord's for the Varsity match; the Hon. Alfred Lyttelton played for Cambridge from 1876 to 1879. Singleton and Lyttelton captained their respective Universities in their final year.

The Varsity Match
Oxford v Cambridge

"Long may the Universities continue to be the stepping stone of 'Cricket' –
long may University cricketers continue to keep up the high tradition handed down
to them by famous cricketers of the past."

[Wisden 1936]

• June 27, 28, 1870 •

ALL CLASSES of visitors were unanimous in praise of the decided improvement to the ground by the addition thereto of the slip of land on the eastern side, hitherto known as "Guy's Nursery Ground", and alike general were the expressions of gratification at the several excitingly close contests that were played during "the three months at Lord's". Among them was that wonderfully effective last over of Mr Cobden's that took three wickets and won, when it was 50 to 1 against Light Blue, the Universities match for Cambridge by 2 runs and caused that madly joyous "rush of shouting thousands" to the Pavilion that never will be forgotten by those who witnessed it.

From the first ball a single was made (3 to win with three wickets to fall).

From the second ball Mr Butler was superbly caught out at mid-off.

The third ball bowled Mr Belcher.

The fourth ball bowled Mr Stewart.

Cambridge: 147 (A. T. Scott Esq. 45; T. H. Belcher Esq. 4–52, C. K. Francis Esq. 5–59) and 206 (J. W. Dale Esq. 67, W. Yardley Esq. 100; Francis 7–102).

Oxford: 175 (A. T. Fortescue Esq. 35; F. C. Cobden Esq. 4–41) and 176 (C. J. Ottaway Esq. 69; Cobden 4–35, E. E. Ward Esq. 6–29).

• June 26, 27, 1871 •

AT A QUARTER TO FOUR the Cambridge first innings was commenced; at twenty minutes past five the innings was completed for 65 runs. Mr Money was first in and fourth out, the score at 35, when he was bowled for 23. Mr Yardley went in at 28 for three wickets; he was fifth out with the score at 62. Mr Butler had all the five wickets then down, and in thirteen more balls he succeeded in obtaining the other five, thus accomplishing the unusual and great bowling feat of obtaining all the ten wickets in one innings. Mr Butler's last three overs and one ball were bowled for 1 run and five wickets – all five bowled. Mr Pelham bowled fourteen overs for 5 runs (all singles), so although it was minus a wicket, this bit of slow bowling of Mr Pelham's was in its way as curious as the fast of Mr Butler's. Oxford won by eight wickets.

Oxford: 170 (B. Pauncefote Esq. 50; W. N. Powys Esq. 4–40, E. Bray Esq. 5–38) and 25–2.

Cambridge: 65 (W. Yardley Esq. 25; S. E. Butler Esq. 24.1–11–38–10) and 129 (F. C. Cobden Esq. 32 not out; Butler 34–14–57–5).

Frank Cobden – hat-trick hero for Cambridge in 1870, the first of his three years at Lord's.

• June 24, 25, 1872 •

THE FIRST DAY of the 38th Inter-University match will be a red-letter day in the history of Cambridge cricket, for on that day two Light Blue colts made over 100 runs before the first Cambridge wicket went down. On that day Mr Yardley hit the highest score ever before hit by light or dark blue, and the Cambridge eleven played the largest innings, by 91 runs, yet chronicled in the 38 matches.

The weather was magnificently bright, warm and genial on the morning of the 24th, and although the opening of the Bethnal Green Museum, by HRH The Prince of Wales, and many other London attractions that morning detracted from the numbers assembled at the commencement of the match, as the afternoon wore on the gathering so materially increased that by luncheon time the crowded Grand Stand, the well-filled Pavilion seats and roof, the closely packed triple rows of charmingly freighted carriages that surrounded the dense ring of lookers-on, and the brilliant crowd that promenaded the old turf during the half-hour set apart for refreshment, told that the Varsity match was yearly increasing in interest and attraction, for when the last visitor had passed through the turnstiles, those "ready reckoners" told that over 1,000 more visitors had that day gone on to the old ground than on any previous day had paid to witness an Oxford v Cambridge match. The actual numbers who paid for admission were on Monday 10,283 and on Tuesday 4,905. Add to these visitors those who passed on in vehicles and the members of the club, who extensively availed themselves of their privilege of free entry, and there can be no doubt but that more than 20,000 visited Lord's during the two days.

Cambridge won by an innings and 166 runs.

Cambridge: 388 (G. H. Longman Esq. 80, A. S. Tabor Esq. 50, W. Yardley Esq. 130; C. K. Francis Esq. 3–133, S. E. Butler Esq. 3–103, A. W. Ridley Esq. 3–49).

Oxford: 72 (W. Townshend Esq. 20; W. N. Powys Esq. 6–26) and 150 (C. J. Ottaway Esq. 41; Powys 7–49).

William Yardley (left) hit the first Varsity match centuries, in 1870 and 1872. A. J. Webbe captained Oxford in 1877 and 1878 and went on to captain Middlesex.

• June 28, 29, 30, 1875 •

THIS WAS the 41st match played by Oxford and Cambridge and, inasmuch as each University was credited with nineteen victories, a more than usually strong interest was felt in the result of the 1875 struggle, which will long be remembered for the unprecedentedly large attendance on the second day; for the magnificent catch made by the Oxford colt, Mr A. J. Webbe; for the plucky, stirring form in which the Cambridge men brought up their second-innings score so near to victory; and for that never-to-be-forgotten last ball bowled by the captain, Mr Ridley, which so excitingly won the match for Oxford by 6 runs.

At 161 for seven, or 14 for Cambridge to win, with the first ball he delivered Mr Ridley bowled Mr Patterson. Mr Macan went in; he made a single (13 to win); Mr Sims then drove one from Mr Ridley for four (9 to win). Then Mr Lang bowled. A leg-bye made it 8 to win; a no-ball made it 7 to win; an especially fine catch at long-on by Mr Pulman (Mr Sims out) left it one wicket to fall and 7 to win.

So the score was 168 for nine when the last of the Cantabs, Mr Smith, went in. He did not appear confident, but stopped two balls bowled by Mr Ridley, who then tossed in one that clean bowled Mr S. and that ball, at four minutes past four, won Oxford the match by 6 runs.

Thereupon all the Oxford eleven threw up their caps in token of their gratification at gaining this much coveted victory over Cambridge. Thousands of excited men rushed to the Pavilion front and roared for "Ridley, Ridley". The longer they stayed the more vigorous became their shouts. At last Mr Ridley came and bowed his thanks, but that would not do so he was forced down the steps on to the turf. There he was hoisted on to men's shoulders and – pushing through the roaring crowd – they carried him to and fro the wickets with all the wild enthusiasm of other days. So ended this memorable contest, which Oxonians will ever recall as "Ridley's Match" with as much pleasure as Cantabs refer to the 1870 contest as "Cobden's Match".

Oxford: 200 (A. J. Webbe Esq. 55; C. M. Sharpe Esq. 5–89) and 137 (W. W. Pulman Esq. 30; Sharpe 6–66).

Cambridge: 163 (G. H. Longman Esq. 40; T. W. Lang Esq. 5–35) and 168 (H. M. Sims Esq. 39; V. Royle Esq. 4–51; A. W. Ridley Esq. 4.3–1–16–2).

JUNE 26, 1876
The great crowd (which had been sitting and standing under a blazing hot sun that had moved the thermometer up to 147) left the ground as best they could, and as they swarmed along in one crowded continuous stream to the neat little railway station, and elsewhere, the sight seen in St John's Wood road for a quarter of an hour was one that will not readily fade from the memories of those who witnessed it. How the thousands from Lord's got on "Underground" that evening this compiler knoweth not, for the Metropolitan Railway was not his way that journey.

• July 1, 2, 1878 •

THIS MATCH was productive of incidents sufficiently interesting to merit a more extended record than it is possible to give them here, owing to the compiler being bound down to complete this year's book in a certain number of pages; nevertheless he will do his best to give a fair chronicle of the features of this curiously finished match, wherein one side commenced their second innings by scoring 117 runs before a wicket fell, and the other eleven concluded their second innings for 32.

At a quarter to five on the second day, the brothers Webbe commenced Oxford's second innings, and at six o'clock that innings was over for the smallest score ever chronicled in these matches. How to account for this is beyond the power of the pen that built up this book, but it seemed as though the brothers Webbe (and Mr Greene) going down when only 7 runs had been scored, crushed the hearts of those who followed, who went to wickets as if it was there written "let all who come here leave hope behind". All three wickets went down from the bowling of Mr A. G. Steel.

In their first innings, Oxford's 127 runs were made from 130 Cambridge overs, 61 of which, for 62 runs and eight wickets, were bowled by Mr Steel, a particularly successful bowling debut to make in the Inter-University match.

Cambridge: 168 (Hon. E. Lyttelton 53, A. G. Steel Esq. 44 not out; A. H. Evans Esq. 5–55) and 229 (A. P. Lucas Esq. 74, Hon. A. Lyttelton 64; Evans 7–86).

Oxford: 127 (A. D. Greene Esq. 35 not out; Steel 8–62) and 32 (E. T. Hirst Esq. 13; Steel 5–11, P. H. Morton Esq. 5–20).

The day before the match, the hot weather of the preceding week was broken by a severe storm. Although the prepared wicket had been protected by "a tarpauling cover", this was objected to and the stumps were pitched on the "then imperfectly prepared wickets" intended for Gentlemen v Players the following week.

All-conquering Cambridge defeated MCC, Oxford and the Australians at Lord's in 1878.
Back (l-r): Hon. Ivo Bligh, Hon. Alfred Lyttelton, D. Q. Steel, L. K. Jarvis, A. F. J. Ford.
Middle: F. W. Kingston, A. P. Lucas, Hon. Edward Lyttelton, P. H. Morton.
Front: Herbert Whitfield, A. G. Steel. The Lytteltons and Steels were brothers.

Family affair: Cambridge captains J. E. K., C. T. and G. B. Studd.

A summer for the Studds

MCC AND GROUND
v CAMBRIDGE UNIVERSITY
• June 19, 20, 21, 1882 •

For the second time in 1882 Cambridge defeated the MCC in very hollow fashion, winning the match by no fewer than 163 runs, despite the fact that the club sent into the field a much stronger eleven than on the first occasion and that Mr Hornby played two masterly innings of 51 and 121 not out for the home team. Though several of the Cambridge eleven batted in splendid style, Mr Hornby's second innings was undoubtedly the feature of the match. The magnificent stand made by Messrs G. B. and J. E. K. Studd in the University's second innings was also a most meritorious performance. Both played in very dashing style and hit with great power and freedom. They scored 86 in the first hour after luncheon and when Mr J. E. K. was out for 67, 163 had been put on for the first wicket in two hours and a quarter. He had not made a mistake; Mr G. B. did not score a run after his brother left, and his grandly played 94 included a couple of hard chances.

OXFORD v CAMBRIDGE
• June 26, 27, 28, 1882 •

In the early part of the season it was very generally thought that the Dark Blues would be strong and the Light Blues weak, and that the result of the Inter-University contest would be a repetition of that played in the previous year; but the seven wickets' victory gained by Cambridge was a vindication of the form displayed by the team in their later trial matches and went far to compensate them for their unexpected defeat in 1881. Much, of course, was expected of the brothers Studd, and most worthily two of them upheld their cricketing fame. Messrs G. B. and C. T. Studd scored 189 out of 408 from the bat made for Cambridge, and Mr C. T. all told bowled 138 overs (84 maidens) for 102 runs and nine wickets and thereby proved himself by far the most successful bowler in the Light Blue team. There were faults in the early part of Mr G. B.'s innings but his 120 was unquestionably a grand performance and was the second-highest score in an Inter-University match after Mr W. Yardley's 130 for Cambridge in 1872.

THE GENTLEMEN
v THE PLAYERS
• July 3, 4, 5, 1882 •

This, the second contest between the amateurs and professionals of England in 1882, was commenced in delightfully fine weather before an exceedingly numerous concourse of visitors, who were well rewarded by witnessing some of the best all-round cricket of the season. The principal feature of the match was the magnificent display of batting by Mr Lucas and Mr C. T. Studd, who together raised the score from 32 for two wickets to 236 for three. Altogether 901 runs were scored during the three days.

When Mr C. T. Studd became associated with Mr Lucas, the best batting display of the season at Lord's commenced. They began very carefully, neither being disposed to hit too freely, the fielding at this point of the game being very good and only 48 runs appearing on the telegraph board after one hour's play. When the luncheon interval occurred the score stood at 95; on resuming the batsmen began to hit more freely. With the score at 235, Flowers and Scotton went on, and this change in bowling brought about the desired parting as, 1 run later, Mr Lucas was well caught at mid-off for a brilliant innings of 107. No less than 204 runs had been put on since the fall of the last wicket. Lord Harris followed, and soon after lost the partnership of Mr Studd, who was thrown out by Shrewsbury. Mr Studd had played a faultless innings of 100.

Late on the final afternoon the Gentlemen commenced their somewhat easy task of getting 77 runs to win. Immediately on the fall of the last wicket of the Players' second innings, rain had come down in torrents, so runs came rather slowly on the dead wicket. With the dismissal of Messrs Grace and Leslie, Mr Lucas and Mr C. T. Studd again became associated and by steady, careful play knocked off the balance of the runs, thus winning the match for the Gentlemen by eight wickets.

THE AUSTRALIANS v MCC AND GROUND
• July 10, 11, 12, 1882 •

The toss resulted in Hornby's favour and at 12.05 he accompanied W. Grace to the wickets to begin MCC's innings. The champion played in his best form and exhibited all his old power of placing the ball out of danger, but Hornby, although he succeeded in making a good number of runs, hit recklessly. Hornby was out at 67 and Lucas took the vacant place. The score was carried to 102, when Grace was bowled by Spofforth and C. T. Studd joined Lucas. When 11 more runs had been totalled, rain came down so heavily that the wicket was under water and no more play that day was possible. Lucas had made 9 and Studd 11. Next day rain fell heavily for several hours in the morning and so saturated the ground that it was decided to postpone play till the following day.

Play began at 11.45 on Wednesday, Lucas and C. T. Studd resuming their innings. When the 200 was hoisted the two batsmen were still together, but 8 runs later Lucas was caught for a most finished and patient innings of 45. He and Studd had put on 106 runs for the third wicket. Lord Harris was soon dismissed for 4, Barnes without

Charles Thomas Studd, the youngest and most famous of three brothers all of whom played for Eton, Cambridge University and Middlesex, died at Ibambi in the Belgian Congo on July 16, 1931. Each of the three brothers enjoyed the distinction of captaining the Cambridge eleven – G. B. in 1882, C. T. in 1883 and J. E. K. in 1884. J. E. K., the eldest – Lord Mayor of London in 1929 – left Eton in 1877 but did not go up to Cambridge until 1881. All three figured in the Eton eleven of 1877 and also in the Cambridge elevens of 1881 and 1882.

. . .

Unhappily for English cricket, C. T. Studd was not seen in the field after 1884. Feeling a call for missionary work, he went out to China in connection with the China Inland Mission and there remained from 1885 to 1895. Invalided home, he engaged in missionary work in England and America and after 1900 with the Anglo-Indian Evangelization Society. Later on, the state of the multitudes of the Belgian Congo, which had not been touched by any missionary agency, made such strong appeal to him that he went out to that uncivilised region and, despite numerous illnesses and many hardships, devoted the remainder of his life to missionary work there.

scoring and Steel for 6; but on G. B. Studd joining his brother another long stand was made. G. B. Studd had extraordinary luck, as in scoring his 25 he was three times missed, twice from easy chances. He helped his brother to increase the total by 46 runs and was then lbw to Garrett, just after C. T. had made his century. The 300 went up at five minutes past four and then, with 1 run added, Studd's masterly innings came to an end. Of the 199 runs put on during his stay he had made 114, and his magnificent innings was marred by no real chance. This was the fourth three-figure innings he had made since the commencement of the season and he was the only English batsman who succeeded in making

two scores of over 100 against the Australians. He followed up this splendid batting display by taking four Australian wickets for 26 runs.

The match ended in a draw greatly in favour of the home team.

ETON v HARROW
• July 14, 15, 1882 •

The feature of the Eton innings was the batting of H. W. Bainbridge and A. H. Studd (31), who both played exceedingly well and added 55 during their third-wicket partnership.

Studd played in the 1885 Freshmen's match but never for Cambridge.

• July 2, 3, 4, 5, 1888 •

THE OXFORD AND CAMBRIDGE match of 1888 will not be remembered for any remarkable display of cricket but simply from the fact that it was the first since 1844 that has not been brought to a definite conclusion. Drenching rain made cricket quite impossible on Monday [the first day] , and in the hope of finishing the match it was arranged on the second day to utilise Thursday. This, though unusual in modern days with the crowded lists of fixtures, was a most sportsmanlike thing to do, but the good intentions were frustrated by the weather, Thursday proving such a hopeless day that there was no choice but to abandon the game.

• July 1, 2, 1889 •

THE PLAY in the London trial matches left little doubt in the minds of impartial judges that Cambridge had very much the stronger side, the presence of Mr Woods being in itself an immense advantage, but few could have been prepared for the utterly one-sided game that was actually seen when the two Universities came together. The match was played on a perfectly good wicket, without anything in the way of luck to favour one side rather than the other, and yet Cambridge won in a single innings with 105 runs to spare. Their team included nine old blues, of whom eight had taken part the previous year. The two newcomers were Mr C. P. Foley, of the Eton eleven in 1886–87, and Mr E. R. De Little, an Australian, both seniors, and it was certainly something of a reproach to the Light Blues that the two fast bowlers in their eleven, Mr Woods and Mr De Little, should both have been by birth Australians. The Oxford side as originally chosen included seven old blues, but the illness of a younger brother, which afterwards proved fatal, kept the Hon. F. J. N. Thesiger out of the match. Among the new choices, Mr M. R. Jardine, the freshman from Fettes, was on hard

wickets very far indeed from keeping up the promise he had shown on slow ones. He was bowled before scoring in each innings.

• June 29, 30, 1891 •

BEFORE LUNCHEON on the first day, the Hon. F. J. N. Thesiger, in trying to field a ball, slipped down and sprained his hand. As he was unable to go on playing, MacGregor, the Cambridge captain, courteously allowed his place to be taken by T. B. Case, a senior from Winchester and a son of the Mr T. B. Case who played in the great Oxford elevens of 1864 and 1865 under Mr R. A. H. Mitchell's captaincy.

Case scored 5 and 2; Cambridge won by two wickets.

• June 30, July 1, 2, 1892 •

IN MANY RESPECTS the Oxford and Cambridge match of 1892 was almost one of the most remarkable in the whole series of engagements. In the first place the aggregate number of runs, exactly 1,100, was by far the largest the contest has produced; secondly, the Cambridge team, though they lost the match by five wickets, tied in their second innings the record total of 388, obtained in 1872; and thirdly, there were three individual scores of over 100.

Though the later stages of the game proved wonderfully interesting, the match was as good as won on the first day, Oxford playing a first innings of 365 and getting two Cambridge wickets down for 34. For the first time – at least within recent experience – the contest took place on the three last days of the week. Oxford's innings opened in a very sensational way, Palairet and Jones being got rid of before a run had been scored. But C. B. Fry, a freshman from Repton, and M. R. Jardine made an invaluable stand for the third wicket and, for a long time, the batsmen always had the upper hand. This was Jardine's fourth year in the Oxford eleven, and by making 140 his previous failures were fully condoned. In second wicket down, he was the ninth man out and so far as could be seen he did not give a chance. His play was marked by very watchful defence and a remarkable power over the stroke which can best be described as the leg glance. No better exhibition of defensive play has been seen in the series since W. H. Patterson's great innings of 107 not out in 1881. In the second innings Jardine made 39, which gave him the best aggregate ever obtained in the University match, the previous best being that of Lord George Scott, who scored 100 and 66 in 1887. As Jardine's fielding was quite as fine as his batting, the Scotch cricketer indeed finished his University career with a complete triumph.

C. B. Fry – Oxford blues for athletics, cricket and soccer.

The luncheon half-hour promenaders "on the famous old historical battle field" in 1898. Background buildings include the ivy-covered tennis court and the Tavern.

• July 2, 3, 4, 1896 •

IN ONE RESPECT at least, the University engagement of 1896 was the most remarkable of the series, the Oxford eleven being left to get 330 in the last innings and hitting off the runs for the loss of six wickets. No such feat had ever been performed before in the University match. It is not so much, however, for this exceptional performance, as for the much discussed incident in regard to the follow-on rule, that the match of 1896 will be remembered. When the MCC, yielding to the fears of some famous players, rejected a drastic alteration of Law 53, and contented themselves with increasing from 80 to 120 the number of runs involving a follow-on, it was easy to foresee that, given the same circumstances, the incident which caused so much angry discussion in the University match of 1893 would inevitably be repeated. After an interval of three years, Mr Frank Mitchell, as captain of Cambridge,

followed the example set him in 1893 by Mr F. S. Jackson and, by palpably giving away runs to prevent his opponents from following on, forced the MCC to reconsider the whole question. Cambridge had occupied nearly the whole of the first day in scoring 319, and at about a quarter to four next day they were leading in the first innings by 131 runs, with only one Oxford wicket to go down. Rightly or wrongly, Mitchell judged that it would be better for his own side to go in again than to field for the rest of the afternoon, and E. B. Shine settled the matter by sending three balls – two of them no-balls – to the boundary for four each.

As they left the field, the Cambridge eleven came in for a very hostile demonstration at the hands of the public, and inside the Pavilion matters were still

worse, scores of members of the MCC protesting in the most vigorous fashion against the policy that Frank Mitchell had adopted. In our opinion this display of passion was altogether illogical and uncalled for. We defended F. S. Jackson and C. M. Wells for what they did in 1893 and, believing that even in its amended form Law 53 is ill-adapted to modern cricket, we think Mitchell was quite entitled in the interests of his side to take the course he did. The incident gave rise to a long correspondence in the columns of *The Times*, and to show the difference of opinion that existed amongst the best authorities, diametrically opposite views were expressed by Lord Cobham and his younger brother, Edward Lyttelton. Lord Cobham strongly supported Mitchell's action, and Edward Lyttelton as strenuously opposed it.

The compulsory element in the follow-on law was removed in 1900, and the run-difference again increased.

• July 5, 6, 7, 1900 •

FOR THE SECOND TIME in its history the Oxford and Cambridge match was left drawn owing to heavy scoring, the bat beating the ball to such an extent that, from the time Cambridge avoided the follow-on, there was no likelihood of arriving at a definite result. In playing an innings of 171 on the opening day, R. E. Foster, the Oxford captain, set up a new record in the match, the best individual score up to last July having been Mr Key's 143 in 1886. Foster's innings was not only a great one in a numerical sense, but was in every way a magnificent display of batting. He took only three hours and ten minutes to get his runs, and so far as anyone noticed he did not give a single chance. Apart, indeed, from the fact that he once failed to bring off a more than usually daring pull, and that just before he was out he made a dangerous stroke beyond mid-off, we did not – watching the game very closely – see any fault in his play. As a matter of record it may be added that he hit 24 fours, three threes and thirteen twos. Hitting more superb than this can scarcely have been seen in the University match since Yardley played his great innings of 130 in 1872. He was strong all round the wicket, driving magnificently on the off, pulling with the utmost certainty, and making any number of late cuts that were as safe as they were effective.

• July 4, 5, 6, 1901 •

FOR THE THIRD YEAR in succession the Oxford and Cambridge match had to be left unfinished. On a superlatively good wicket, the bat so beat the ball that even with three full days' play it was found impossible to arrive at a definite result. In order to avoid a draw, play began half an hour earlier than usual each day, and the game went on until seven o'clock on the last day but, as it happened, all to no purpose. Only in the last stage of the match did the bowlers assert themselves, and with

a little luck Cambridge would certainly have won, Oxford at the finish being 149 runs behind with only three wickets to go down.

Oxford's seventh wicket fell at 145, 40 minutes then being left for play. At this point a curious, and from Cambridge's point of view an unsatisfactory, incident occurred. Hollins, before he had scored, played a ball from Johnson to the slips. E. R. Wilson took the ball close to the ground and – clearly under the impression that he had made a catch – threw it up. On appeal to the bowler's umpire, however, W. Hearn could not give Hollins out, owing to Johnson having obstructed his view, and Phillips, on being appealed to, was also unable to give a decision, the wicket-keeper, standing back, having exactly covered Wilson when he secured the ball. Whether or not a catch was really made it is impossible to say, but the Cambridge men certainly had reason to consider themselves unlucky in the fact of both umpires having had their sight of the ball obstructed.

Wilson was quite the hero of the match, playing an admirable innings of 118 on the opening day, and bowling with rare steadiness. Considering the state of the ground, and the fact that 1,175 runs were scored in the match, it was a fine performance to take, as he did in Oxford's first innings, five wickets for 71. In getting his 118 he withstood the Oxford bowling for four hours, going in first and being out, seventh wicket down, at 251. In making a hundred against Oxford he followed in the footsteps of his brother, C. E. M. Wilson, who scored 115 in 1898. There is only one other instance of two brothers making hundreds in the University match – H. K. Foster scoring 121 in 1895, and R. E. Foster 171 in 1900.

Rockley Wilson hit a hundred against Cambridge in 1899 when playing as a last-minute locum in A. J. Webbe's XI, so lining himself up for a blue while a freshman. He made 118 against Oxford in 1901, and next year captained and bowled Cambridge to victory.

Philip Le Couteur, an Australian Rhodes Scholar,
followed his 1910 *tour de force* with eleven Cambridge wickets
in Oxford's 1911 victory.

• July 4, 5, 1910 •

THANKS to the all-round cricket of P. R. Le
Couteur, who by scoring 160 and taking
eleven wickets [for 66 runs] beat all records
for the match, Oxford beat Cambridge by an
innings and 126 runs. Nothing in the trial games had
suggested such a one-sided result, but those who saw
Le Couteur bowl a fortnight earlier against the MCC at
Lord's felt tolerably certain that, if he got the right
length to his leg-breaks, his efforts would turn the
scale. For his triumph as a batsman, however, no one
could have been quite prepared. His batting was very

modern in style, a vast proportion of his runs being
obtained by on-side hitting, and his 160, made after
Oxford were four wickets down for 30, is the third-
highest score in the whole series of matches. As a
bowler, Le Couteur owed his success chiefly to his
quick leg-break, but he occasionally sent down a
googly, and the uncertainty as to what they had to
expect had no doubt a good deal to do with the
downfall of the Cambridge team. Great as Le
Couteur's performance was, the match ought not to
have been so one-sided, Cambridge paying a
desperately high price for dropped catches.

• July 8, 9, 10, 1912 •

THE UNIVERSITIES have not often been more
evenly matched than in 1912. After a
strenuous fight, Cambridge won by three
wickets and, apart from a very unfortunate
circumstance, the result in all probability would have
been even closer. G. E. V. Crutchley scored 99 not out
for Oxford on the first day, but at the end of his
innings he was found to be suffering from an attack of
measles. He could, of course, take no further part in
the match, the loss of his batting in Oxford's second
innings making a considerable difference. He was
very unwell before the game began, but naturally had
no idea what was the matter with him. It was stated
that while he was scoring his 99 not out, his
temperature went up two degrees.

Gerald Crutchley held another distinction,
for he was the last man to play cricket during the
Canterbury Week and to act at night for the Old Stagers.
As a lieutenant in the Scots Guards during the First
World War, he was wounded and held prisoner-of-war
in Germany for almost four years. [1970]

• July 10, 11, 12, 1922 •

SO MUCH RAIN had fallen in London during
the previous week, and the weather was so
unsettled, that the outlook for the University
match was dubious in the extreme. Happily,
things turned out far better than anyone could have
expected. The weather, almost at the last moment,
underwent a startling change and, except that on the
first day the wicket was very soft and dead, there was
not much cause for complaint. G. T. S. Stevens,
though not quite himself
after his sharp attack of
jaundice, was well
enough to take charge of
the Oxford side, but it
was not thought safe to
play Jardine, who had for
weeks been suffering
from a damaged knee,
the Dark Blues thus
losing their most dep-
endable batsman. As
regards the result, the
match proved an almost
exact repetition of that of
1921, Cambridge declar-
ing after hitting up a big
score, having everything
their own way from start
to finish, and winning in
a single innings. The
margin of runs this time
was larger than before –
exactly 100 as against 24.
    The finest cricket of
the match was seen on
the second morning,
Hubert Ashton and
Chapman, by superb
play, taking the score to

1913
There was a very
impressive incident on
the second day. At noon
– the hour of the
memorial service to
Alfred Lyttelton at
St Margaret's,
Westminster – the flags
were lowered to half-
mast, and for two or
three minutes the players
stood with bared heads
in solemn silence.

403 and being still together when, at ten minutes past one, rain and a wretched light caused the players to leave the field. Nothing more could be done for some time, and after the luncheon interval it became known that Hubert Ashton had declared. Though he needed only 10 runs to rival William Yardley's 1870s' feat of getting two hundreds in the University match, he was far too keen on winning to let any personal consideration weigh with him. His 90 not out was quite worthy of comparison with his 118 in 1921. A. P. F. Chapman, who had been very disappointing in the trial matches, happily found his best form on the all-important occasion. His 102 not out – a delightful innings to watch – included eleven fours.

Hubert Ashton

Robertson-Glasgow's stories regarding the game he loved were many and various, but never ill-natured. One against him concerned the occasion when he was in the Pavilion at Lord's during the match following the University game of 1922.
A friend introduced him to a certain celebrated pressman who, as was his wont, paid little attention to his name. When the friend left them, the pressman, endeavouring to make conversation, enquired: "Did you see Chapman's wonderful innings in the Varsity match?" For once "Crusoe" was speechless.
A big proportion of A. P. F. Chapman's brilliant 102 for Cambridge had come at the expense of Robertson-Glasgow, who sent down 43.1 overs for 97 runs and did not take a wicket. [1966]

The sensation of the match came when Oxford followed on against a balance of 181. The pitch was faster than at any previous time during the match, and Wright and Allen proved irresistible, getting seven wickets down for 17. Stevens stayed in for an hour, but his plucky cricket only delayed the inevitable end. Hubert Ashton, in finishing with Cambridge cricket, had reason to congratulate himself – alike as captain, batsman and fieldsman. No one in England except Hitch could have fielded at short leg as he did.

• July 9, 10, 1923 •

THERE HAS NEVER been a more tragic Oxford and Cambridge match. Oxford won in two days by an innings and 227 runs – the most overwhelming victory in the whole series of contests. Without detracting in any way from the excellence of their all-round cricket, it must be said that they were favoured by fortune to an extraordinary degree. They were batting the whole of the first day on a beautiful wicket, and on Tuesday they bowled on a pitch ruined by the most violent thunderstorm experienced in London for twelve years. Nor was this all. G. O. Allen, the one Cambridge bowler who might have been expected to do well on a good wicket, was rendered practically useless by a strained muscle in his side. He had hurt himself, it was understood, while playing at Eastbourne, and the trouble came on again when he went out to practise in the morning. He was quite incapable of doing himself justice and, though he sought surgical advice during the luncheon interval, he sent down only fifteen overs in Oxford's innings of 422. The outstanding feature of Oxford's innings was the beautiful batting of C. H. Taylor. Never before had a freshman made a hundred in his

first innings on the big occasion and his style of batting was so good as to recall memories of A. P. Lucas. He missed nothing on the leg side and brought off some fine hits in front of cover point. In Jardine he found a partner who, though in other respects excellent, let the off side alone entirely.

Oxford: 422 (Mr C. H. Taylor 109, Mr R. C. Robertson-Glasgow 53, Mr E. P. Hewetson 57; Mr P. A. Wright 4–113).

Cambridge: 59 (Mr C. T. Ashton 15; Mr G. T. S. Stevens 6–20, Mr R. H. Bettington 3–19) and 136 (Mr G. O. Allen 28; Bettington 8–66).

• July 6, 7, 8, 1925 •

A DRAWN MATCH was rendered memorable by the performance of H. J. Enthoven, who followed up his score of 104 in the preceding year with an innings of 129. In so doing Enthoven equalled the record of William Yardley, who made 100 in the match of 1870 and 130 two years later, and in playing three-figure innings in the great contest in two successive years Enthoven achieved a distinction which is his alone. While in the previous summer Enthoven had not been regarded as a batsman likely to do a big thing, his second triumph had in it no element of surprise, his batting during May and June showing him to be the most consistent run-getter in the eleven. Finely caught in the end by the wicket-keeper, Gilliat, on the leg side, he withstood the Oxford attack for four hours. Strong in defence and possessed of plenty of power, if of no particular grace of style, Enthoven was, of course, very lucky to be let off twice in making his first 50 runs, but going in when the wicket was kicking, he faced the only crisis of the match in resolute fashion. In a Cambridge innings of over 400, I. A. W. Gilliat did not give a single bye.

• July 6, 7, 8, 1931 •

BEATING CAMBRIDGE by eight wickets, Oxford not only registered their first victory over the Light Blues for eight years but, considering the circumstances in which the win was gained, accomplished by far the finest performance credited to either University since the war. Fielding out for the whole of the first day, they had to go in against a total of 385. For the loss of eight wickets they headed that score by 68 and, in registering 453 runs, put together the second-highest innings on record in the long history of games between Oxford and Cambridge. Furthermore, although when the concluding day's cricket was entered upon the Light Blues had all ten wickets standing, the Oxonians followed up their batting triumph with such a workman-like display of bowling and fielding that the match was all over by a quarter to four. D. N. Moore, the Gloucestershire amateur, should have led the Oxford team, but illness kept him out of the field after the first few weeks of the season and the responsibility fell to A. Melville, a South African.

For the sixth consecutive year, the spin of the coin gave the Light Blues choice of innings. And when Cambridge turned the opportunity of batting first to such good purpose, Oxford's prospects of victory seemed to have disappeared. The

The University match probably has lost something of its old interest and popularity, but this idea may be more apparent than real. Before the Mound Stand was built, a ring of ten or fifteen thousand people was about as many as Lord's could hold. Given fine weather you might get ten thousand spectators a day at the University match, but with the accommodation at Lord's increased to Test-match requirements, this is a mere sprinkling and the ground looks somewhat empty. But, while this contrast is not much to go by, it remains true that there are not the coaches and carriages, the arbours and the luncheons, that there once were. It is curious that the attraction of matches like Eton and Harrow, or Eton and Winchester, seems to increase as the years go by; as opportunities for social gatherings they become more patronised every season. But, if as a cricket spectacle it holds its own, as a society function the University match is not what it used to be.
[H. D. G. Leveson Gower, 1937]

great piece of luck enjoyed by Cambridge, however, consisted not in the advantage conferred by choice of innings but rather in an accident which affected the composition of their eleven. In making up the side, Kemp-Welch had given a place to J. G. W. Davies, a freshman from Tonbridge, and had dropped A. T. Ratcliffe, a member of the 1930 team. A few days prior to the big match Davies sprained his ankle and when, on the morning of the match, he was still unable to take the field, the vacant place fell to Ratcliffe.

Ratcliffe not only helped his captain to put on 149 for the first wicket but went on to complete his hundred, then to beat the record innings of the match – 172 not out by J. F. Marsh in 1904 – and finally to bring his score to 201. Steady, confident and skilful from start to finish, he played a truly admirable innings, his triumph being so well deserved that he gave no chance until he had brought his figures to 179. The extent to which Ratcliffe's batting dominated the first day's play is suggested by the score. Latterly, no doubt, there appeared to exist no strong reason for restraint on the part of the Cambridge batsmen, but there remained the fact that, apart from Ratcliffe and Kemp-Welch, no one put together an innings of five-and-twenty.

While Ratcliffe's big innings would, in the special circumstances in which he came to play, have rendered the match memorable, his score was not

allowed to stand as a record for the University match for 24 hours. Next day the Nawab of Pataudi not only equalled Ratcliffe's total in 80 minutes less that that player had been at the wickets but went on to raise his figures to 238, and was still unbeaten when Melville declared. Batting altogether for nearly five hours, without giving an absolute chance, Pataudi made runs all round the wicket in masterly fashion. His 238 not out, it may be added, was his fifth hundred in the course of his last six innings and – for those innings – brought his aggregate to 892 and his average to 223. In addition, he joined that very selected band of cricketers who have put together two separate hundreds in that encounter, the other members being William Yardley in 1870 and 1872, and H. J. Enthoven in 1924 and 1925.

• July 6, 8, 9, 1946 •

OXFORD WON by six wickets. M. P. Donnelly, with the experience of having played for New Zealand against England in 1937, created a personal record for a Test player in scoring a century in the Varsity match when a freshman. In the previous season, by scoring 133 and 39, this fine left-handed batsman was mainly responsible for the Dominions beating England; and at the age of 28 he held a distinct advantage over the other players, apart from his captain, D. H. Macindoe, who, by virtue of his bowling when a freshman in 1937, appeared that season for the Gentlemen against the Players.

On Monday morning, with the pitch unimpaired, though the ball sometimes lifted appreciably, Donnelly reigned supreme; in an hour and three-quarters he added 113 to his not out 29 before an extra-fast ball from Griffiths, that looked to turn a little down the slope, sent his off stump flying. No words would exaggerate the beauty and effectiveness of Donnelly as a batsman in this perfect innings of 142. Of moderate height and build he played the left-handed game in a

Martin Donnelly's 142 at Lord's was his sixth hundred for Oxford in 1946 and equalled the Nawab of Pataudi's 1931 record. That winter he was fly-half for the University's unbeaten rugby XV.

manner comparable to the best we have known. Never looking in doubt or difficulty, he usually played forward in defence, and his watchful back play made the forcing stroke look simple, as he invariably kept the ball on the turf as it sped away from his bat. Some drives, off, on and straight, were grand. The hook, genuine leg hit and cut were done with equal facility. No one scored more than 19 while Donnelly was at the wicket and he retired amidst an ovation.

• July 2, 4, 5, 1949 •

CAMBRIDGE WON by seven wickets. This result provided one of the biggest surprises of the season. Whereas Oxford alone beat the New Zealanders, and also claimed victories over Yorkshire and Middlesex, Cambridge's solitary

win had been against a weak Somerset eleven. There was no question that the Light Blues deserved success. Under the inspiring captaincy of Insole, they played as a team with a will, but Oxford gave such a wretched display of batting that many people expressed the opinion that better talent must have been passed over. As the Lord's pitch on many previous occasions during the summer proved very helpful to bowlers on the first morning and gradually eased, the feelings of the Cambridge captain when he won the toss must have been mixed. He decided to bat, and had to thank the Dark Blues for their generosity in allowing his side to occupy the pitch for the whole of the first day while they scored 339 for eight. Before tea Oxford missed six catches, two chances of stumping and one run-out.

• July 4, 6, 7, 1953 •

CAMBRIDGE WON by two wickets. The Light Blues had only three minutes to spare at the finish, but they thoroughly deserved their first success in the University match since 1949. For a long time they fought a losing battle until fine performances by Marlar, their captain, and Silk, who saw his side to victory with a splendid century, turned the fortunes of the game. Oxford, for whom Cowdrey hit the first century made against Cambridge in the series for five years, looked assured of honours when they led on the first innings by 121, but their subsequent display against the skilful off-spin bowling of Marlar showed them in poor light. In eight overs and one ball he sent back Williams, Cowdrey – this time out for a duck – and Dowding for 11 runs out of a score of 29 for four. Luckily for Oxford, Fellows-Smith was not so easily disposed of and at the close, with half their wickets standing, they were 222 ahead.

Another change of fortune came on the last morning. At once the rest of the Oxford batsmen were nonplussed by Marlar, who played on their unwillingness to come out and kill the spin, and in half an hour the whole side was out for the addition of

Robin Marlar's off-breaks so impressed in his freshman year at Cambridge, 1951, that he was invited to join the Gentlemen at Lord's. "Experienced batsmen faced him with respect," *Wisden* noticed.

15 runs. Marlar, in five overs of deadly bowling, took four wickets for 5 runs [innings figures, seven for 49; match figures, twelve for 143]. Cambridge, set to make 238 to win in five hours and twenty minutes, were left with a fair chance, but Silk, losing partner after partner to steady pace and spin bowling, had little option but to concentrate on defence. The match, indeed, seemed as good as lost when, with 35 minutes left for play and eight men out for 186, Marlar joined Silk. At first the Cambridge captain gave no indication of wanting to hurry and a section of the crowd clapped in slow rhythm, but soon there came a startling transformation in the tactics of Silk. Opening his shoulders he took 19 from the tempting left-arm bowling of Allan in nine balls, reached his century and raised the crowd to a high pitch of excitement. With five minutes left and two more overs likely,

Cambridge needed 5 more runs to win. Silk, now perfectly confident, cut Allan for four and levelled the scores. Then a neat deflection to square leg off the fifth ball settled the issue. He hit only ten fours, but he batted without a mistake and, more to the point, he adopted his policy to the needs of his side in a highly commendable manner.

• July 6, 8, 9, 1957 •

CAMBRIDGE WON by an innings and 186 runs. The margin was their biggest since the series began in 1827. Other records were the score of 211 by Goonesena, the Light Blues captain – the highest individual innings by a Cambridge man in the University match – and the Cambridge seventh-wicket stand by Goonesena and Cook of 289, which was the highest for any wicket by either side in the series. It was also the highest for the seventh wicket by Cambridge in any match.

Oxford: 92 (J. A. Bailey 21; O. S. Wheatley 5–15) and 146 (I. M. Gibson 63; C. S. Smith 4–42, G. Goonesena 4–40).

Cambridge: 424–7 dec. (Goonesena 211, G. W. Cook 111 not out; Gibson 3–48).

• July 6, 7, 8, 1960 •

DRAWN. Rain, which prevented play on the final day until after lunch, helped Cambridge to save the match after they had been led by 157 on first innings, but their own determined batting also did much to earn them a draw. For Oxford, Burki and the Nawab of Pataudi, immediately looking completely at ease, batted in splendid fashion on the second day and were not parted until they had added 190 runs at one a minute. Burki, eminently sound in defence, cut fiercely at times and batted chancelessly for three and a half hours, hitting eleven fours in his 79. Pataudi emulated the feat of his late father by hitting a century in his first University match for Oxford. This is the only

Light Blue all-rounder Richard Hutton, his father Sir Leonard and the Nawab of Pataudi, Oxford's captain, before the 1963 Varsity match.

instance of father and son reaching three figures in this fixture. Though he escaped from hard chances at 42, 46 and 86, Pataudi batted with memorable grace and skill, using a wide range of strokes with particular strength to the on. He batted just under four hours and his 131 contained one six and eighteen fours.

• July 11, 12, 13, 1962 •

DRAWN. For the third successive year the University match was left undecided and again this was due mainly to the Light Blues concentrating on making themselves safe instead of thinking in terms of victory from the very first ball. Indeed, this game has become so uninteresting in recent years that it has lost its appeal even to past and present members of the two Universities. The attendance on all three days was

Edward Craig – "first Cambridge cricketer in 50 years to be placed in the first class in three Triposes".

• July 6, 8, 9, 1968 •

DRAWN. A magnificent attacking innings by Goldstein provided the 124th University match with a wonderful start, and the game was notable for fighting, spirited cricket throughout, though, unhappily, only 2,033 spectators paid to see it. Goldstein gave Oxford a firm grip on the match with a breathtaking succession of strokes. He hit 100 runs in fours, as well as three sixes. Most of his boundaries came from fierce on-drives and pulls, played early. His 155 occupied only three and a half hours, and at one stage during his stand of 131 with Walsh for the second wicket he contributed all 53 runs as the score moved from 125 to 178. He was in exhilarating form again in Oxford's second innings, hitting 32 of the first 34 runs before touching a bumper from Jorden into his face. He retired, but returned and completed 50 in 52 minutes. Set 242 in two and three-quarter hours, Cambridge looked a beaten side at 78 for six, but Cosh and Jorden saved the match by staying for the last 70 minutes. Oxford bowled the remarkable number of 26.3 overs during the last hour in their attempt to split this pair.

• June 26, 28, 29, 1982 •

CAMBRIDGE WON by seven wickets. For the first time in its 138 years' history the University match was won on a declaration. After Ellis had set Cambridge to score 272 in 210 minutes, a dashing 100 by Boyd-Moss helped them home with five overs to spare. This departure from the uncompromising combat of former years was dictated partly by the modern approach to the match and partly by the loss through rain of seven hours' play on the first two days. Though the Cambridge captain, D. R. Pringle, had preferred to play for England against Pakistan in the Second Test, Cambridge had promised to be the stronger of two sides of modest bowling. John Varey, bowling for

Oxford, gave the 1982 match another place in history by taking the wicket of his twin brother, David.

• June 29, 30, July 1, 1983 •

DRAWN. Three declarations were not enough to produce a result to the 139th University match. Little time was wasted, however, in the search for one, and for Boyd-Moss the occasion brought rare distinction. With innings of 139 and 124, he became the first batsman ever to have scored two separate hundreds in the same University match and the first in the history of the fixture to have scored three successive hundreds, having made exactly 100 when Cambridge won in 1982. He also passed, by 12, M. J. K. Smith's record aggregate for the match of 477 runs, and took seven Oxford wickets for 68 with his orthodox left-arm spin. Being the better, more confident side, Cambridge held the initiative almost throughout, being threatened with defeat only briefly when Ellis was making 83 as Oxford attempted to score 304 in 265 minutes to win the match.

• June 30, July 1, 2, 1992 •

CAMBRIDGE WON by seven wickets. John Crawley led Cambridge to an unexpected victory, the first decisive result in the fixture for six years, when he scored an unbeaten 106 on the final day. Containing thirteen fours and a six, it was his maiden century for Cambridge, and the first in the University match since his brother Mark's 140 for Oxford in 1987; by coincidence, Mark made 102 not out for Nottinghamshire at Maidstone the same day. Oxford might have had the upper hand if Crawley had not been dropped twice on 20. For the fifth year running the match was seriously disrupted by rain, and it took the good will and determination of both captains to make a match of it. The third declaration set Cambridge 238 to win in 52 overs.

---

extremely small. The pattern for a drawn game was set by Cambridge after Lewis had won the toss. In four hours before tea they scored only 180 runs from 85 overs. Craig occupied two hours for 35, and Brearley needed four hours and twenty minutes for his not out 113. Clearly Brearley's tempo was affected by Craig's slowness. Many admirable cover drives were among the eighteen boundaries hit by Brearley, who not for the first time showed that he possessed the big-match temperament. He was the third wicket-keeper (all from Cambridge) to hit a century in the University match since the First World War, following J. T. Morgan in 1928 and P. A. Gibb in 1938.

• July 2, 3, 4, 1996 •

RAWN. Oxford's total of 513 for six, a record for the Varsity match, was the game's most notable feature. But when that score was combined with the loss of three hours to rain on the second day, the draw, always a favourite given two teams stronger on batting than bowling, became near inevitable. Curiously, Cake put Oxford in, giving them a licence to amass 390 for four in 106 overs on the first day. Gupte and Sutcliffe opened with 107 and were only separated by a run-out. Ridley made 155, his highest score, with seventeen fours and seven sixes, and next day Kendall also reached a career-best, an unbeaten 145; he hit sixteen fours and one six. Oxford added 123 in eighteen overs on the second morning, passing the previous Varsity record, their own 503 in

1900, through a six from Wagh. Cambridge replied by scoring at 6 an over in the time permitted by the weather, and after negotiations they declared at their overnight 164 for three and Oxford knocked up 63 in half an hour, leaving Cambridge a target of 413 from 86 overs. That seemed unlikely even before more rain wiped out another thirteen overs.

• July 11, 12, 13, 2000 •

RAWN. First-class university cricket at Lord's quietly petered out, with no play surviving the weather on the final day. In 2001, these two teams were scheduled to meet at Lord's only for a one-day game, with the three-day match held at Fenner's. Cambridge had the better of what play there was – damp and drizzle had also

Fred Goldstein's 1967 half-century was an *hors d'œuvre* for the 155 he served up a year later as Oxford captain.

threatened the opening day, which finally got under way at 4.10 p.m. Pyemont chose to bat and, coming to the crease on the second morning, scored a maiden first-class hundred, having fallen just short the previous year. As in 1999 he shared a century partnership with Hughes, who hit his second successive hundred in this fixture. Together they added 187 for Cambridge's third wicket: Hughes hit thirteen fours in his 119, Pyemont twelve fours and two sixes in 124, and each faced 213 balls. There was time for a brisk 50 from Howitt before the declaration at 382 for four. Oxford's openers were undaunted, however, putting on 71 before bad light ended play.

Wisden at Lord's

90

Up from Down Under

Australians at Lord's

"Lord's is to Australia what it is to this country. We would refuse to contemplate
a world in which there would be a jurisdiction over Lord's
which would prohibit the playing of Test matches."
[John Curtin, Prime Minister of Australia, Wisden 1945]

v MCC and Ground

THE SHOWERY MORNING of the 27th of last May, the day on which the Australians were to commence their first match at Lord's, and in London, was most discouraging to admirers of outdoor attractions, and when the Colonials were driven on to the ground at 11.30 there were not 500 visitors present, those who were there failing to recognise the team and, consequently, to welcome them with that hearty good old English cheer that of a surety would have rang out clear and loud had they known who those dozen or so men were who at that time were being driven up to the Pavilion in so quiet and unpretentious a way.

Ten minutes after their arrival, another sharp rainfall wetted the ground. That downpour over, the sun shone out in good old-fashioned early-summer form and, continuing to shine the remainder of the day, visitors flocked on to the ground so continuously that by four o'clock there was an excellent attendance grouped round the players. When the tell-tale at the money-taker's box had been finally consulted, it told of 4,742 visitors having paid, the whole of the money then taken (£119 7s.) being subsequently handed over to the Australians, the MCC also paying all expenses attending the match.

This, one of the most remarkable matches ever played at Lord's, was commenced at three minutes past twelve and concluded at twenty minutes past six the same day. Only 128 overs and two balls were bowled and but 101 runs, from the bat, scored in the match. One Australian bowler (Allan) got the crack bat of England caught out from the second ball delivered in the match. Another Australian bowler (Spofforth, left) clean bowled the said crack for 0 in the second innings. Another Australian bowler (Boyle) finished his bowling with eight overs and one ball for 3 runs and five wickets – four bowled. The aforesaid Australian bowler (Spofforth) made a distinct mark in the bowling of the match by delivering six overs (less one ball) for 4 runs and six wickets – three bowled. Alfred Shaw characteristically led off his bowling with seventeen overs for 1 run and two wickets (both bowled); another English bowler, Morley, obtained the first three Australian wickets ever captured at Lord's. And the decisive victory of the Australians, by nine wickets, was earnestly applauded by the members of MCC, and tumultuously so by the thousands of other Englishmen present, whose bones will have mouldered to dust long, long before the cricketers of the future – Colonial and English – cease to gossip about the marvellous short-time match played by the Australians at Lord's on the 27th of May, 1878.

MCC and Ground: 33 (A. N. Hornby 19; H. F. Boyle 3–14,
F. R. Spofforth 6–4) and 19 (W. Flowers 11; Boyle 5–3, Spofforth 5–16).

The Australians: 41 (W. Midwinter 10; A. Shaw 5–10, F. Morley 5–31) and 12–1.

Dave Gregory's 1878 team to England. Back (l-r): T. P. Horan, F. R. Spofforth, Jack Conway (manager), F. E. Allan. Middle: G. H. Bailey, T. W. Garrett, D. W. Gregory, A. C. Bannerman, H. F. Boyle. Front: Charles Bannerman, W. L. Murdoch, J. M. Blackham. They were joined in England by W. E. Midwinter, but in June, immediately before the Middlesex game, he was "abducted" from the Lord's Pavilion by W. G. Grace and transported to The Oval by cab to honour his Gloucestershire commitments.

v Cambridge University

• July 22, 23, 1878 •

THE AUSTRALIANS came to play this, their third and last match at Lord's, prestiged up by their two brilliant victories previously achieved on the old ground; one, of nine wickets, over as strong an MCC and G. eleven as could well be got together; the other, a 98 runs success, over a county of Middlesex team that included such front-rank cricketers as I. D. Walker, the two Lytteltons, the two Webbes, W. H. Hadow, etc.; and there were many who took those victories as their stand-point in anticipating success for the Colonials over the Cantabs. On the other hand there were those who duly reckoned up the

natural wear and tear of travel, cricket and unrest on the strangers consequent on their having played eighteen matches between the 19th of May and the 22nd of July, and, coupling all this with the comparative freshness and known cricket excellence of their more youthful opponents, foretold victory for the undefeated Cambridge men.

Neither side played full strength. The Australians were virtually without an eleventh batsman – the damaged hand (hurt at Swansea) of A. Bannerman prevented his scoring more than 1 run in his first innings and altogether precluded his batting in the second – and the Cantabs lost the valuable aid of Mr A. P. Lucas, whose illness barred his playing his part in this last brilliant success of his University's famous team, who won every match they played in 1878.

My thoughts in their hazy wanderings had fixed on one particular hit – never by me to be forgotten. Charley Bannerman was the striker, P. H. Morton the bowler, and the match Cambridge v Australians at Lord's, 1878. Half-asleep I seemed to see again that sturdy striker raise his massive shoulders and hit the ball a warrior's knock; the ball flew low, over the bowler's head, struck the iron-bound ground twenty yards in front of the outfield, and bounded right over the awning of Lord Londesborough's drag and struck the wall behind. Truly a mighty hit. I could almost hear the cheers and shouts that greeted it.

[A. G. Steel, 1891]

v MCC

• June 12, 13, 1868 •

MCC

Earl of Coventry, N. C. Allix Esq., C. Gee Esq., C. F. Buller Esq., Lt-Col Bathurst, R. A. Fitzgerald Esq., H. W. Fellows Esq., Captain Trevor, A. W. Fitzgerald Esq., Viscount Downe and T. Smyth Esq. *Scores:* 164 (R. A. Fitzgerald 50; Mullagh 5 wkts, Cuzens 4 wkts) and 121 (Buller 23; Mullagh 3 wkts, Cuzens 7 wkts).

The Australians	1st innings		2nd innings	
Bullocky (maroon)	b Buller	11	absent	0
Tiger (pink)	b Smyth	0	b Smyth	0
Cuzens (white)	b Buller	0	c Bathurst b Buller	21
Redcap (black)	b Buller	13	c Allix b Buller	5
Mullagh (dark blue)	b Buller	75	c Downe b Buller	12
Lawrence (captain)	b Fellows	31	run out	1
King Cole (magenta)	run out	7	b Smyth	0
Dick-a-Dick (yellow)	c and b Buller	8	b Buller	0
Twopenny (drab)	b Buller	6	b Smyth	3
Peter (green)	b Smyth	3	c Trevor b Smyth	0
C. Dumas (brown)	not out	0	not out	0
Extras	(byes 18, l-b 3, w 7, n-b 3)	31	(byes 1, l-b 1, w 1)	3
		185		**45**

MCC winning by 55 runs.
Umpires – Grundy and Farrands

Some of the pioneering Aboriginal players who toured England in 1868, photographed two years earlier in Melbourne. Back (l-r): Tarpot, T. W. Wills, Johnny Mullagh. Front: King Cole, who died from pneumonia on the tour, Dick-a-Dick, Jellico, Peter, Redcap, Harry Rose, Bullocky, Cuzens.

double-barrelled success of the young bowler, whose fast bowling ever and anon shot in down the incline in wonderful form. When the match ended at ten minutes past one on the Tuesday, Cambridge winning by an innings and 72 runs, Morton had taken twelve wickets, nine bowled, for 90 runs.

Cambridge University: 285 (Hon. A. Lyttelton 72, A. G. Steel 59; H. F. Boyle 3–82, F. R. Spofforth 3–85).

The Australians: 111 (W. L. Murdoch 47; P. H. Morton 7–45) and 102 (Charles Bannerman 26; Morton 5–45).

v England

• July 21, 22, 23, 1884 •

ENGLAND WON this match by an innings with 5 runs to spare, and the main elements of this success were the magnificent batting of A. G. Steel and the bowling of Ulyett. The Australians batted first, and despite a capital innings of 63 by Giffen they lost nine wickets for 160 runs. Then Scott, admirably supported by Boyle, once more proved how well he merited a place in the team, and before a parting was effected 69 runs were put on for the last wicket. Scott played cool, confident, skilful cricket for his 75. When time was called on the opening day England had lost three wickets for 90 runs, so the match then stood in a fairly even position.

Next morning Steel commenced his remarkable innings, joining Ulyett, the overnight not out. At 135 for five Barlow came to Steel's aid, 98 runs being put on before the professional was caught in the slips for 38. Read came in and, until he was bowled at 272, runs were scored at a rapid rate. Just previous to Read's dismissal, Steel had completed his hundred, and now he was joined by Lyttelton, 76 runs being put on before Lyttelton was bowled for 31. Only 3 runs were added and then Steel's magnificent innings came to a close. He had been at the wickets while 261 runs had been scored, and a hard chance to Boyle when he had made 48 was the only blemish in his

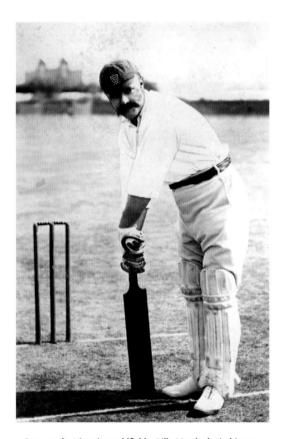

Born on the Victorian goldfields, Billy Murdoch "in his own day had no serious rival among Australian batsmen and, except for W. G. Grace, scarcely a superior in England... Few batsmen have been better worth looking at."

The Cantabs' 285 runs were made from 105 overs bowled by the Australians, six of whom took a turn with the ball, some of them twice. The Australian batting was commenced by Charles Bannerman and Murdoch, to the bowling of A. G. Steel (with the wind) and P. H. Morton (from the Pavilion end). Morton settled down to real good form and at 23 bowled Chas. Bannerman and Horan with successive balls, a shout akin in intensity to an Indian war-whoop greeting this

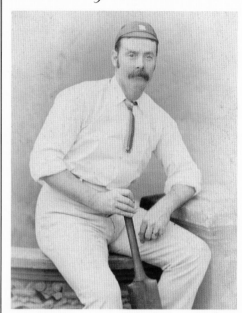

Ulyett's catch

It was on that eventful Tuesday afternoon that Ulyett caught and bowled Bonnor in a way that no one who was present will ever forget. Bonnor's mission was to knock the fast bowler off, and he did his best. He drove a half-volley with all his force, but the ball – travelling faster than an express train – went into Ulyett's right hand instead of to the boundary. Bonnor wandered disconsolately back to the Pavilion, and the England players gathered round Ulyett, curious, perhaps, to know what manner of man he was, and anxious to congratulate him on his escape from imminent danger. One can remember, even now, the look of wonder on the faces of A. G. Steel and Alfred Lyttelton. Ulyett himself was very modest about the matter. Complimented on the catch, when the day's play was over, he said simply that if the ball had hit his fingers instead of going into his hand, he should have played no more cricket that season. [1899]

148, the highest score made against the Australians during the season.

Before play ceased that day the Australians had lost four wickets in their second innings for 73 runs. On the last day Scott made a gallant effort to save the innings defeat but without avail. He was the highest scorer in both innings of the Australians, and his total of 105 for once out was a very fine performance. Ulyett's second-innings bowling figures of 39.1–23–36–7 speak for themselves, but he was undoubtedly helped by the ground.

v Gentlemen of England

• June 3, 4, 1886 •

ON THE OPENING DAY of this contest, Spofforth, in attempting to stop a ball hit hard back to him by Lord Harris (inset), dislocated the third finger of his bowling hand. The great Australian had immediately to leave the field, and he did not appear again until the match at Chichester on June 28. He afterwards continually complained of the weakness of the finger that had been injured, and the difficulty he found in imparting anything like the old spin to the ball. This was the first of two matches between the Australians and the Gentlemen, and the home side was distinctly less powerful than previous elevens that had represented the Gentlemen of England. Mr Steel had only just been married, and had therefore perfectly legitimate excuse for being absent. But the composition of the eleven, and also of the team that afterwards played at The Oval, showed the cricket public perhaps more clearly than anything else could have done the comparative weakness of the amateur element last season.

The Australian team that Billy Murdoch brought to England in 1890, the last of his five UK tours. He had previously led the 1880, 1882 and 1884 sides. Back (l-r): J. E. Barrett, S. P. Jones, H. F. Boyle (manager), G. H. S. Trott, E. J. K. Burn, Hugh Trumble, J. M. Blackham. Middle: C. T. B. Turner, J. J. Lyons, W. L. Murdoch, F. H. Walters, J. J. Ferris. Front: P. C. Charlton, S. E. Gregory.

v Players of England

• June 19, 20, 21, 1890 •

IN SOME RESPECTS this was the most remarkable match of the Australian tour. The fact that the Players scored 526 – the biggest total hit against the seventh Colonial team – would in itself have been sufficient to lend distinction to the fixture, but this performance on the part of the

English eleven was quite put into the shade by the personal achievement of Gunn, who played an innings of 228, the highest individual score ever obtained against Australian bowling in England. The Nottingham batsman went in first for the Players at five minutes past twelve on the opening day, and was not out till long after lunch on the second, his being the ninth wicket to fall. Altogether he was at the wickets for rather more than nine hours and a half, and so correct was his play that during the whole of

that time he did not give a chance. On the first day he scored 147 not out, and on the second he was batting four hours for 81 runs. It could certainly be urged against him that, on the second day at least, he played with undue caution, but he was no doubt pardonably anxious to beat the previous record score against Australian bowlers in England – Maurice Read's 186 for Surrey at The Oval in 1886 – and we at least shall not blame him. For finish and grace of style his batting was equal to anything we have seen.

*With regard to this match, rather a good story
has been told. Asked in an interview whether he had
ever felt tired of cricket, Sydney Gregory said he thought
not, except perhaps when he heard Billy Gunn say
"No" at Lord's for seven hours and a half. [1922]*

WE SHOULD SAY without hesitation that the finest performance of the 1893 tour was the first match with the MCC – a match which certainly deserves to go down to cricket history as one of the most remarkable games ever played. Going in against a total of 424, the Australians had to follow their innings with an adverse balance of 181 runs, and yet, in spite of this enormous disadvantage, they almost succeeded on the Saturday afternoon in snatching the game out of the fire, only the resolute play of Attewell and J. T. Hearne saving the MCC from defeat. Remarkable in many ways, this particular match will be remembered, more than anything else, for the most extraordinary display of hitting ever seen at Lord's. Lyons and Bannerman opened the second innings of the Australians, and before they were separated the balance of 181 was hit off, Lyons' share of this number being 149. So tremendous was the pace at which the big hitter scored that his first 100 runs were obtained in an hour. This beat the never-to-be-forgotten 100 in 80 minutes scored at Lord's for Middlesex against Yorkshire in 1889 by T. C. O'Brien, but in comparing the two performances it is important to bear in mind that the English amateur made his runs against time in the last stage of the match. [1894]

v MCC and Ground

• June 11, 12, 1896 •

SO FAR the Australians had had a career of uninterrupted success, but in this match – perhaps the most sensational of the whole tour – they met with a rude check, the MCC beating them by an innings and 18 runs. The game is already a historical one, the Australians being got rid of in their first innings by J. T. Hearne and Pougher for 18, the smallest score for which an Australian team has ever been dismissed in this country. George Giffen's illness compelled them to bat one short, but, though his absence of course made a difference, it is hardly likely he would have been able to save his side from disaster. By winning in such sensational style, the

v England

• June 22, 23, 24, 1896 •

THE FIRST of the three Test matches proved an enormous attraction, the official return showing that on the opening day no fewer than 25,414 people paid for admission. The full attendance was estimated at nearly 30,000, but while this great crowd was in itself a compliment to the Australians, it had a grave disadvantage. The field of play was seriously encroached upon, and it is to be feared that a good many of the people saw very little of the cricket. Under the circumstances it would hardly be fair to criticise the conduct of those present, but there was certainly an absence of the quiet and decorum usually characteristic of Lord's ground.

J. T. Hearne rocked the 1896 Australians.

MCC at last took their revenge for the never-to-be-forgotten defeat in 1878. Pougher, who went on with the total at 18 for three, took five wickets and not another run was scored. [Only the first three Australians scored.] Nearly 24 hours' rain had considerably affected the ground, and the MCC gained a decided advantage in winning the toss.

MCC and Ground: 219 (Mr A. E. Stoddart 54, Mr F. S. Jackson 51; H. Trumble 6–84).

Australians: 18 (J. J. Kelly 8; J. T. Hearne 4–4, A. D. Pougher 5–0) and 183 (J. Darling 76; Hearne 9–73).

When the Australians came again in 1899, the Mound Stand had been built on the site of the ivy-covered tennis court, with the clock in the middle.
[Sir Pelham Warner, 1955]

UNLIKE most of the previous teams, the 1899 Australians were seen at their very best at Lord's. Playing there four times they gained four brilliant victories, defeating – in addition to England – the MCC in June and July, and Middlesex in August. The MCC were not so well represented as they ought to have been, but inasmuch

Monty Noble – known to some as "Mary Ann".

as they won the toss on both occasions the crushing defeats they suffered were somewhat humiliating. In the return match the Australians were seen to extreme advantage, for, though the first day's cricket went all against them, they had the game in their hands when stumps were drawn on the second evening. In the later part of this match, Noble always looked extremely difficult to play, but I am bound to add – somewhat reluctantly – that the fairness of his delivery was often questioned by those who played against him. No one alleged that his action was habitually unfair, but that he threw now and then scarcely seemed to be disputed. In this connection I may mention that on the first morning the team practised at Lord's at the beginning of May, I had not been on the ground ten minutes before three people – quite independent of one another – told me that Noble's action was questionable. [*Sydney H. Pardon, 1900*]

v MCC and Ground

• May 26, 27, 28, 1902 •

THOUGH IN THE END left drawn, this was one of the most interesting matches played at Lord's last season. The MCC managed for once to put into the field a team worthy of their reputation, and got on so well that on the third day W. G. Grace declared the second innings closed. The task set the Australians was that of making 250 runs in three hours. Subsequent events proved that Grace had been rather premature in adopting the closure. Owing to rain, the Australians did not go in till after lunch, and yet, though a further fall of rain caused a delay of half an hour, they were only 33 runs short of victory with seven wickets in hand when the game had to be given up. So fierce was Darling's hitting at the finish that 56 runs were obtained in twenty minutes. Trumper was the hero of the match, playing superbly in both innings.

MCC and Ground: 240 (K. S. Ranjitsinhji 67; W. P. Howell 4–54) and 280–8 dec. (Mr P. F. Warner 50, Mr F. Mitchell 55 not out).

Australians: 271 (V. Trumper 105; W. G. Grace 5–29) and 217–3 (Trumper 86, J. Darling 42 not out).

v Gentlemen of England

• May 18, 19, 20, 1905 •

ON FEW OCCASIONS were the Australians seen to greater advantage than in this match against the Gentlemen of England. They lost the toss and had to field out for more than four hours and a half, yet at no time was their bowling mastered and on Saturday morning they gained a wonderful victory by an innings and 189 runs. The performance was the more remarkable from the fact that, on going in to bat, the Colonials lost their first four wickets for 94. Duff, who played a fine,

---

Mr Perkins grasps the nettle

The annual meeting of county secretaries for the arrangement of fixtures for the 1891 season was held on Tuesday, December 9, in the dining-room at Lord's Cricket Ground. Mr Henry Perkins, Secretary of the Marylebone Club, presided over a representative gathering. Before the ordinary routine of the business was entered upon, Mr Perkins rose and said he desired to draw attention to a matter of the greatest importance to the cricket community, and especially the counties, and that was the question of umpires.

Under the present system, each county nominated one or two representatives, who were not to stand umpire in any match in which their own county was engaged, and so far the system was an extremely good one. It seemed to him, however, that the counties had each nominated two persons with the idea that two bad umpires would make a good one. There were some people who were never satisfied, and had he received merely an individual complaint he should not have mentioned the matter, but complaints had come in wholesale. The Marylebone Committee could not stand this continuous succession of complaints, and the system must be improved. How was

that to be done? It would not be improved by the generous feeling that seemed to exist among the committees of counties that, because a man was a good cricketer and a deserving man, he was qualified to stand umpire in good matches. An umpire had been compared to a signalman in a box but, apart from the questions of danger and risks, the latter's duties were nothing compared to those of an umpire, who had to watch every single thing connected with the game.

It had been suggested by one county that every umpire should pass a written examination before him (Mr Perkins), but if that was the case there would not be an umpire at all. There were very few umpires who had got the Laws of Cricket at their fingers' ends, but he did not know that that was absolutely necessary. A man might not be clever, and might not have a great knowledge of the Laws, but he nevertheless might do fairly well and give good decisions. The Australians, who were the chief grumblers, told him at the end of the match played for the benefit of the Cricketers' Fund that the umpiring was the worst they had seen, though quite as many decisions had been given in their favour as against them. [1891]

determined game, helped to add 176 in 100 minutes, but the feature of the match was the brilliant and resolute hitting of Armstrong and Darling, who put on 273 in two hours and 40 minutes. Armstrong, whose 248 is the third-highest score ever obtained in a first-class match at Lord's, scored all round the wicket, except that he made no late cuts, and did not give a chance until he had put together 188. Though overshadowed by his colleague, Darling cut and drove in splendid form. The Englishmen shaped in most unglorious fashion in the final stage of the match, making only 48 runs in an hour and twenty minutes and during that time they lost eight wickets. It should be noted that the Gentlemen were without Jackson, Jones, Jessop and Bosanquet.

Gentlemen of England: 300 (P. F. Warner 85, Capt. E. G. Wynyard 61; C. E. McLeod 3–50) and 66 (C. B. Fry 26; F. Laver 4–13, W. P. Howell 3–1).

Australians: 555–6 dec. (R. A. Duff 94, W. W. Armstrong 248 not out, J. Darling 117 not out; W. Brearley 5–169).

v Gentlemen of England

· June 23, 24, 25, 1919 ·

IN THIS MATCH, the most important of the whole programme played by the Australian Imperial Forces, the Australians at last met with defeat, the Gentlemen beating them in uncompromising fashion by an innings and 133 runs. Though a little rain fell late on the first afternoon, there was nothing in the condition of the ground to account for the one-sided result. One may safely say that the Gentlemen were the better side, but whereas they were at the top of their form at every point, the Australians for once lost all their fighting spirit. The Gentlemen's victory was made certain on the second day when Douglas and Falcon, by means of really wonderful bowling, got the Australians out in two hours. Falcon made the ball swerve in deadly fashion, and Douglas had a little swerve to help his

W. W. ARMSTRONG (The Australian Cricket Team 1909.)

irreproachable length. Though the Australians' batting was better in the follow-on, there never seemed the slightest chance of avoiding defeat.

v England

· June 26, 28, 29, 1926 ·

IN MARKED CONTRAST to the dismal experience at Nottingham, the Test match at Lord's was favoured with splendid weather on all three days, while so great was the public interest in the struggle that, even with the gates closed on Saturday, when several more thousand people could

have been safely admitted, the ticket-holders and those passing through the turnstiles numbered 72,976 in all. The game, although drawn, produced a great batting triumph for England who, going in against a total of 383, headed that score by 92 runs and lost only three wickets. Australia, indeed, were saved from disaster only by a masterly display on the part of Warren Bardsley who, carrying his bat right through the tourists' first innings, put together a score of 193 – the highest registered in a Test match at Lord's.

v Public Schools XV

· August 11, 12, 1926 ·

A VERY HAPPY IDEA was this match, but rain on the first day limited play to 75 minutes. Collins to begin with objected to the Schools fielding fifteen, and four of the boys retired, but they were soon allowed to resume their places. The Australians, who left out five leading members of the team, lost Collins and Taylor for 16, but Ponsford and Woodfull added 174 in two hours. May, a slow-medium bowler, separated them, and the other seven wickets fell for 66, May sending down seven overs for 24 runs and five wickets. The Schools lost three wickets for 16, but Killick, the captain, and Tegner put on 50. Tegner remained until the hundred appeared, but the last seven wickets went down for 14 runs.

Australians: 264 (W. H. Ponsford 97, W. M. Woodfull 84; Mr W. D. S. May 6–53, Mr R. C. C. Whittaker 3–76).

Public Schools XV: 114 (Mr F. M. S. Tegner 45; C. V. Grimmett 4–26, J. Ryder 4–9) and 105–2 (Mr C. J. Wilson 57 not out).

Public Schools XV: P. G. T. Kingsley (Winchester), I. D. K. Fleming (Winchester), G. A. Rimbault (Dulwich), E. T. Killick (St Paul's), F. M. S. Tegner (Clifton), S. A. Block (Marlborough), C. M. Andreae (Harrow), W. D. S. May (Wellington), H. Taylor (Mill Hill), N. A. Doggart (Bishop's Stortford), L. P. Le Marchand (Beaumont), G. M. Hay (Highgate), R. C. C. Whittaker (Eton), W. H. V. Levett (Brighton) and C. J. Wilson (Repton).

v England

• June 27, 28, 30, July 1, 1930 •

BEATING ENGLAND, after a memorable struggle, by seven wickets Australia took an ample revenge for their overthrow a fortnight previously at Trent Bridge. The batting of the Australians and particularly that of Bradman will assuredly live long in the minds of those who saw it but, while giving the visitors the fullest praise for winning so handsomely after having to face a first-innings total of 425, it is only proper to observe that to a large extent England played right into the hands of their opponents. Briefly, the Englishmen lost a match which, with a little discretion on the last day, they could probably have saved.

Records went by the board. Australia, in putting together a total of 729 before declaring with only six wickets down, broke four – the highest score by Australia in England, 551 at Kennington Oval in 1884; the highest score in this country, 576 by England at The Oval in 1899; the highest score by Australia, 600 at Melbourne in 1924; and the highest score in the whole series of Test matches, 636 by England at Sydney in December, 1928. Bradman himself, with a score of 254, played the second-highest individual innings in the whole series of Test matches between England and Australia, while Duleepsinhji not only made a hundred on the occasion of his first appearance in a Test against Australia but scored the highest number of runs ever obtained by an England player in these matches at Lord's. There was one other notable point, A. P. F. Chapman, after leading England to victory six times, captaining the losing side. As some set-off against that, he enjoyed, for the first time in his career, the distinction of making a hundred in a Test match.

The Australians batted to a set plan, Woodfull and Ponsford steadily wearing down the bowling for Bradman later on to flog it. Nearly three hours were

Don Bradman, the man and the bat.

occupied over the first 162 runs, but in another two hours and three-quarters no fewer than 242 came. While in the end Bradman made most runs, very great credit was due to Woodfull and Ponsford. Curiously enough their partnership terminated almost directly after a break in play while the members of both teams were presented to The King in front of the Pavilion, Ponsford, who had batted very soundly, being caught at slip. Bradman, who went in when Ponsford was out and the bowling had been mastered, seized his opportunity in rare style and, hitting all round the wicket with power and accuracy, scored in two hours and 40 minutes 155 runs and was not out at the close.

On the Monday, Australia kept England in the field for another four hours and a half and added 325 runs, for the loss of four more batsmen, before declaring their innings closed at the tea interval. The partnership between Bradman and Kippax, which did not end until ten minutes to three when Bradman was caught right-hand by Chapman at extra mid-off, produced 192 runs in less than three hours. In obtaining his 254, the famous Australian gave nothing approaching a chance. He nearly played on at 111, and at 191, in trying to turn the ball to leg, he edged it deep into the slips, but apart from those trifling errors no real fault could be found with his display. He scarcely ever lifted the ball and, while his defence generally was perfect, he hit very hard in front of the wicket. Altogether he batted five and a half hours, his chief strokes being 25 fours, 3 threes, and 26 twos.

In the course of the four days, 110,000 people watched the cricket, the takings being roughly £14,500.

v Middlesex

• May 26, 28, 1934 •

UNTIL THE SECOND day Middlesex fought hard, but then they broke down badly and the Australians won easily by ten wickets. Hendren (115) and Robins (65) carried off the county batting honours on Saturday, scoring all but 78 of their side's total of 258. An amazing innings by Bradman overshadowed everything else in the Australian reply. After the quick fall of two wickets he hit the bowling all over the field. He and Len Darling put on 132 and he and Kippax 84, while altogether he obtained 160 out of 225 in just over two hours. For all his freedom, Bradman gave no chance. Enthoven accomplished the hat-trick after lunch on Monday, but the Australians led by 87 and, Middlesex losing eight wickets in clearing the arrears, the result was soon beyond doubt. Grimmett, main cause of the collapse, took five wickets for just over 5 runs each.

v England

• June 22, 23, 25, 1934 •

FOR THEIR DEFEAT at Trent Bridge, England took an ample revenge at Lord's, winning in three days in an innings with 38 runs to spare. This was England's first success in a Test match against Australia at Lord's since 1896 when Lohmann and Tom Richardson in a memorable struggle swept the Australians off their feet. While everyone in England was jubilant over the triumph of the Englishmen, it could not be denied that they were helped in a pronounced degree by the weather.

Winning the toss, England stayed in until nearly three o'clock on the second afternoon and put together a total of 440, but before the end of the day Australia had 192 on the board with only two men out. In view of this splendid start by the visitors there existed no sound reason why they should not have closely approached, if not even passed, the England total, but they suffered the cruellest luck, rain falling during the weekend and rendering their chances almost hopeless. Fortunately England had in the team a bowler capable of taking full advantage of the conditions that prevailed, and Verity, obtaining seven wickets in the first innings for 61 runs, followed this up with eight in

---

Hedley Verity's fourteen wickets in the day at Lord's in 1934 – Not a really bad wicket; just a patch as big as a tray where the rain had seeped under the covers, but he kept hitting it all the time. [*Frank Chester, 1954*]

---

the second for 43 to be the chief factor in giving England such a pronounced success. With his full record for the match, fifteen for 104 runs, he excelled Rhodes' performance at Melbourne in 1904 when that even more famous left-hander took fifteen wickets for 124 runs. By a singular coincidence, Rhodes was

"Judged by any standard, Verity was a great bowler... the high ease of the left-handed action, the scrupulous length, the pensive variety, all proclaimed the master."

present at Lord's to see his brother Yorkshireman accomplish his wonderful performance. Verity had taken one of the Australian wickets which fell on Saturday, and on the Monday he dismissed fourteen men for 80 runs, six of them after tea at a cost of 15. This amazing achievement would probably have been possible only to a man possessed of such length and finger-spin as Verity, because although the wicket helped him considerably it could scarcely be described as genuinely "sticky", except for one period after lunch. Verity's length was impeccable and he made the ball come back and lift so abruptly that most of the Australians were helpless. The majority of them had no experience in England of such a pitch, and they showed no ability or skill in dealing with bowling like that of Verity. Those who tried to play forward did not get far enough, and their efforts at playing back were, to say the least, immature.

England: 440 (Mr C. F. Walters 82, M. Leyland 109, L. E. G. Ames 120; T. W. Wall 4–108).

Australia: 284 (W. A. Brown 105; H. Verity 7–61) and 118 (W. M. Woodfull 43; Verity 8–43).

v England

• June 24, 25, 27, 28, 1938 •

DRAWN. A match of many fluctuations and fine personal achievements ended with Australia needing 111 runs to win and with four wickets to fall. In the Nottingham game, the scoring of a double-hundred on each side had been unprecedented, and yet in the very next Test match the same thing was done again. Hammond, who with able assistance from Paynter and Ames rescued England from a deplorable start, played an innings of 240 – the highest in England against Australia. Brown batted through the whole of Australia's first innings, scoring 206 not out and equalling the performances of Dr J. E. Barrett, Warren Bardsley and W. M. Woodfull by carrying his bat through a Test innings against England. Brown was on the field from the start of play until five o'clock on the fourth day.

The total number of spectators admitted to the ground on payment was 100,933 – a record for Lord's – and the receipts were £28,164 11s. 9d. On Saturday, the cricket was seen by the largest crowd ever to assemble at headquarters – the attendance was officially returned as 33,800. The gates were closed before the start and, after hurried consultations between officials, spectators were permitted to retain positions they had taken up on the grass, the boundary ropes being moved forward a few yards, thus reducing the playing area.

WALTER HAMMOND

Don Bradman meets King George VI and Queen Elizabeth in 1948, when he led the Australians through England, Scotland and Wales without defeat. Out for 98 against MCC in May, for 38 and 89 against England in June, for 6 against Middlesex in July, Bradman set the record straight in August with 150 against the Gentlemen on his farewell appearance at Lord's. His sixth hundred at headquarters, it took his aggregate there to 1,510 runs at an average of 79.47. At the end of the tour he and his "Invincibles" were the guests of The King and Queen at Balmoral.

At Lord's in 1938, England won the toss v Australia. In next to no time the fierce fast bowling of McCormick overwhelmed Hutton, Barnett and Edrich for 31. Then we saw the most memorable of all Wally's walks from the pavilion to the crease, a calm unhurried progress, with his jaw so firmly set that somebody in the Long Room whispered, "My God, he's going to score a century." Hammond at once took royal charge of McCormick, bouncers and all. One cover drive, off the back foot, hit the palings under the Grand Stand so powerfully that the ball rebounded halfway back.
[Neville Cardus, 1966]

v MCC

• May 22, 24, 25, 1948 •

AUSTRALIANS WON by an innings and 158 runs, a most convincing victory against the strongest opposition met so far. They excelled in run-getting, and the bowling of Toshack and Miller, in the first innings, and of McCool and Johnson, in the second, proved too much for the MCC batsmen. Barnes shared with Bradman in a stand of 160. Though at times subdued, Bradman obtained eleven fours in his 98 before giving slip a catch. Afterwards Miller was the dominating batsman, making 163 in four hours ten minutes with three sixes and twenty fours among his strokes. He drove and hit to leg gloriously. Johnson (three sixes and eight fours) helped him to add 155 in 105 minutes. On the second morning, when rain deadened the pitch, Laker was punished for nine sixes over a short boundary.

Hutton tried hard to check a collapse, but MCC had to follow on 363 behind, and though Hutton again batted well he received little support. The total attendance was nearly 60,000, the gates being closed on the first day.

v Gentlemen

• August 25, 26, 27, 1948 •

AUSTRALIANS WON by an innings and 81 runs. Bradman celebrated his farewell appearance at Lord's with his ninth century of the tour, in the course of which he became the first overseas cricketer to score 2,000 runs during each of four visits to England. Once again the Australians' big total robbed the match of much competitive interest. Brown, who hit his eighth century in his most attractive innings of the season, showed even more freedom than Bradman, with whom he shared a second-wicket stand of 181. Bradman (nineteen fours) threw away his wicket after

Paul Wilson Brookes, a member of the Lord's groundstaff, died in St Mary's Hospital on January 27, 1946, from the effect of wounds received when with the Coldstream Guards in Italy. As a County of London schoolboy he headed the batting averages and played against both Eton and Harrow for selected schoolboy teams. When sixteen years of age, in 1938, he became famous by bowling Don Bradman in the nets at Lord's during practice before the season began. Hooking at a left-hand delivery, Bradman missed the ball, which took his middle stump.

reaching 150, but Hassett and Miller took part in the third century stand in succession, the Australians finishing the first day with 478 for three. After hooking the second and third deliveries next morning for four and six, Miller gave deep square leg a catch off the fourth, but Hassett continued effortlessly and reached 200 in the last over before lunch, when Bradman declared at 610 for five.

v England

DRAWN. One hour remained for play on the fourth day when England began the last innings, needing 343 to win. That was an hour to make Australia happy and England miserable. Lindwall struck two shattering blows at once, getting Kenyon caught at mid-on and Hutton at slip, and when Langley made a thrilling diving catch off Graveney three men were out for 12. Although Watson stayed with Compton to the close, he might have been caught at short leg in the last over. The costliness of that miss was to be seen on the last day.

The general view of England's prospects of saving the game was shown by the size of the crowd which gathered for the final stages. In contrast to thousands having to be turned away earlier in the match, it numbered only 14,000. Few of those could have imagined they would witness anything approaching the gallant resistance by which England escaped defeat. Compton held out for 95 minutes before being leg-before to a ball that kept low. This brought in Bailey, the last of the recognised batsmen. Nearly five hours remained for play. At first Australia did not appear unduly worried, but, as Bailey settled down to his sternest defence, the bowlers produced all they knew. Still Bailey went on playing a dead-bat pendulum stroke to every ball on his wicket. His batting was far from attractive to the eye but it was thoroughly efficient and founded in first principles.

Peter Burge and Ken Mackay look on as Keith Miller flips the bails into the crowd after taking ten wickets in the 1956 Test.

Watson, too, met the ball with the full face of the bat. The most testing period came midway through the afternoon when Lindwall and Miller took the new ball. Three times Bailey was struck on the hand by a bouncer, but after each he paused only to wring his hand. Then the struggle was joined anew.

When Australia's fast bowlers went off after an all-out spell of 40 minutes, the total had risen by only 12 runs. As a result any visions of England snatching a sensational win had disappeared, but by now Australia showed their anxiety. The batsmen, unmoved and seemingly immovable, pursued their determined course. Their mood so infected spectators that often cheers broke out for purely defensive strokes. At the end of five and three-quarter hours, Watson's vigil came to an end. Soon afterwards Bailey, who stood in the breach for four and a quarter hours, shook off his self-imposed shackles and essayed a cover drive which resulted in a fairly easy catch. His annoyance was plain for all to see.

At the fall of the sixth wicket, 35 minutes were left for play, and the way the ball turned to Brown and

Evans gave rise to thoughts that, after all, Australia might finish England's resistance in time, but, riding his luck, Brown struck out boldly. Even so, feelings were such that when Brown was out in the last over, the prospects of Benaud taking three wickets in the last four balls to win the match were discussed seriously. Wardle soon brought speculation to an end.

v England

AUSTRALIA won by 185 runs and gained their first Test victory in England since 1948 at The Oval. After nearly three weeks of intermittent rain, the weather improved shortly before the match and the pitch rolled out firm and easy-paced, but throughout the game fast and fast-medium bowlers were able to make the ball move appreciably off the ground and this resulted in many snicks. No fewer than 21 wickets fell to catches behind the stumps. Evans did well at the wicket for England, holding six catches and making one stumping, but Langley achieved an even better performance for Australia. He established a new Test record for a wicket-keeper by helping to dismiss nine men in the match. His five victims when England batted a second time equalled the Test record for one innings by W. A. Oldfield in 1924-25 and himself in 1955 in Jamaica.

Ted Swannell was MCC head groundsman from 1955 to 1969, years when the problems of the Lord's pitch entered national folklore, and the alleged ridge at the Nursery end became the most famous since Vimy. He battled manfully with the problems in the manner of the old-fashioned Lord's retainer, relying on deference towards his superiors and a deep knowledge of the grass and soil. [2000]

v England

• June 22, 23, 24, 26, 1961 •

AUSTRALIA WON by five wickets. Almost throughout, batsmen were worried by the fast bowlers on a lively pitch and there were several cases of knocks and bruises, although fortunately none serious. There were talks from the first day of a ridge at the Nursery end, and immediately the match ended MCC called in a team of experts to survey the pitch. They discovered several depressions, and MCC stated that they would make an attempt to put things right before the start of 1962. Most of the time the ball flew at the Nursery end, but even at the other end the fast bowlers were able to get plenty of lift, and anyone who stayed at the crease a long time needed plenty of good fortune, besides determination and courage.

The only century of the match was 130 by Australia's W. M. Lawry, who batted for six hours ten minutes.

v England

• June 22, 23, 24, 26, 1972 •

AUSTRALIA WON by eight wickets on the fourth day with nine and a half hours to spare. So they soon avenged their defeat at Manchester in a contest which will be remembered as Massie's Match. The 25-year-old fast bowler from Western Australia surpassed all Australian Test bowling records by taking sixteen wickets for 137 runs [8–84 and 8–53]. In all Tests, only J. C. Laker, nineteen for 90 for England against Australia in 1956, and S. F. Barnes, seventeen for 179 for England against South Africa in 1913-14, stand above him. Moreover, Massie performed this wonderful feat on his Test debut, the previous best by

Squaring the pitch

I thought the Lord's pitches in 1968 were uncommonly indifferent. One expects something better at the headquarters of the game and it was, for the Australians, a blessing in disguise that rain so often intervened there, or else the Australians would have suffered several more defeats on their tour. I was watching play there one day, with the ball bringing up dust, when the idea occurred to me how little use is made of the middle of the pitch, which gets just as much rolling as the business ends. My thoughts led me to imagining a pitch made up of "middles" which, at the very least, would be thickly turfed with no bare spots – and I suggested this in the London *Sunday Times* as an experiment well worth trying.

One of the Lord's assistant-secretaries, Jack Bailey, was absent in Holland at the time I wrote my suggestion, and I still think it had much merit and the spirit of experiment in it. It would have turned play about, with the bowlers running from Father Time one end and the late Tavern the other. Even the traditions of Lord's, I thought, could have withstood what would have been an interesting innovation. But Mr Bailey seemed to think I had gone berserk when he approached me about my suggestion. He thought I was not taking Lord's seriously. [Jack Fingleton, 1969]

Jack Bailey – not impressed.

Dennis Lillee, John Gleeson and Ross Edwards give Bob Massie pride of place after his sixteen wickets. Bruce Francis adds his congratulations.

a bowler on his first appearance for his country being as far back as 1890 when, at The Oval, Frederick Martin, a left-arm slow to medium-pacer from Kent, took twelve for 102 for England against Australia on a pitch that had been saturated by rain. Of the 36 bowlers *Wisden* lists who have taken eight wickets in a Test innings, only A. E. Trott, for Australia against England at Adelaide in 1895, and A. L. Valentine, for West Indies against England at Manchester, 1950, had previously accomplished the performance on their Test debuts.

During the first three days, the atmosphere was heavy and ideally suited to swing. Massie maintained excellent length and direction, and his late swing either way always troubled the England batsmen. The conditions would also have suited Arnold, but England's best bowler at Manchester was suffering from hamstring trouble and on the morning of the match was replaced by Price, who proved rather disappointing. One must also stress the important part Lillee played in Australia's victory. Perhaps he was inspired by his six for 66 in England's second innings at Manchester. Anyhow, although this time his reward was confined to two wickets in each innings, he looked a far better bowler. He had tidied his long, fast approach of 22 strides, he was truly fast and he sent down far fewer loose deliveries. Massie capitalised on the hostility of his partner.

v MCC

• July 2, 3, 4, 1975 •

AUSTRALIANS WON by seven wickets with sixteen overs to spare. Despite MCC's defeat, this was a successful match from the England selectors' point of view because the young men on trial like Woolmer, Gooch, Slocombe and Bairstow all proved themselves in exalted company. Gooch excelled on the first day after Lillee had taken the first three wickets in eleven balls. He pulled full pitches from Gilmour and Thomson each for six, but most of his runs came from splendid square cuts and powerful off-drives. Woolmer enjoyed all-round success in scoring 55 and 85 and performing the hat-trick when the last four Australian first-innings wickets went down in four balls. It was the first hat-trick in England against the Australians since H. J. Enthoven did it at Lord's for Middlesex in 1934, and now it was on the day of Enthoven's funeral. The Australians made light of getting 270 to win, Greg Chappell (86 not out) and Walters (103 not out) seeing them home in an unbroken stand of 166 in two hours. It was Walters' first hundred at Lord's in three tours.

v England

• July 2, 3, 4, 6, 7, 1981 •

DRAWN. Lord's and Test-match time in recent years have become synonymous with bad weather, controversy and abysmal public relations, redeemed only partially by isolated individual performances. The Second Test followed this morbid trend. At the end of a personally disappointing match, which concluded a fruitless year as captain, Botham resigned as leader.

Left: Lord's line-up. Bruce Laird, Mike Gatting, Rod Marsh and Greg Chappell go through the motions as the 1980 Centenary Test lingers on to a tepid draw. Organised with great expectations, the match was ruined by rain and remembered for an unseemly scuffle involving the umpires and angry MCC members.
Right: Bye bye, Warnie! Ian Healy enjoys a close-up of the Ben Hollioake show.

Controversy came when the umpires took the players off for bad light during the extra hour of the second day. The sun reappeared, but Messrs Oslear and Palmer were under the false impression that no resumption could be allowed once play had stopped in the extra period. In protest at what happened, the crowd jeered and threw their cushions on to the ground, and next day the TCCB issued a statement regretting the misunderstanding.

v England

• May 23, 1993 •

AUSTRALIA WON by 19 runs. England slumped to their seventh successive defeat in a one-day international after apparently being in complete control. Chasing 231, they were 96 without loss and 159 for three. The collapse was engineered by the young left-arm fast bowler, Julian, who tore through England's middle order. Though Gooch made 42, he was sufficiently worried about his form to announce that he would play for the Essex second eleven later in the week for the first time in nineteen years. The day was enlivened by one great one-handed catch – taken by Hayden, leaping backwards in the deep, and worthy of a more distinguished victim than Jarvis – and by the Band of the Coldstream Guards playing "Happy Birthday" to Denis Compton on his 75th. The great man stood on a balcony and raised a glass, grinning.

v England

• May 25, 1997 •

ENGLAND WON by six wickets, making a clean sweep of the one-day series with their third consecutive victory by this margin. Every match began with Atherton winning the toss and ended with a stroke from Adam Hollioake. But it was Adam's nineteen-year-old brother Ben who stole the show here, on his debut, as he thrilled Lord's with an audacious half-century. Australia, captained by Steve Waugh because Taylor had dropped himself, had set England 270, their most demanding target yet. Hollioake junior made his entrance when the reply stood at 21 for one, and drove his third ball back past McGrath for four. He lasted just 45 more balls, but

some glorious strokes – including a swept six off Warne – and some streaky edges had already taken him to 63, with another ten fours. England still needed 157 when he fell, but the run-rate was down to 5 an over. Stewart, Crawley and Thorpe cruised along with few alarms.

v England

• July 19, 20, 21, 22, 2001 •

AUSTRALIA WON by eight wickets, ending England's run of three Lord's victories with a display of all-round brilliance that approached perfection. For the home side, events had a depressing familiarity. As in the First Test, the batting, notably the middle order, fractured – quite literally –

under pressure. At Edgbaston, Hussain broke a finger; at Lord's, Thorpe a bone in his right hand. Once again only the weather dragged play into a fourth day. And so, for the fifth time in seven Ashes series, England found themselves 2–0 down after two Tests.

Beforehand, though, England's quest was for a locum captain to replace the brittle-boned Hussain. Stewart declined the post after leading them to seven straight international defeats, while Butcher, dropped after his only foray into Test captaincy in 1999, ruled himself out. Gough optimistically volunteered his services, but Atherton, for a record 53rd time, was preferred. Despite Hussain's injury, England's selection worries had eased slightly. Fit again were Surrey colleagues Ramprakash and Thorpe. It meant the entire middle order, from Nos 3 to 7, came from one county, an unprecedented event.

Springboks and Proteas
South Africans at Lord's

*"The challenge of South Africa to English cricket is serious
and likely to call for a strenuous answer. The pioneer work of years is about to receive
fitting rewards and prizes – and what worthy pioneers!"*

[Wisden 1955]

v MCC and Ground

• June 4, 5, 1894 •

THIS WAS at once the sensational match of the tour and the most notable victory of the South African team. Rain prevented a ball being bowled on the opening day, and on the second morning W. G. Grace, for some inscrutable reason, put the South Africans in after he had won the toss. By playing on beyond the time for drawing stumps, the game was completed in one day and the finish proved highly exciting. In the last innings the MCC wanted 84 to win, and it seemed any odds on them when, at twenty to seven, they had scored 63 with only three wickets down. From this point, however, Middleton and Rowe carried all before them and in another half-hour the match was over, the South Africans gaining a thoroughly well-earned victory by 11 runs.

v Middlesex

• June 20, 21, 22, 1904 •

THIS PROVED the sensational match of the tour, the result being a tie. Middlesex did not have anything like their best team, MacGregor, Moon and the two Beldams being all away.

Opposite: South Africa's captain, Kepler Wessels, celebrates their four-day win on his country's return to Lord's after a 29-year absence. Above: The 1904 South Africans were soon sick of the sight of Bernard Bosanquet. He took nine in an innings against them for MCC, then hit a century for Middlesex a few weeks later.

Bosanquet took the batting honours of the match, hitting splendidly in both innings. The finish was exciting to a degree, the South Africans wanting only 11 runs to win with two wickets to fall. "Tip" Snooke was leg before wicket with the score at a tie, and directly afterwards Kotze was bowled by a fine ball from Trott.

Middlesex: 272 (Mr B. J. T. Bosanquet 110; Mr J. J. Kotze 5–94) and 225 (Bosanquet 44; Mr R.O. Schwarz 5–48).

South Africans: 287 (Mr W. A. Shalders 56, Mr F. Mitchell 66; A. E. Trott 4–80) and 210 (Mr L. J. Tancred 75, G. C. B. Llewellyn 60; Trott 6–75).

v MCC and Ground

• May 27, 28, 29, 1907 •

SO COMPLETELY did the South Africans outplay their opponents that shortly before lunch time on the second day, the MCC with only three wickets to fall required 46 runs to escape a single-innings defeat. The match, of course, looked as good as over but, Tarrant receiving useful assistance from Thompson and Hubble, the three wickets produced 138 runs. Even after this improvement on the part of the home side, no reason existed to doubt the ability of the Colonials to make 93. Tarrant and Trott, however, bowled in great form and when stumps were pulled up, six wickets had

The South African team that toured England in 1907.
Back (l-r): "Dave" Nourse, Harry Smith, William Shalders,
Maitland Hathorn, Aubrey Faulkner, Mr G. Allsop (manager).
Middle: Jimmy Sinclair, Reggie Schwarz, Rev. Cyril Robinson,
Percy Sherwell (captain), Louis Tancred, Bert Vogler, "Kodgee"
Kotze. Front: "Tip" Snooke, Gordon White, Stanley Snooke.
"A side so rich in bowlers has perhaps never gone on tour,"
Wisden remarked, adding that South Africa's googly bowlers
"Schwarz and Vogler, and in a lesser degree Faulkner
and White, were the talk of the season."

fallen for 58. Thanks mainly to Sinclair the remaining
runs were speedily obtained next morning, but instead
of winning in brilliant fashion the South Africans had
to be content with a narrow victory by three wickets.
Vogler in the second innings of the MCC took his first
seven wickets for 12 runs.

v England

• June 28, 30, July 1, 1924 •

THE SECOND Test match made it clear that,
whatever their merits, the South Africans had
no hope, under normal conditions of weather
and wicket, of beating England. The result was
overwhelming, England declaring with two wickets
down for 531 and winning by an innings and 18 runs.
They had twenty minutes batting at the end of the first
day, Hobbs and Sutcliffe carrying the score to 28.
Monday was a day of sensations and record-breaking.
Very seldom in a Test match has bowling been so
mercilessly knocked about. In two hours and a half
before lunch Hobbs and Sutcliffe added 200 runs, and
in all their partnership for the first wicket produced
268, this being a record in England for a Test match
and only once surpassed – by Hobbs and Rhodes in
1912 – in Australia. The running between the wickets

was daring to the point of audacity, but the two batsmen understood one another perfectly and never
looked to be in danger. Woolley was sent in first wicket
down to keep up the pace and most brilliantly he
played, his driving being magnificent. Before four
o'clock, Hobbs completed his 200 but he did not stay
much longer. When, with the total at 410, he lifted the
ball and gave cover point the easiest of catches, he had
not the faintest idea that another run would have given
him the record innings in Test matches in England. As
it was, he tied with Murdoch's 211 for Australia at The
Oval in 1884. The figures of his great innings were 15
fours, 6 threes, 24 twos and 85 singles, the large
proportion of singles speaking volumes for his
running between the wickets.

v England

• June 29, July 1, 2, 1929 •

LIKE that at Birmingham, the Second Test was drawn, but the cricket proved vastly more interesting, the game being brimful of incident and varying fortune. Bell, who came into the South African side, accomplished a great bowling performance, taking the last six England wickets after Morkel had led off with the first four. Morkel, bowling from the Pavilion end, obtained such pace off the ground that the first three England wickets fell for 18 runs in the first half-hour's play. O'Connor of Essex, who was playing in his first Test, was bowled first ball. The total was only 39 when the South African should have taken his fourth wicket, Sutcliffe, with his score at 14, being missed by Mitchell at slip. The consequences of that blunder were, from the South African point of view, deplorable, for Sutcliffe, after he and Hendren had added 93 in 75 minutes, went on to make a hundred.

South Africa were left with 293 to get to win. When, at 25 minutes past five, they had lost five wickets for 85, victory for England seemed certain.

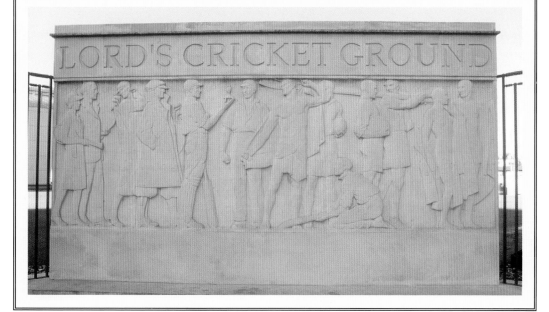

Bas-relief

Representations having been made by the local authorities as to the danger to traffic occasioned by the blind corner at the junction of St John's Wood Road and Wellington Road, the MCC Committee have agreed to a few feet of the club's leasehold property being cut off at this corner and dedicated to the public. By the generosity of Mr David Isaacs, a panel in bas-relief executed by Mr Gilbert Bayes, the sculptor, depicting "Athletics", is being placed on the angle wall. [1935]

PLAYER'S CIGARETTES

H. LARWOOD (NOTTINGHAMSHIRE)

The blow to the head that Harold Larwood inflicted on "Jock" Cameron at Lord's in 1929 prevented the South African wicket-keeper from playing for more than three weeks. Cameron's return to head-quarters in 1935 was memorable for a much better reason: his first-innings 90 put South Africa on course for their first Test victory in England.

A most unfortunate accident followed, Cameron being hit on the head by a fast, rising ball from Larwood and being knocked senseless to the ground. Cameron was carried off and the unhappy incident damped everybody's spirits; all real interest vanished. With 4 runs added, the players, owing to defective light, went in at a quarter to six and not a murmur of dissent was heard.

v England

• June 29, July 1, 2, 1935 •

BEATING ENGLAND by 157 runs, South Africa, after striving for 28 years, won a Test match in England for the first time. Although undoubtedly fortunate in winning the toss, they richly deserved their victory. In batting and bowling they were definitely superior, and brilliant fielding, notably by Wade, the captain, in the silly mid-off position, also played a conspicuous part in the success. From an early point in the match the wicket

Leather-jackets

The match ground has been attacked by a plague of "leather-jackets", the larvae of the crane fly commonly known as "daddy long-legs". They have destroyed the roots of the grass in places, and bare patches are to be seen, especially in the centre of the ground. Every effort is being made to exterminate the grubs. [1936]

. . .

Harry White, head groundsman at Lord's for 26 years before retiring on pension at the end of the 1936 season, performed the difficult task of preparing "natural" pitches with marked skill. The MCC Committee would not allow the use of "dope", but White contrived to keep the turf fit to withstand the wear of three-day matches throughout each season, and the centre for Test matches was his special pride. In 1926, during the England and Australian match, he overcame a severe trial. On the Monday morning, part of the ground, including a narrow strip across the middle of the pitch, was saturated with water from the hose, turned on in some way that always remained a mystery. By careful drying White and his staff got the ground in order so satisfactorily that the game was resumed only ten minutes late. A greater cause for worry was the plague of leather-jackets during the 1934 winter. With the help of Austin Martin, of The Oval, and his son, who eventually succeeded Harry White at Lord's, this trouble was dealt with satisfactorily. White played regularly for Hertfordshire from 1894, and after a modest start became the best all-round player for the county, taking many wickets each season and scoring freely for a side that often showed marked weaknesses. Bowling medium-pace right-hand, he was very good on sticky wickets. [1944]

Herby Wade introduces King George V to the 1935 South Africans before the start of the Lord's Test. "Chud" Langton, next in line beside openers Bruce Mitchell and "Jack" Siedle, contributed six wickets and 48 runs to a momentous win.

lent an appreciable amount of help to bowlers who could turn the ball, which in addition frequently came off the ground very low. Much was said and written during the match about the vagaries of the pitch. South Africa's bowlers, however, without a shadow of doubt, were by far the better, and Xenophon Balaskas marked his Test debut in England with a most skilful piece of work by taking in the two innings nine wickets for 103 runs.

South Africa: 228 (H. B. Cameron 90; H. Verity 3–61) and 278–7 dec. (B. Mitchell 164 not out; Verity 3–56).

England: 198 (Mr R. E. S. Wyatt 53; X. Balaskas 5–49) and 151 (H. Sutcliffe 38; Balaskas 4–54, A. B. Langton 4–31).

v England

· June 21, 22, 23, 1951 ·

ENGLAND WON by ten wickets. This Test will be remembered as "Tattersall's Match". Whereas rain helped South Africa to their victory in the First Test at Trent Bridge, this time it provided a wet pitch for the England bowlers, and Tattersall exploited the conditions to such an extent that he took twelve wickets for 101 runs. A thunderstorm in the early hours of Friday morning, after England had scored 311 on the opening day, transformed the pitch, but in the absence of powerful sunshine it never became a "glue-pot" like that in 1934 when Hedley Verity took fourteen Australian wickets in one day. The previous month, when appearing at Lord's for MCC, Tattersall upset the South Africans by taking eight wickets for 51 runs, and now, on his first appearance in a Test at cricket's headquarters, he carried almost everything before him.

For the most part he bowled over the wicket at medium pace to a cluster of short legs and a silly mid-off and silly mid-on. He varied his pace and used the seam as an alternative to finger-spin. Tattersall owed much to the excellent support he received from the fielders and particularly Ikin, who with Hutton, Watson and Brown made some brilliant catches.

With the match finishing so early on Saturday afternoon, a short time-limit game was played to entertain the spectators.

v MCC

• May 21, 23, 24, 1955 •

SOUTH AFRICANS won by 93 runs. This was a most auspicious occasion for the touring team to gain their first victory of the tour, and it was achieved mainly by sound bowling supported by excellent fielding. The task was made easier owing to Hutton, the MCC captain, taking no part in the match after the opening day because of an attack of lumbago. In his absence the MCC batting proved woefully weak. Although holding a substantial lead at the close on the second day, the South Africans could add only 8 runs while losing their last five wickets next morning. They broke down completely in the face of really splendid off-spin bowling by Titmus, who took those five wickets in seven overs and one ball while conceding only 3 runs. Titmus's analysis of eight wickets for 43 runs was the best of his career so far.

Fred Titmus, aged 22, made his England debut when the South Africans returned to Lord's in June for the Second Test.

v MCC

• May 21, 23, 24, 1960 •

DRAWN. An even match ended with the South Africans having to fight hard to save the game. It was notable for the no-balling of Griffin for throwing on Saturday. Lee called him first in his fifth over, and when Griffin returned for a second spell Langridge called him twice from square leg. Once Griffin was called simultaneously for throwing and dragging. No further action was taken against him during the match, but afterwards a special meeting was held to discuss the point, the umpires saying that his basic action was all right. According to the *South African Cricket Annual*, Griffin had been called twice before, in February and March 1959 while playing for Natal.

v England

• June 23, 24, 25, 27, 1960 •

ENGLAND WON by an innings and 73 runs with over a day to spare and placed themselves two-up in the series. The game was made memorable by the several incidents which occurred while Griffin was bowling. He became the first South African to achieve a hat-trick in a Test match, and the first man for any country to accomplish that feat in a Test at Lord's, when he dismissed M. J. K. Smith with the last ball of one over and Walker and Trueman at the start of his next. He also gained a less enviable record, for he became the first player to be no-balled for throwing in a Test match in England. There had been two previous instances abroad, E. Jones of Australia against England at Melbourne in 1897-98 and G. A. R. Lock of England against West Indies at Kingston in 1953-54.

Griffin was called eleven times during the course of the England innings, all by F. Lee at square leg.

Griffin's action

If Gover, the former Surrey and England bowler, said that he found that Griffin's main trouble, apart from any bent arm [the result of a childhood accident], was an early opening up at the wicket and a tendency to bowl from the edge of the crease. This had the effect of getting the right shoulder in front of the left at the moment of delivery. There was little or no follow-through and to get his speed there was a late acceleration of the bowling arm which caused the umpire's doubt as to the fairness of the action. When he changed his style and turned his left shoulder to the batsman on arriving at the wicket, there was loss of pace. At Lord's, Griffin put all he could into his bowling and slipped back into his old way. [Norman Preston, 1961]

Then, when the match ended at 2.25 p.m. on the fourth day, an exhibition game took place and Griffin's only over consisted of eleven balls. S. Buller no-balled him for throwing four times out of five. On the advice of his captain, McGlew, who had spoken to Buller, Griffin changed to underarm bowling but was promptly no-balled again by Lee for forgetting to notify the batsman of his change of action. Griffin's last three balls were bowled underarm.

These events tended to overshadow the match itself, which provided England with an easy victory against a disappointing South African side. Taking eleven wickets for 97, Statham achieved the best Test match figures of his career and became the first English fast bowler to take eleven wickets in one game since the war. To avoid the possibility of the supposed ridge near a length at one end interfering with the game, the pitch was moved a yard nearer the Pavilion.

v England

· July 21, 22, 23, 24, 1994 ·

SOUTH AFRICA won by 356 runs. The first Test between the countries for 29 years began with the word "historic" being used to the point of monotony but ended with controversy engulfing the England captain, Mike Atherton, and threatening his future. The Atherton affair took over all discussion of the match and the genuinely historic outcome – a devastating South African victory – was all but forgotten amid the fuss.

Normally, England being bowled out for 99 on a sound wicket might have caused a great deal of anguish. However, everyone was preoccupied by the fact that Atherton, fielding on Saturday afternoon, was seen by the TV cameras taking his hand out of his pocket and rubbing it across the ball before passing it back to the bowler. He was called before the referee, Peter Burge, to explain what the official statement

called his "unfamiliar action" and answer suspicions that he had broken Law 42.5 by using an artificial substance to alter the condition of the ball. Burge said he had accepted Atherton's explanation without saying what it was. But the following day, after further TV pictures were shown that looked even more sinister and England's batsmen had crumpled to a humiliating four-day defeat, Atherton admitted publicly that he had not told Burge the truth by saying that he had nothing in his pocket. In fact, he said, he had some dirt there that he picked up to keep his hands dry and prevent moisture getting on the ball while Darren Gough was trying to reverse-swing it; the second set of pictures clearly showed some of the dirt falling off it.

Ray Illingworth, the chairman of selectors, immediately fined Atherton £2,000 – half for using the dirt, though that was not a breach of any law, and half for the lie. He hoped that would close the matter. But over the next 48 hours there was a tidal wave of public emotion in which almost everyone from the cricket correspondent of the BBC to people who had never seen a match in their lives demanded Atherton's resignation. Illingworth and the TCCB remained staunch in their support, though. The umpires said the condition of the ball had not been changed and the South Africans made no complaint, except to grumble that their triumph had been ignored.

v England

· July 12, 2003 ·

ENGLAND WON by seven wickets, demonstrating a ruthlessness many felt beyond them and inflicting a record-breaking defeat upon South Africa in an unexpectedly – and gruesomely – one-sided NatWest Series final. In their first one-day appearance at Lord's, South Africa were asked to bat and were promptly bowled out for 107, the lowest score in 34 one-day internationals at the ground. Not one of their batsmen reached 20.

The obvious conclusion, that the toss decided the match, was unfair on the head groundsman, Mick Hunt, who produced a pitch which had a little moisture to start with, but displayed even bounce throughout. The fault lay instead with a sequence of flat-footed strokes from South Africa, some of them batting on the Lord's slope for the first time. England's discipline with the ball was exemplified by Gough, whose opening burst of seven overs cost just 9 runs. The wicket that symbolised England's dominance was that of Kallis, who came into the match with a tournament average of 164.50, but was out for a twelve-ball 0 when he edged Gough through to Read, one of five catches by the wicket-keeper. Kallis flew home to Cape Town immediately after the game to be with his dying father.

The South African innings lasted just 32.1 overs, and England's reply was even quicker. Solanki overcame a cautious start to hit a 58-ball half-century and take England to the brink of victory with the help of Vaughan. McGrath and Flintoff supplied the finishing touches. At the end of the match Smith gathered his players around him on the outfield, a sight more usually associated with winning teams. He told his players to "remember the hurt" of this defeat. It was a neat way of converting humiliation into motivation and, as far as England were concerned, it worked all too quickly.

v England

• July 31, August 1, 2, 3, 2003 •

SOUTH AFRICA won by an innings and 92 runs. The new smiling face of English cricket, which Michael Vaughan presented to the cameras in the Long Room on the eve of the game, lasted less than 24 hours – indeed only about 65 hours from the moment he was handed the captaincy when Nasser Hussain resigned on the Monday night. Normally, even England captains get a honeymoon longer than that. But by Thursday lunchtime, England were in crisis for the second Test in succession. And this time there was no escape. South Africa, having scored 682 for six, smashed the record for their highest total and inflicted on England their biggest-ever first-innings deficit – 509, five more than at Brisbane in 1946-47.

The disaster was, at least in part, attributable to the unplanned handover, and the brutal scheduling of Tests with only two days in between. England were too distracted to absorb the lessons of Edgbaston and evolve a plan to combat Smith's relentless, but not infallible, batting. By the end of this game, a man being patronised ten days earlier as a young inadequate was being compared to Bradman – indeed he had surpassed him by scoring 259, five more than the Don's 73-year-old record for an overseas player in a Lord's Test, and reaching 621 in the two games, which was beyond even Bradman.

England's first-day batting certainly was gormless. They nearly all looked at home but got out needlessly, for no good reason crashing to 118 for nine. Then the last pair, Gough and Anderson, had some fun; their 55 was the highest stand of the innings, an oddity last achieved for England 133 Tests earlier, by Phil DeFreitas and David Lawrence at Trent Bridge against West Indies in 1991. But the spectators' cheers were more ironic than delighted, and if there were a trace of happiness left in Vaughan's smile, it was wiped out

Graeme Smith has 250 on the board, and Sir Donald Bradman's record at Lord's is within his grasp.

when Smith was dropped horribly by Hussain at cover on 8. His opening stand with Gibbs was worth 133; he put on 257 with the uncompromising and unflashy deflector Kirsten, then 123 with Dippenaar. At 3.02 on the second afternoon, Smith reached 500 for the series, only eight days after it had begun. Night fell

again, and he was still there, Brian Lara's 375 apparently at risk. By then bowlers and spectators alike began to forget there was ever an existence without Smith at the centre of it.

The interminability of his innings had a drawback for him – observers began to sniff out his technique, which involved biffing anything straightish into the leg side and keeping the face closed to avoid nicks. A line outside off stump had possibilities. But as the weather grew hotter, the pitch ever blander and their spirits weaker, England had no way of executing a plan even if they had one: the old-new pairing of Gough and Anderson, so hyped during the one-day series, was a disaster (except with the bat). Both were knackered: Anderson by overwork; Gough, terminally, by the passing years. And what chances came were mostly dropped, four in all.

After nine hours (or maybe years) and 34 minutes, 370 balls and 34 fours, Smith was bowled by Anderson for 259. South Africa improved their highest total against England for the second match running, but Smith declared, kindly, just short of the wholly demoralising 700 mark and England, in their second innings, batted far better than in their first. No one ever imagined they could save the game but they did put down markers for the weeks ahead. Butcher and Hussain put on 126, and later came Flintoff, who finally played the sensational innings in front of an English Test crowd that he had long threatened. He smashed 142 off 146 balls, with eighteen fours and five sixes, crashing the ball with a power that may even have surpassed Ian Botham, and enchanted a packed house (who feared they would watch only another collapse). Just as importantly, he dispelled the panic in the England camp. It was the highest score by a No. 7 in a Lord's Test, beating Les Ames' 137 against New Zealand in 1931. Ntini became the first South African to take ten wickets in a Lord's Test, just reward for his pace and zest, though he was helped by the tightness of the other bowlers and the looseness of the batting – half his wickets came from misjudged pulls, hooks and swats.

Omnium-gatherum

"Dr Gaye made some remarks about the permission being refused or granted
to charitable bodies for festivities at Lord's ground. He had appealed to the Secretary for permission
for a band of clown cricketers to play at Lord's on behalf of a charitable corporation,
but had received an answer which he thought was scarcely polite."

[Wisden 1876]

Right Handed v Left Handed

• May 9, 10, 1870 •

THIS WAS the opening match of the 84th season of the Marylebone Club. So brilliant an array of the cricketing talent of the country on no prior occasion appeared in an opening match at Lord's, the match being moreover interesting from its not having been played since 1835, and for its being the first match Carpenter, Hayward and Smith had played in at Lord's since 1866. The weather was bright, but nippingly cold for May. The Left were comparatively weak as batsmen, and were without a professed wicket-keeper, so they were defeated by an innings and 8 runs.

The Left: James Lillywhite, H. Killick, A. Rylott, G. Griffith, G. Wootton, T. Emmett, E. Willsher, C. Martin, J. West, G. Howitt and J. C. Shaw. *Scores*: 73 (Lillywhite 26; Grace 6–24) and 104 (Killick 55; Grace 3–44).

The Right: W. G. Grace Esq., H. Jupp, Richard Daft, T. Hayward, R. Carpenter, John Smith (Cambridge), C. F. Buller Esq., T. Hearne, Alfred Shaw, Walter Price and S. Biddulph. *Score*: 185 (Smith 45; Shaw 4–49).

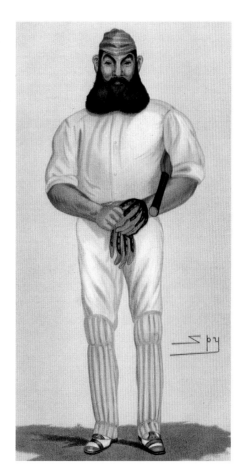

Two of I Zingari's founders – J. Loraine Baldwin (in the bath chair) and, on his right, the Hon. Spencer Ponsonby Fane – with the eleven who played for "the Gypsies" at Lord's in their Golden Jubilee match of 1895.

North v South

• May 17, 1875 •

WHIT MONDAY was most enjoyably fine, the bright, hot sun that beamed down upon the millions of holiday folks out that day pleasure-taking, being agreeably tempered by a cool and brisk breeze from the east. Lord's was thronged, so many as 8,342 having paid for admission to the old ground, which, as evening drew near, presented all the familiarly free and easy appearance of a great match day on a great holiday. The Tavern balcony was as full as the many bottles of champagne that were uncorked there on that day. The top of Mr Frank Dark's garden wall was covered by those "who could climb and did not fear to fall". The reporters' stall was filled by an unusually large number of the gentlemen of the press, and around the ground the people sat or stood five or six deep, crowding in front of the score box throughout the afternoon and evening as they were never before allowed to crowd and, it is to be hoped, will never again be allowed to crowd. For the angry disputations, the noisy chaff, the frequent question-asking to the scorers and the (at times) interception of all sight of the wickets by that upstanding throng of men – some of them six-footers – rendered the perfect fulfilment of the scorers' duties next door to an impossibility.

The match – as a fair trial of the cricketing strength of North and South – was a thorough failure, owing to the absence of many of the best cricketers of the North. Mr A. N. Hornby did not play; Richard Daft, William Oscroft, Martin McIntyre, J. C. Shaw, Mycroft, Flint and Frost were playing at Nottingham in the Notts v Derbyshire match; Ephraim Lockwood, Andrew Greenwood, Pinder, Allen Hill, Emmett and Ulyett were playing against a 22 at Hallam (or thereabouts); Watson – the Southerton of the North – was playing at Old Trafford; Rylott was absent and F. Randon was playing at Leicester. So the North team had to be made up from men engaged on the ground, colts, veterans, etc. Consequently the surprise was not that the Northerners were so emphatically licked, but that they were enabled to get that very strong batting eleven of the South out for an innings of 123 runs, the match being then half played out with an advantage of 33 runs to the South.

The North's second innings was indeed a brief affair; commenced at 5.12, it was done with at 6.40. Under the impression there would be no more play that day, hundreds of visitors left the ground and thereby lost a brief but busy bit of batting. A consultation was held and a decision to play out the match that evening promptly come to. The clear-the-ground bell rang out forthwith, the people settled down in their places and at 6.50 out came Mr W. Grace and Jupp to get the 40 runs. They got them in dashing form.

The North: 90 (Alfred Shaw 26 not out; J. Southerton 9–30) and 72 (R. Clayton 27; Southerton 7–22).

The South: 123 (H. Charlwood 24; Shaw 4–52, F. Morley 5–55) and 41–0.

A Contrast

• September 8, 1875 •

AT THE North of the Thames Licensed Victuallers' Annual Fête, held on the old ground on the above day, a match at cricket was played between twelve of the Licensed Victuallers' Sons and twelve boys of the Licensed Victuallers' School. Each side played out their innings, with this result:

North of Thames Licensed Victuallers' Sons: 6; **Boys of the Licensed Victuallers' School**: 234.

Smokers v Non-Smokers

• September 15, 16, 1884 •

THIS MATCH was played for the benefit of the Cricketers' Fund Friendly Society, and, contrary to the anticipations of many, proved one of the most attractive contests of the season. Though it occupied only two days, no less a sum than £561 16s. 6d. was handed to the treasurer of the Fund after all the expenses were paid. The match owed its origin to Mr V. E. Walker, whose desire was in the first place to promote the welfare of a very deserving charity, and in the second to see members of the redoubtable Australian team opposed to each other. That this object was effected, a glance at the teams will show. The sides were not as strong as could have been wished as several prominent amateurs were unavoidably absent and, owing to the early departure of Shaw and Shrewsbury's team for the Antipodes, many of the most celebrated professionals were prevented from taking part. The two elevens, however, were undoubtedly strong, though the Smokers laboured under the disadvantage of going into the field without a thoroughly reliable wicket-keeper, Blackham, owing to a bad hand, being unable to render any assistance. Bonnor's remarkable hitting

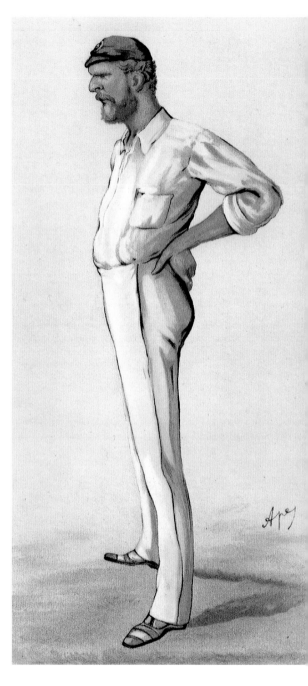

Above: Close inspection reveals that cigarettes and a pipe separate the Smokers from the Non-Smokers. Even umpires Tom Hearne (left) and Edgar Willsher have an affinity with the rival camps. Left: Six feet six in his boots and weighing in at just under 17 stone, neither smoker nor drinker, Australia's George Bonnor was just the man to render smoker Spofforth ashen. He hit him for six to reach his hundred, and another mighty drive landed on the Pavilion roof.

was of course the feature of the match. His 124 is the highest score he has made in England, and the manner in which he punished the bowling of Spofforth was perhaps the most extraordinary part of it. The great bowler had certainly never been hit with such astonishing freedom in this country before.

Non-Smokers won the match easily by nine wickets.

Non-Smokers: W. G. Grace, A. C. Bannerman, W. L. Murdoch, G. J. Bonnor, R. G. Barlow, E. M. Grace, H. J. H. Scott, T. C. O'Brien, W. Wright, S. Christopherson and R. Pilling. *Scores*: 250 (Bonnor 124; Peate 6–30) and 15–1.

Smokers: C. I. Thornton, P. S. McDonnell, G. Giffen, Lord Harris, W. Gunn, M. P. Bowden, G. E. Palmer, F. R. Spofforth, C. C. Clarke, T. Emmett and E. Peate. *Scores*: 111 (Bowden 29; W. G. Grace 5–29) and 152 (Gunn 43 not out; Barlow 5–24, W. G. Grace 3–63).

Colts of the North v Colts of the South

• May 21, 22, 1888 •

IT BEING quite impossible now-a-days to get representative teams for a North and South match at Lord's on Whit Monday, the MCC Committee, at the meeting of secretaries in December , submitted to the inevitable and arranged a fixture between the Colts of the North and South. The result was an interesting game, though bad fielding had much to do with the long scoring. The Northern team won by 73 runs.

Government v Opposition

• July 29, 1893 •

A MATCH BETWEEN members of Parliament representing respectively the Government and Opposition was played, but did not prove the attraction expected. However, the weather was most unfavourable. The Opposition, which included several well-known cricketers, won very easily, declaring their innings at an end when three wickets had fallen for 243 runs.

Government: Mr J. A. Pease, Mr J. F. Leese, Hon. Mark F. Napier, Mr H. J. Gladstone, Mr George Newnes, Mr A. E. Hutton, Mr William Allen, Mr R. K. Causton, Mr C. E. H. Hobhouse, Mr J. M. Paulton and Mr R. T. Reid.
Scores: 104 (Napier 40; Forster 7–49) and 41–3.

Opposition: Mr H. W. Forster, Viscount Curzon, Viscount Chelsea, Mr Walter Long, Mr W. Bromley-Davenport, Mr Ernest W. Beckett, Hon. Sidney Herbert, Mr A. F. Jeffreys, Captain Grice-Hutchinson, Mr G. Whitelaw and Sir William Walrond.
Score: 243–3 dec. (Forster 81, Curzon 97, Chelsea 44).

Right: The Unknown Zingaro, dated June 20, 1866, since when the colours black, red and gold have appeared in I Zingari's records.
Far right: J. L. Baldwin, flanked by the Ponsonby brothers, Sir Spencer Ponsonby Fane and Lord Bessborough (right), who founded I Zingari over dinner in July 1845. R. P. Long "under mesmeric influence assisted at the séance" and woke for long enough to give the new club its name.

Mos!

I Zingari v Gentlemen of England

• June 20, 21, 22, 1895 •

FOR THE MATCH arranged to commemorate their Jubilee, the Zingari put a splendidly powerful side into the field while, on paper, that of the Gentlemen of England was far from representative. But, despite the absence of several famous names, the latter unexpectedly proved the stronger and defeated the Zingari in decisive fashion by ten wickets. It was a batsman's match all through, and partly for that reason, and partly from the fact that it was contested in delightful weather, drew large and appreciative crowds on each of the three days. Among those who were present, and subsequently photographed with the Zingari eleven, were Mr John Loraine Baldwin and the Hon. Spencer Ponsonby Fane, two of the original founders of the famous amateur organisation.

England v The Rest

• June 29, 30, July 1, 1911 •

FOR THE SECOND of the Test Trials, the Selection Committee (Lord Hawke, P. F. Warner and G. L. Jessop) could not secure the elevens that had been chosen. F. L. Fane would not captain The Rest, Barnes declined his invitation, Hobbs begged off on the ground that he was not quite fit, and Rushby was kept away by a bad heel. These little points involved a good deal of rearrangement in the sides and it cannot be said that the match afforded sufficient compensation for the serious disturbance of county cricket that it caused. England beat The Rest very easily by ten wickets.

Navy v Army

• June 3, 4, 1913 •

THE OUTSTANDING feature of the first day's cricket was the batting of Capt. Fowke, who, going in first for the Army, scored 113 out of 207 – being sixth man out – in two hours and a half. He did not give a chance, and among his figures were fifteen fours. Despite his performance the Navy dismissed their opponents for 255, but they could get only 103 themselves with the consequence that they had to follow on. Major Fawcus accomplished a remarkable bowling feat. He took four wickets in five balls at the close of the Navy's first innings, and altogether dismissed nine batsmen in the match for 32 runs. The Army, easily the stronger side, won by ten wickets.

Surrey v Kent

• August 10, 11, 1914 •

TRANSFERRED TO LORD'S – The Oval being in the occupation of the military authorities – and finished off in two days, Hobbs' benefit match did not yield anything like the sum which could have been confidently expected in normal circumstances. Outplaying their opponents at all points, Surrey gained a well-earned victory by eight wickets.

PLAYER'S CIGARETTES

J. B. HOBBS (SURREY)

The Kent match, as a benefit to Hobbs, was such a failure that the Surrey committee have decided not to treat it as a benefit. They will give Hobbs another match as soon as circumstances permit, his subscription list in the meantime remaining open. This generous action on Surrey's part – not hitherto made known – will please everyone. Hobbs is not only the best bat in England at the present time, but also the most attractive and popular.
[*Notes by the Editor, 1915*]

The Surrey opening pair of Tom Hayward (left) and Jack Hobbs.

Surrey v Yorkshire

• August 13, 14, 15, 1914 •

YORKSHIRE prior to this match having won eight games in succession, there seemed every reason to expect a close struggle, but Surrey rose to the occasion in great style and gained a brilliant victory by an innings and 30 runs. A wonderful stand by Hayward and Hobbs was the outstanding feature of the match, the famous batsmen withstanding the Yorkshire bowling for three hours and 40 minutes and taking the

score to 290 for the first wicket. Hayward, 116, played almost faultless cricket until, having completed his hundred, he began to hit out wildly. Hobbs, in playing his tenth three-figure innings of the season, gave chances when 87 and 186. Second out for 202 at 349, he hit splendidly even if he scarcely reached his highest standard.

Test Trial Match

• June 8, 10, 11, 1929 •

CONTESTED a week before the first of the five Test matches for the purpose of assisting the Selection Committee in choosing the England eleven for that encounter, the Test Trial game produced some very interesting cricket but could not be brought to a definite issue. Probably the great hope of the Selection Committee was that the match would show some of The Rest bowlers to be possessed of the ability necessary to dispose of the powerful England batting side for a moderate score. If that were the chief desire, the opening day's cricket must have been a considerable disappointment to the authorities for – much to the delight of the spectators – the England team scored with refreshing freedom. Admittedly the pitch was in favour of run-getting; if the bowlers could at times make the ball turn, they were unable to get any pace out of the ground. Possibly, too, the ordinary-sized stumps used for the occasion may have made some difference to men who in matches during the previous weeks had had the larger at which to bowl, and this view, whether correct or not, was strengthened by the fact that not once during the day did a bowler hit the stumps.

In 1929 the Advisory County Cricket Committee agreed as an experiment to make the wicket one inch wider and one inch higher in that season's inter-county matches.

William H. Slatter, son of the better known "Steevie" Slatter, was engaged at Lord's for 57 years, originally as a Pavilion dressing-room attendant in 1863 and working his way up to become clerk of works. Some idea of the changes which time wrought during his long association with the ground can be gauged from the fact that he could recall seeing wild rabbits there. He designed and built the luncheon arbours surrounding the practice ground. [1930]

• • •

Harry George Burton, a slow right-handed bowler, did not play for Middlesex until 30 years of age, but in his first match – against Surrey at Lord's in 1881 – he bowled Harry Jupp with the second ball he sent down and in the second innings (in which he secured five wickets for 20) he dismissed John Shuter, the Surrey captain, with his first ball. At The Oval in 1888 he took all ten wickets for 59 in the Surrey first innings. A member of the MCC groundstaff from 1883 to 1904, he in 1894 against Oxford City again took all ten wickets in an innings. A coachsmith by trade, Burton, even when assisting Middlesex regularly, put in, as a rule, several hours' work before taking the field. For many years he scored for Middlesex, and he was honorary secretary to the Cricketers' Fund Friendly Society. [1931]

• • •

Alfred John Atfield, a versatile cricketer of much experience, known chiefly as a very efficient umpire in first-class cricket, was a member of the groundstaff at Lord's from 1901. He scored 121 not out on that ground in a Cross Arrows match after his marriage earlier in the day at Hanover Square. [1950]

Royal Navy v Royal Air Force

• August 12, 13, 1953 •

RAF WON by eight wickets. The Navy, having beaten the Army at Portsmouth, were upset by Trueman who, just chosen for the last Test, took ten wickets for 112. At first he caused no trouble and was punished for 40 in eight overs. Ainsworth hit him for 17 in one over, including four sparkling boundary strokes, but later the England fast bowler claimed three victims in six overs from the Pavilion end and the Navy were all out for 169. The airmen took the lead with half their wickets in hand and, declaring first thing on the second morning, they were soon in sight of success. Hurst, a left-arm spinner who was not used on the first day, dismissed the first three batsmen, after which the pace of Trueman proved too much for the rest.

Lord's 1956: Fred Trueman (right) in conversation with Australia's Ray Lindwall, the cricketer Trueman once described as "my one and only fast-bowling idol. To me he was the greatest of them all." Between them, they took 535 Test wickets.

Army v Royal Air Force

• August 22, 24, 1953 •

DRAWN. Bowlers generally held the upper hand until torrential rain put an end to the proceedings at 2.35 p.m., when the Army appeared to be in a hopeless position. With only three wickets left, they were no more than 28 runs ahead. In gaining the upper hand, the RAF were mainly indebted to Trueman who, fresh from his part in England winning the Ashes, took seven wickets in the match for 32 runs. On Monday, when seven Army wickets were captured for 81, Hurst formed a deadly partner to Trueman, and he finished with six for 46.

Lord's Taverners v Old England XI

• June 16, 1962 •

OLD ENGLAND won by two wickets. Former Test cricketers and stars of stage and television provided sparkling cricket in this one-day match organised by the Lord's Taverners for the National Playing Fields Association.

Joseph W. Filliston, who died in hospital on October 25, 1964, aged 102, five days after being knocked down by a motor-scooter, acted as umpire to the BBC Cricket Club for many years. In his younger days he played cricket with Dr W. G. Grace and he helped Gentlemen of Kent defeat the Philadelphians by six wickets at Town Malling in 1889. He also played as a professional in the Staffordshire League. He liked to tell of the occasion when he gave W. G. out leg-before in a London County game at the Crystal Palace. The Doctor, he said, refused to leave the crease and, as nobody had the courage to contradict him, he continued his innings.

A crowd of 12,000 saw 640 runs scored in six hours and Old England won in an exciting finish. During the afternoon a centenarian, Joe Filliston, stood as umpire.

As many as thirteen sixes were struck in the region of the Tavern, the example being set by Keith Miller who hit the ball five times over the ring. Comedians Norman Wisdom and Roy Castle provided plenty of laughter when they went in to bat, but generally the cricket was of a high standard, with Cyril Washbrook and Jack Robertson the outstanding artists in their opening partnership of 126 in 48 minutes. Jack Ikin kept up the rapid scoring and landed the ball three times on the Mound Stand roof. When it seemed that Old England would romp home, the Rev. David Sheppard dismissed Doug Insole, Denis Compton and Godfrey Evans, but the Taverners were thwarted by those old stalwarts, Doug Wright and Alec Bedser, who got the last 30 together. Wright smacked Norman Wisdom to the Pavilion for the winning hit.

1964 Single-Wicket Competition

BARRY KNIGHT, the Essex all-rounder, won the Carling Single-Wicket competition at Lord's on July 30 and 31, defeating Colin Milburn of Northamptonshire by 1 run in the final. The only difference in the laws which operated when this form of cricket – popular at the beginning of the nineteenth century – was revived at Scarborough in 1963 was that each of the sixteen competitors was allotted eight overs instead of ten. The sponsors awarded prizes of £250 to the winner, £100 to the runner-up, £50 each to the beaten semi-finalists, and £10 each to the losers of the second round. R. Benaud and G. S. Sobers both went out in the first round, as did K. E. Palmer, the winner at Scarborough. Knight beat Horton in an evenly matched semi-final, and had to bowl at his best to overcome Milburn in the final.

The Laws of Cricket were in force, there being the

usual two sets of stumps. The bowler, changing ends after each six-ball over, had the assistance of a first-class wicket-keeper (K. V. Andrew and J. T. Murray shared the duties) and nine fieldsmen from the MCC groundstaff. Two chalk marks, each side midway along the pitch, indicated a point of no return if passed by the batsman, who could be run out only at the end to which he was running.

Contestants: T. E. Bailey (Essex), R. Benaud (Australia), D. B. Close (Yorkshire), M. C. Cowdrey (Kent), B. L. D'Oliveira (Worcestershire), W. W. Hall (West Indies), M. J. Horton (Worcestershire), R. Illingworth (Yorkshire), B. R. Knight (Essex), C. Milburn (Northamptonshire), J. B. Mortimore (Gloucestershire), K. E. Palmer (Somerset), P. H. Parfitt (Middlesex), W. E. Russell (Middlesex), G. S. Sobers (West Indies) and F. S. Trueman (Yorkshire).

The single-wicket competition was held at Lord's until 1967, and again in 1969.

Extempore

• April 30, May 2, 3, 1966 •

MCC drew with Yorkshire, who thought they had won when the ninth wicket went down, with MCC still 48 runs short of the winning target of 254. But Mr S. C. Griffith, the MCC Secretary, ruled otherwise. He said that it was a draw as David Gibson, who had taken no part in the game after the first day because of an injured leg, did not have time to reach the wicket.

. . .

• August 13, 15, 16, 1966 •

Middlesex drew with Lancashire. The game concluded in dramatic fashion. On the fall of their ninth wicket, Lancashire needed 3 runs to win but, with 90 seconds remaining, the umpire, Fagg, took off the bails. Fagg said: "There was a minute and a half left by the Nursery clock, and under the two-minute rule – the time allowed for a batsman to come in – I decided the match was at an end when Statham was out. Had he played the ball (the last of an over from Price) I would have allowed another over." Thus both sides were denied the chance of a success they had done little to deserve. Not a moment was lost to the weather over the three days, but only 692 runs were compiled at an overall rate of 38 an hour.

. . .

• April 29, May 1, 2, 1967 •

Yorkshire beat MCC by 157 runs. For the second year running, this fixture ended in some confusion. When MCC, set to score 347 to win, lost their ninth wicket at 189 with Walker apparently unfit to bat, the players and umpires trooped off. A minute or so later D. R. Smith, the not out batsman, reappeared with Walker, who was padded up. The umpires came, too, despite the fact that the groundstaff had commenced to sweep the pitch. There

followed a brief discussion in which the head groundsman took part, after which all returned to the Pavilion. From there it was learned from D. B. Carr, the MCC assistant-secretary, that Mortimore, the MCC captain, had agreed that Walker should be recorded as "absent injured". Even the MCC batsman had been under the impression that he would not bat. Yorkshire would no doubt have won in any case, for plenty of time remained, and they well deserved the victory.

. . .

•July 20, 21, 22, 1977 •

Middlesex drew with Gloucestershire. An extraordinary match with two distinct halves reached a controversial, tense climax after seeming all over on the second afternoon. Brearley batted all the first day for his 145 and declared at 343 for six. After tumbling from 48 for no wicket to 80 all out, Gloucestershire came back strongly with an opening stand of 145 between Sadiq Mohammad and Stovold on the second day, and the middle order fought tenaciously after the first three had fallen in the opening hour of the last day. While Edmonds and Emburey toiled through a vast number of overs – Edmonds' 77 has rarely been surpassed in the Championship – their colleagues gradually showed the strain and substitutes were needed, including coach Don Bennett, for Brearley, Smith, Featherstone and Selvey. The last wicket fell at 5.12 p.m., but umpire Alley allowed Middlesex only twelve overs to make 75 (as five had already been bowled since 5.00), seeming to ignore the regulation that, when a new innings starts inside the last hour, it should contain one over for every three minutes: 38 minutes should have meant thirteen overs, but a note from Brearley to the umpires as Middlesex vainly tackled their task proved fruitless. Against Procter at his fastest, Middlesex sacrificed wickets recklessly but finished 12 runs short.

World Cricket Cup, 1966

THE Rothman World Cup, introduced for the first time and well won by England, provided three one-day matches of considerable interest at the end of the season. A Rest of the World side gathered from far and near were beaten by both England and West Indies in the first two matches. The South African, Graeme Pollock, played a fine knock of 65 against West Indies, and Nadkarni, the Indian left-arm spin bowler, tied the batsmen down with his nagging length, but generally it was clear that much of the great talent lay dormant because of lack of match practice.

So the destination of the trophy lay on the last game, between England and West Indies. Sobers put England in to bat and maybe felt satisfied in tying down the opening pair, Edrich and Parfitt. With half the permitted 50 overs, a maximum of eleven per bowler, gone, 78 runs were on the board. Only one wicket had been lost, too, and with the sensible use of a longer handle subsequently, the very respectable average of 4.34 runs an over resulted.

West Indies could never challenge such a rate, largely because Dexter, captain while Cowdrey sat in the Pavilion with a strained leg muscle, brought to bear the considerable knowledge gained in leading Sussex successfully in the Gillette Cup. After the first few overs he dispensed with his slips, bringing back an attacking field only for a short time as each batsman arrived at the wicket. Against such tactics, the West Indies were always struggling. Over the three days [September 10, 12, 13], 13,036 people paid at the turnstiles.

England XI: 217–7 (50 overs)
(J. H. Edrich 33, J. M. Parks 33; P. D. Lashley 3–46).

West Indies: 150 (40.4 overs)
(S. M. Nurse 58; K. Higgs 4–50).

Women at Lord's

THE MOST memorable event in a Women's Cricket Association Golden Jubilee season packed with cricket as well as social functions was the falling, to women cricketers, of the last stronghold of cricket, Lord's. With the blessing of the MCC and amidst a considerable flurry from the press, England played Australia on Wednesday, August 4, 1976, in a 60-over match and history was made. Fate had also played a certain part as this match, originally scheduled for Sunbury, was moved to Lord's when Middlesex failed to reach the Gillette Cup quarter-final. There was a good crowd which swelled during the day, many spectators coming from a distance to be present at this unique event on a flawless summer day. A centrally pitched wicket was provided, and countless press, broadcasting and television personnel took an active interest.

The sight of Australia's opening pair emerging from the Pavilion door and of their players sitting on the familiar dressing-room balcony heightened the atmosphere, and the tension rose even more when Lorraine Hill, with 1,000 runs and five centuries to her credit on the tour, lost her wicket in the first over. This prompt success on England's part certainly affected the final outcome. Australia seemed over-conscious of the fact that they were playing in the hallowed atmosphere of the most famous ground in the world, and their usual batting liveliness was lacking. England, set 161, celebrated the day fittingly with an eight-wicket victory in the 56th over. Chris Watmough provided a first-class display and was well partnered by a quieter-than-usual Rachael Flint, visibly feeling her responsibility as captain.

Despite winning this match, England forfeited the St Ivel Jug, Australia having achieved the faster scoring-rate in the combined Canterbury and Lord's limited-overs matches. The scene in the Long Room afterwards was one to be remembered. Many spectators, most of them women, stood there to watch

A ground-breaking day for the ladies at Lord's: England's Rachael Heyhoe Flint flips the coin and Australia's captain, Anne Gordon, calls to determine which country bats first in the maiden women's match at headquarters. Mrs Heyhoe Flint wrote more Lord's history 28 years later when, in 2004, she became the first woman on the MCC Committee. The club had voted in 1998 to admit women as members – a grave-turning decision for dyed-in-the-wool opponents of the "Monstrous Regiment".

the President of the MCC, Mr C. G. A. Paris, present the trophy to Australia, and players of both teams received from the sponsors a specially manufactured blue cricket ball in commemoration of the historic occasion. [*Netta Rheinberg, 1977*]

National Village Finals

• August 28, 1983 •

QUARNDON of Derbyshire won the village championship for the first time when they beat Troon, victors three times previously, by eight wickets when Hibberd, a bank clerk, hit the last two balls of the final over to the long-leg boundary for four. Troon, put in, were restricted to 155 for six in their 40 overs, Quarndon using left-arm spin from both ends for much of the innings. Taylor, a police constable, and Butcher, a postal engineer, had five wickets between them for 52 runs. When Quarndon batted, Farmer, a Rolls Royce engineer, joined Hibberd at 53 for two and their unbroken third-wicket partnership of 104 saw them home.

• September 1, 1985 •

FREUCHIE beat Rowledge by virtue of having lost fewer wickets with the scores level, so becoming, in the bicentenary year of Scottish cricket, the first Scottish village to win the final. Rowledge had won the toss and batted first, but against tigerish Scottish fielding the runs came slowly and they managed only 134 in 39.3 overs. Freuchie's captain and president, David Christie, saw their score to 134 for seven, when he was run out off the last ball of the 39th over, whereupon in great excitement in the gloaming of St John's Wood, the ninth-wicket pair played out a maiden 40th over to ensure victory. Freuchie, with kilts swirling and their piper skirling at their head, had marched into Lord's, where the national dress, including tie and jacket, was permitted wear in the Pavilion.

• August 25, 1990 •

GOATACRE beat Dunstall by 50 runs. Iles, grandson of the Wiltshire village club's founder, played one of the finest innings seen at Lord's for many a day and by virtually monopolising this nineteenth village final he gave Goatacre their second title. Having decided to bat, he saw Leavey out to the first ball, Spencer at 23 and the punishing Turner at 100 before he joined Hunt. After that it was all Iles. His hundred took only 45 minutes and included seven sixes – four in succession – and six fours in 39 balls received. He added two more sixes and a four in his total of 123 (49 balls) and came back to a standing ovation from MCC members and the supporters of both clubs. Iles' hundred was the first, and Goatacre's 267 for five the highest total, in a village championship final. Dunstall, a tiny Staffordshire village who had done their share of giant-killing *en route* to Lord's, faced a near-impossible target but stuck bravely to the task.

Harry Philip Hugh Sharp was an old-fashioned kind of cricketing stalwart who spent his entire adult life at Lord's except for the interruption of war, when he was an able seaman – which is why he was known as "The Admiral". He joined the Lord's groundstaff in 1934 and stayed on as player, coach, MCC umpire and Middlesex scorer for 60 years. He did not make his Middlesex debut until he was back on dry land in 1946, when he was already 28, but in 1948 he was capped and he became the regular opener in 1950. In all his roles he was genial, humorous, knowledgeable and helpful and he was a much loved figure on the circuit. [1996]

• September 9, 2001 •

YNYSTAWE beat Elvaston by 99 runs. Paul Discombe crushed Elvaston with six for 18, the best analysis in 30 village finals. His first three wickets reduced the defending champions to 33 for five; later, he ended Robert Torry's counter-attack, having him caught on the boundary, and swiftly bowled two tailenders to clinch victory. Elvaston were not even halfway to a target of 191. They could not have expected to

Spotting the wrong-'un at Lord's

In August, wide publicity was given to the claim that some of the oil paintings hanging at Lord's, mostly in the Memorial Gallery, were fakes. Started in 1864 by Sir Spencer Ponsonby Fane, the MCC Collection contains a wide variety of pictures, of which something like 300 were, at the time, on display. Of these, some 150 were oils. Those of doubtful origin formed a part of a valuable bequest made in the 1940s by Sir Jeremiah Colman. For many years MCC have presented the game and its history by exhibiting the most comprehensive display of cricketing memorabilia in the world. Fourteen of their pictures have now been taken out of circulation. [Notes by the Editor, 1984]

I always thought it was a fake, it's nothing like Boycott's stance at the crease!

chase so many when Ynystawe were 94 for two in 30 overs, but with wickets in hand the Welshmen were well placed to make a vigorous final assault. Their last ten overs more than doubled the score, with Andrew Beasley (48 in 47 balls) and Gareth Bishop adding 67 in six.

Cheam's team in the 1990 National Club final contained a future England cricketer in eighteen-year-old Mark Butcher (front row, right). Seven years later he would open the batting against Australia in his first Test at Lord's.

openers were back in the Pavilion, Mark Butcher, eighteen-year-old son of Glamorgan's captain, enlivened proceedings with two sixes, one of them taking Cheam past 100 in the 29th over. Blackpool, chasing 194 in 45 overs, saw Lawton run out in the first over by Butcher. However, Hesketh lifted his side to victory with an unbeaten 86 after he and Ashton added 70 for the sixth wicket to rescue Blackpool from a parlous position at 95 for five.

• September 4, 2003 •

SANDIACRE TOWN beat Bath by 1 run. Sandiacre's captain John Trueman summed it up best when he said, with a smile, "We weren't winning it at any stage, were we?" And, right until the last ball, he was probably right. With ten overs to face and six wickets in hand, Bath needed 54. Quick bowler Irfan-ul-Haq – known in Sandiacre as "Cyril" – scattered the stumps of the key remaining batsman, Tom Hankins. But Stuart Barnes hit two successive fours: 26 needed from four overs. Barnes ran himself out: 10 needed from twelve balls. Two more wickets fell to Irfan: 2 runs from four balls. Even with the last pair at the crease, Bath were favourites. But in the final twist Simon Gwilliam set off for what looked, and proved, a suicidal single – and, after one of the best finals in the competition's 35-year history, Sandiacre had pickpocketed a win. It all looked very different when Sandiacre, from Derbyshire, had crawled to 124 in 35 overs on a pitch with none of the usual September-at-Lord's zip. But Trueman picked up the pace, Rob Attwood swung at everything and Sandiacre managed 90 from their last ten overs. It proved just enough.

National Club Finals

• August 28, 1987 •

OLD HILL beat Teddington by five wickets. A commanding half-century by Morgan, a Minor Counties cricketer for Suffolk, was the feature of the morning's play. But having reached it in the over before lunch by driving Mushtaq Mohammad for the second of his two sixes, he was bowled around his legs next ball. Dean Headley, seventeen-year-old son of R. G. A. and grandson of G. A., had made the initial breakthrough, bowling at a brisk pace, and it was his direct hit from near the third-man boundary to run out Holliday which further checked Teddington's progress. A partnership of 109 between Mushtaq and Hemsley put Old Hill well on the way to victory, and captain Wilkinson saw his side become national club champions for the third time in four years.

• August 24, 1990 •

BLACKPOOL beat Cheam by three wickets. After successive washouts at headquarters in the two previous years, the last National Club Championship final under the sponsorship of Cockspur Rum was played in glorious weather. Indeed, it was so hot that drinks were taken after the first 45 minutes. Cheam chose to bat and, after the

In a Class of their Own
Other schools games at Lord's

"After watching so much first-class cricket, in which the object of far too many players seemed to be the expenditure of time by devious devices and without commensurate expenditure of energy, I found the cricket of the boys at Lord's exhilarating."

[Wisden 1961]

Rugby v Marlborough

• June 23, 24, 1869 •

CURIOUS INCIDENTS cropped up in this match. Rugby lost two wickets before a run was made, three wickets for 1 run, and seven for 24. Then Mr Walker went in and took his bat out for 53, a busy, timely innings that deserved all the applause it gained. At a quarter to two, the Marlborough innings commenced; at twenty minutes to four it was over for 51 runs. In Rugby's second innings, Mr Pearson made 20 runs in eighteen minutes, but the feature of the match was the effective fast bowling of Mr Francis that, in 24 overs, took all the ten wickets in Marlborough's second innings (nine bowled). In his first, second, fourth and fifth overs Mr Francis had a wicket; he then bowled six successive maiden overs, having a wicket in his eleventh. In his eighteenth over he had two wickets, another in his 21st, and with the second and third balls of his 24th over he had the other two. Rugby won by 179 runs.

Two years later, C. K. Francis was a member of the Oxford team when S. E. Butler took all ten Cambridge wickets in the first innings. In 1870, Francis had taken twelve Cambridge wickets in Cobden's Match.

Rugby v Marlborough

• August 1, 2, 1906 •

Rugby
Mr R. C. Brooke b Wyer . . . 0

Marlborough
Mr E. Clover c Brooke b Cole . . . 1

Rupert Brooke with Virginia Stephen in 1911.
"He had gained considerable reputation as a poet,"
said *Wisden* after his death in 1915.
Miss Stephen made waves as a novelist.

Charterhouse v Westminster

• July 14, 1869 •

PLAY COMMENCED about 11 a.m.; before the clock struck six the match was played out. Mr Nepean, the Carthusian captain, scored a good-hitting innings of 59 runs; the Westminster eleven joined heartily in the applause that greeted his return to the Pavilion. In the second innings of Westminster, nine wickets were down for 9 runs. Mr Saunders and Mr Vidal then increased the score to 38. In that innings Mr Dunn had bowled three overs for five wickets but no runs, and Mr Kirby's first seven overs were bowled for 1 run and four wickets. Charterhouse won by ten wickets.

Rugby v Marlborough

• July 29, 30, 1885 •

RUGBY went in for the second time at ten minutes past three and when stumps were finally pulled up, and the game left drawn at seven o'clock, the score was 338 for six wickets. The hero of this startling performance was E. H. F. Bradby, the Rugby captain. He went in first and was the fifth man out, the total when he left being

335. Out of this number, by some very dashing and resolute hitting, he made no fewer than 170, his figures being 23 fours, 7 threes, 14 twos and 29 singles. The wicket was very easy and the bowling by no means difficult, but still it was a very big thing for a school batsman to make 170 runs at Lord's.

Lord's Schools v The Rest

• August 6, 7, 1923 •

THE LORD'S SCHOOLS proved altogether too strong for The Rest and won in the easiest fashion by nine wickets. Duleepsinhji, of Cheltenham, was the hero of the game. He played a beautiful innings of 108, completing his hundred in an hour and three-quarters, and in the follow-on by The Rest he bowled high-tossed leg-breaks with surprising success, taking five wickets for 41 runs. For the most part the batting of The Rest was very disappointing, but E. R. T. Holmes, of Malvern, hit up a brilliant 83 in an hour and a half.

Cheltenham v Haileybury

• July 29, 30, 1927 •

BATTING VERY BRIGHTLY and bowling with considerable skill, Haileybury won by an innings and 3 runs, and in so doing gained their first victory over Cheltenham since the year 1913. They had four wickets down for 75 and yet in little more than three hours put together a score of 278. E. M. Wellings, bowling unchanged, took seven wickets for 113 runs and followed up that performance by carrying his bat right through the Cheltenham innings. Unfortunately his colleagues failed him so badly that he had to exercise extreme care and, although withstanding the Haileybury attack for two hours and three-quarters, he scored no more than 44.

Spooners dish it out at Lord's

RUGBY v MARLBOROUGH
• July 27, 28, 1898 •

There was some capital batting on both days – on the Wednesday by R. H. Spooner, who made 139 out of 215 in a couple of hours for Marlborough, and on Thursday by Hannay, Grylls and Parton for Rugby. Spooner's innings was one of the finest hit by a schoolboy at Lord's, being characterised by great brilliancy throughout. He was especially strong on the off side, and made no fewer than 27 fours.

• • •

CHELTENHAM v HAILEYBURY
• July 29, 30, 1898 •
Haileybury
Mr A. H. Spooner c Clayton b Hutton 94 – b Clayton 58

• • •

RUGBY v MARLBOROUGH
• August 3, 4, 1899 •

In R. H. Spooner of Marlborough was probably seen one of the best schoolboy cricketers. In the first innings he made 69 out of the total of 197, and after Rugby had been dismissed for 134 he went in first again and was 98 not out when stumps were drawn with five wickets down for 154. On the Thursday Spooner made his innings into 198, a brilliant display of batting, which lasted three hours and a half and contained only two chances. He hit wonderfully well all round the wicket, but the best feature was the powerful play on the off side. Marlborough declared at 318 for eight wickets and, getting rid of Rugby for 156, won by 225 runs.

Reggie Spooner graced the Golden Age of English cricket. His batsmanship, Neville Cardus wrote, "was all courtesy and breeding".

Haileybury may certainly be classed as equal with Rugby and Marlborough, having in Smith and A. H. Spooner (brother of the Marlburian) two really fine bats, though the latter was inclined to take too many risks. [1899]

Lord's Schools v The Rest

• August 6, 7, 1928 •

LORD'S SCHOOLS narrowly missed a handsome victory, The Rest, who had followed on 230 behind, being only 14 runs on with two wickets to fall when the game was left drawn. Batting first, Lord's Schools kept their opponents in the field for nearly the whole of Monday and put together the big total of 394. The chief contributor was Akers-Douglas of Eton, who followed up his 158 against Harrow on the same ground a few weeks earlier with a delightful innings of 111. Hitting with fine judgment in front of the wicket and cutting in splendid style, this young batsman gave no chance during a stay of two hours and a quarter.

Going up to Oxford, I. S. Akers-Douglas hit hundreds in the 1929 Freshmen's match and the 1930 Seniors' match but was never awarded a blue.

Lord's Schools v The Rest

• August 1, 2, 1932 •

OVERSHADOWING everything else in this match was the slow spin bowling of J. H. Cameron of Taunton School, a son of Dr J. Cameron who toured this country with the West Indies team in 1906. Cameron, varying his legbreaks with googlies, took all ten wickets in the first innings of the Lord's Schools for 49 runs and secured the only two wickets which fell in the second innings of that side – twelve in all for 6 runs apiece.

Army v Public Schools

• August 8, 9, 1934 •

IN ANOTHER good sporting match the Army tried to get 200 runs in 90 minutes despite poor light which became so bad that the umpires pulled up stumps at twenty past six. N. W. D. Yardley, of St Peter's, York, stood out as the great batsman of the game. He scored 180 runs in his two innings, and his 117 on the first day showed him sound in judging the ball to punish, powerful in the drive besides clever in hitting to leg in the genuine sweeping style, seldom seen in these days.

Norman Yardley (above) graduated from schools cricket to lead Cambridge, Yorkshire and England, but the game had other plans for Henry Blofeld (right) – fame as broadcaster and author.

Combined Services v Public Schools

• August 8, 9, 1956 •

COMBINED SERVICES won by two wickets. With the weather improved, a keen, interesting match was played out, and in a thrilling finish the Services, set to score 175 in 100 minutes, won in the last over. Subba Row led the way in some free hitting and 104 came in the first hour. Among several splendid batting displays, the century on the first day of H. C. Blofeld, the sixteen-year-old Eton wicket-keeper, was notable. For one so young he showed remarkable confidence against experienced bowlers, and employed a wide range of strokes which brought him thirteen fours and one five, all run, in his not out 104, made in two and a quarter hours. Blofeld's aggregate for three innings in schools matches at Lord's during the week was 179 for once out [run out 41 in this game].

During the dozen years I have been writing public schools cricket for *Wisden*, some notable players have emerged and there have been some stirring events in the representative matches. Among them the most memorable has been the win by the Public Schools in 1951, when the Services set them to score 188 in 115 minutes. A. C. D. Ingleby-Mackenzie of Eton set off so brilliantly – his own 50 in twenty minutes, and altogether 58 out of 77 in a few overs – that they were home very comfortably.

. . .

Peter May played at Lord's in 1945, when he was only fifteen and routed by the pace of T. E. Bailey, and 1947, but he was omitted from the representative side in the middle year. His fielding then did not satisfy the selectors. In 1947 May was a highly accomplished player of whom I wrote that he "stood out far above the other boys". And those others included David Sheppard, whose part against Combined Services was small and who developed his powers largely after leaving school. That year May scored 146 against the Services, having previously made 148 for the Southern Schools against The Rest. Three years later Colin Cowdrey had scores of 126 and 55 against the Services. Hence in *Wisden* appeared, "We have now seen two unusually gifted schoolboy batsmen in the five post-war years." Both have gone on to still bigger things.

. . .

Those who follow public schools cricket may well have felt that 1956 was the most rewarding season of any since the war. During it, five amateur batsmen occupied the first five batting positions in a Test against Australia. Four of them, Bailey, May, Sheppard and Cowdrey – to put them in the order of seniority – played for the Schools at Lord's between 1942 and 1950. Not since the middle ages of cricket has amateur batsmanship been so prominent, nor public schools batsmanship. [*E. M. Wellings, 1957*]

Public Schools
v English Schools CA

• August 5, 6, 1970 •

DRAWN. The Eton captain and off-spin bowler, J. R. T. Barclay, showed excellent command of length and flight on a firm surface. He took all nine English Schools' wickets to fall, hitting the stumps six times, taking a return catch, and twice having the assistance of the

Easter classes

The MCC Secretary has authority to arrange cricket classes for the instruction of the sons of members in the Easter Holidays of 1902 and after. A charge sufficient to cover the cost of professional tuition will be made. [1902]

Cheltenham Ladies' Sian Davies and Sally Slowe prepare to break the gender barrier at the traditional Easter coaching classes in April 1970.

wicket-keeper. Even so, English Schools amassed a reasonable total of 199, in answer to which Public Schools were 45 for two when rain came soon after tea on the first day and washed out any further play in the match.

MCC Schools v NAYC

• July 23, 24, 1980 •

DRAWN. Batting first in warm sunshine, the National Association of Young Cricketers were restrained by an attack which was accurate but, apart from several difficult chances going to ground, rarely threatened. Bailey's elegant forcing drives and good running between the wickets hastened them to their declaration at 180 for one wicket. MCC Schools declared overnight at 170 for one, thus depriving Little (94 not out) of a century at Lord's, but after inroads by Neil Foster's pace and the slow left-arm of Spiller, hopes of a result were thwarted by a sixth-wicket stand of 74 between Bailey and Settle. Foster's three wickets were caught by substitute wicket-keeper A. J. Stewart.

MCC Schools v NAYC

• August 6, 7, 1986 •

DRAWN. The outstanding performance was that of the sixteen-year-old Middlesex schoolboy, Mark Ramprakash, who on the opening day scored his second hundred of the week in representative cricket, 116 not out – having hit 117 for English Schools against Scotland at Dartford – and followed it with a half-century on the second day. Schools captain Michael Atherton scored 37 and 15 not out. At the close of the first day, the Young Cricketers were 27 for two, with Graham Lloyd, son of the former England and Lancashire left-hander, not out 16. He went on to a neat 59.

Wisden at Lord's

Sitting Tenants
Middlesex at Lord's

"The Middlesex home matches were all played at Lord's ground in 1877.
The county programme consisted of the usual match v Oxford University,
and out and home matches with Notts, Surrey and Yorkshire."

[Wisden 1878]

v Surrey

• July 12, 13, 1869 •

THERE WAS NO HOME for Middlesex county cricket in 1869, so this match was played at Lord's. Stephenson was too ill, Humphrey too lame, Mr Potter unable and Buckle sent for too late to play for Surrey. In one hour and 50 minutes Middlesex's first innings was over for 96. In about one hour Surrey was out for 37. In about one hour and 45 minutes the second innings of Middlesex was over for 89 runs. Then Mortlock and Mr Mayo scored 43 without the loss of a wicket for Surrey's second innings, and so ended the first day's cricket. Next day Hearne bowled thirteen overs for 1 run; Howitt in one over bowled Street and Bristow and, despite the hitting of Mr Mayo (whose 20 included two fives), Middlesex won by 43 runs.

Opposite: There were "sold out" signs and jam-packed bleachers in the setting sun when Middlesex Crusaders brought Twenty20 cricket to Lord's in 2004. Left: V. E. "Teddy" Walker, "top of the tree as an all-rounder" in the 1850s and 1860s, was a driving force behind Middlesex CCC and their first captain.

the two Webbes played out their four innings for an aggregate of 38 runs (Mr A. J. making 32); Mr I. D. Walker (in fine hitting form just then) made but 9 and 14; and 24 wickets were got down at the cost of a trifle over 8 runs per wicket, and all this owing to that frightful wet weather that so seriously flooded the country at that period.

v Gloucestershire

• June 9, 10, 11, 1879 •

THIS WAS the first match played by those two great hitting counties, Middlesex and Gloucestershire, much public interest being felt in cricketing circles as to its result. But it turned out a most unfortunate match, the stormy weather entirely preventing play on two days [the first and third] and causing the wickets to play so untruthfully on the other day that correct-timing the ball was difficult. The two Graces [W. G. and G. F.] were out for an innings of 6 runs each; the two Lytteltons played their four innings for a gross total of 33 runs;

v Surrey

• May 27, 28, 1880 •

THIS WAS the first county v county match played in London in 1880. When time was called on the second day, and the match declared drawn, eight Middlesex wickets had fallen in the second innings for 310 runs [a lead of 266], Mr C. T. Studd 65 not out. Expressions of regret were universal that this important and interesting match should be abandoned in order that the Saturday might be devoted to a contest of no interest whatever to cricketers. The object of the match between the Huntsmen and Jockeys being a charitable one was to be commended, but it is earnestly to be hoped that it will not be necessary to sacrifice the third day of a first-class match should the fixture find a place in any future programme of the Marylebone Club.

v Gloucestershire

• June 13, 14, 1881 •

THE INTEREST on the second day centred in the extraordinary and brilliant hitting of Mr Vernon for Middlesex. A ball from Midwinter was driven for five, and from one over of Woof's he scored 12 runs by three drives of four each. Then from the other wicket he drove Midwinter for a five. Mr Vernon's next important hit was off Woof, through the open door of the tennis court, and as a light had to be obtained to find the ball, "lost ball" was called and a six scored. When Clarke, the last man, came in, nine wickets were down for 159 and Mr Vernon continued his extraordinary hitting. He drove Mr Grace for five, and shortly afterwards scored 11 runs from one over from the same hand. At 195, however, Midwinter bowled him for a magnificent innings of 88, made up of a six, three fives, nine fours, four threes, four twos and eleven singles. In the end the visitors won by six wickets.

Gloucestershire 160: (Dr W. G. Grace 64, Dr E. M. Grace 47; G. Burton 6–45) and 114–4 (Dr E. M. Grace 35, J. Cranston 35 not out).

Middlesex: 77 (G. Law Esq. 19; W. G. Grace 7–30) and 195 (G. F. Vernon Esq. 88; W. Midwinter 6–53).

v Australians

• June 24, 25, 26, 1886 •

THE GROUND was in splendid condition, and the company was very large. It must be mentioned as a matter of record that Captain Hyde, a retired captain of the Peninsular and Oriental Company's service, died suddenly on the ground during the game. The deceased gentleman was a well-known frequenter of Lord's Cricket Ground, and his face and figure were doubtless familiar to hundreds of people.

The interior of the tennis court into which G. F. Vernon hit his "lost ball" six against Gloucestershire. This court was demolished in 1898 to make way for the Mound Stand.

v Yorkshire

• June 20, 21, 22, 1889 •

PERHAPS the most remarkable match of the season, and one that will always be remembered for the marvellous batting display on the part of Mr T. C. O'Brien (right), which enabled Middlesex to win within ten minutes of time on the last day. That Yorkshire had extraordinarily bad luck in meeting Mr O'Brien in such wonderful form was abundantly proved by the fact that, though their totals amounted to 259 and 388, they still lost by four wickets. Could the end have been anticipated, probably Lord's ground would have been hardly big enough to accommodate the spectators.

Middlesex were left with 280 runs to get to win, and only three hours and 35 minutes remaining for play. Under any circumstances, 280 in the last innings

against a first-class team would have been a tremendous task, but its difficulties were very much increased when the runs had to be obtained at the rate of nearly 80 an hour. At first the Middlesex men appeared to have made up their minds not to attempt to force the game. Indeed, so slowly were runs put on at the outset that by half-past five the score was only 129, and there were four of the best men out. Then Mr O'Brien, joining Mr Nepean, commenced his hitting. From the first he seemed able to do practically as he liked with the bowling, but it was a long time before the spectators began to realise that his efforts might bring about the success of his county.

By the time Mr Vernon came in at a quarter past six [197 for six], 83 runs had to be made in three-quarters of an hour and people had ceased to think about a drawn game, the pace at which Mr O'Brien had been scoring having made it clear that a win was possible. Of course the attempt to get 83 runs in the time that remained might have cost Middlesex the match, but the idea of losing apparently never entered Mr O'Brien's mind. Once Mr Vernon played a ball on to his wicket without removing the bails, and once Mr O'Brien hit a ball up in the long field, which Hall might perhaps have caught. At twenty minutes to seven, 32 runs were wanted and at ten minutes to seven the winning hit was made. Mr O'Brien just made his hundred before the close, and his innings was ranked by many of the best judges at Lord's as one of the finest displays of hitting ever seen on the ground. His effort was one that required brains as well as executive ability, and his achievement was one of which too much cannot be said. To get 100 in 80 minutes was in itself a great achievement, but to make the number without giving a real chance and hardly making a bad hit was truly marvellous. The figures of the innings were fourteen fours, six threes, five twos and sixteen singles.

In the whole match no fewer than 1,295 runs were scored for the loss of 36 wickets, this being a record aggregate in a first-class match in this country. It has once been beaten in Australia, in the famous inter-colonial match at Sydney in 1882 when 1,411 runs were obtained for 30 wickets. Then, however, the game extended over five days. In the contest between Middlesex and Yorkshire, five balls were bowled to the over. Under the old rule [four balls an over], 1,295 runs in three days would have been almost impossible.

Yorkshire's bowlers were R. Peel, W. Middlebrook, E. Wainwright, G. Ulyett and L. Whitehead.

v Lancashire

• June 11, 12, 1891 •

THE DISPLAY of the Lancashire eleven must have been extremely disappointing to their many supporters, as no one could have expected that on a fast ground such a strong batting side would be dismissed in an hour and a quarter for the paltry total of 63. Of this number, Mr Hornby, Briggs and Sugg scored between them no fewer than 42; except for them, the Lancashire team could do absolutely nothing against Hearne, the majority of them being beaten by the great pace of the ground. The young Middlesex professional bowled in quite his best form and actually dismissed eight men for 22 runs, hitting the wicket on each occasion. He narrowly missed the hat-trick, for in one over he took three wickets with the first, third and fifth balls, and he bowled another batsman with the first ball of his following over.

v Nottinghamshire

• June 20, 21, 22, 1892 •

THIS MATCH will always be remembered for its remarkable finish, the result only being arrived at within four minutes of the call of time and the great change in the game being brought about by the unexpected success that attended the bowling of Sherwin, the Notts wicket-keeper. Middlesex had begun the day in a thankless position, their only hope being to remain in for the whole day and draw the game. Their first innings was finished off for 195 and just before the luncheon interval they had to follow on against a majority of 271. The wicket, which had worn wonderfully well, was still in excellent condition, but at the outset matters went badly and four wickets were soon obtained. At half-past six, however, Webbe and

Middlesex's doings in 1891 had gained them a great following among the public, and during last summer at Lord's the Middlesex matches attracted bigger crowds than they had ever done before. It was quite a common thing for five thousand people to be at an ordinary match, and on the Whitsun Bank Holiday the game against Somerset was witnessed by over ten thousand people. [1893]

Stoddart were still together and the score had reached 244 for five. It did not appear possible for five wickets to fall in half an hour, but there came one of those turns of fortune that make the charm of cricket. The regular bowlers having been mastered, a trial was given to Sherwin and this change was attended with

"I'm Mordecai Sherwin," the young man told the Notts secretary. "I want to keep wicket for the Coonty." He never said anything about his bowling.

extraordinary success. He clean bowled Webbe at 247 and, with the score unaltered, Stoddart was out leg before wicket to Attewell. Thus the whole position had changed, 25 minutes remaining for play and there being three wickets to go down. Amidst tremendous excitement Thesiger was bowled by Sherwin at 250, and Rawlin by Attewell at 252, while at 257 Hearne was caught by the stand-in wicket-keeper, Robinson, the ball only being held at the second attempt. Notts had won the match by an innings and 14 runs.

Nottinghamshire: 466 (A. Shrewsbury 212, Mr J. S. Robinson 72, W. Attewell 59; J. T. Hearne 4–117, Mr E. A. Nepean 4–133).

Middlesex: 195 (Mr S. W. Scott 55, Nepean 61; F. Shacklock 5–103) and 257 (Mr A. E. Stoddart 130, Mr T. C. O'Brien 57; Attewell 4–38, M. Sherwin 2–9 in seven overs).

v Nottinghamshire

• June 5, 6, 7, 1893 •

IN MATCHES between the MCC and Sussex, the MCC and the Australians, Middlesex and Gloucestershire, and Middlesex and Yorkshire, Stoddart had already given proof of being in splendid form, but his previous efforts in 1893 were completely thrown into the shade on this particular occasion when he scored 195 not out and 124. By obtaining two separate hundreds in the same game he accomplished a feat which previously had been performed in first-class matches only by W. G. Grace and George Brann, and his 195 not out proved, so far as important cricket was concerned, to be the highest individual innings of the year. In making his two long scores he showed some wonderful cricket, playing throughout both innings in his finest and most attractive style. On the Monday he went in first and took out his bat. Everyone hoped that Stoddart would crown his performance by making 200, but he was still five short of the coveted number when J. T. Hearne, his last partner, was bowled.

Middlesex won by 57 runs, with ten minutes to spare.

Middlesex: 327 (Mr A. E. Stoddart 195 not out; R. J. Mee 6–120) and 304 (Stoddart 124, Mr C. P. Foley 68; W. Attewell 4–100).

Nottinghamshire: 301 (W. Gunn 120; J. T. Hearne 4–93) and 273 (Mr C. W. Wright 61; Hearne 5–98).

v Sussex

• July 14, 15, 16, 1898 •

SUSSEX were unable to place their full strength in the field and, after having the worst of the game all through, were beaten by 235 runs. Some capital all-round cricket was shown on the opening day; on the second, Fry increased his not out innings of 56 to 104, and moreover carried his bat right through the innings. He batted splendidly but met with poor support. Trott finished off the innings by taking five wickets for 18 runs. Fry was bowled first ball by him in the visitors' second innings, and with his dismissal went all chance of saving the game. On the second afternoon Fry was no-balled for throwing.

Middlesex: 258 (Mr A. E. Stoddart 60; C. H. G. Bland 7–100) and 377–9 dec. (Mr H. B. Hayman 59, Mr F. G. J. Ford 78, J. T. Rawlin 56, Sir T. C. O'Brien 62).

Sussex: 197 (Mr C. B. Fry 104 not out; A. E. Trott 5–36) and 203 (F. W. Marlow 45; Trott 6–72).

Nothing new

On the hard wickets in June and July, one or two bowlers were sadly needed to assist Hearne and Rawlin. Of course, the prospect in this respect is now much brighter for Middlesex, as in the summer of 1898 Albert Trott (above), the famous Australian, will have become qualified by residence. Judged by the many fine performances he accomplished in small matches for the MCC last season, he looks like proving a tower of strength to the county. In the following season, Middlesex will have the services of Roche, another Australian, who has decided to throw in his lot with English cricket. On this question of qualifying colonial professionals, there is no need to enter here, but the fact of Trott, Roche and O'Halloran being at once retained on the groundstaff at Lord's, with the idea of ultimately appearing for Middlesex, undoubtedly aroused some ill-feeling and dissatisfaction amongst the other counties. [1898]

v Yorkshire

• May 29, 30, 31, 1899 •

MIDDLESEX did many brilliant things last season, but nothing finer than their victory over Yorkshire by an innings and 2 runs. Just at this period, the long spell of fine weather began and, for the first time for nearly three weeks, cricket was played at Lord's on a firm pitch and under really pleasant conditions. As regards both the play and the attendance, the change was magical, the spectators on the opening day numbering, at a rough guess, nine or ten thousand. After losing four wickets on the first evening for 121, Middlesex gave a wonderful display of batting, P. F. Warner and Albert Trott playing better than they had ever played before. Warner's 150 was emphatically the innings of his life. He took two hours and twenty minutes to get his first 50 runs, an hour and 40 minutes to make his second 50, and then, with the bowling mastered, finished up by making 50 in just an hour. So far as could be seen he did not make a mistake. Trott was very careful up to a certain point, but afterwards hit in such tremendous form that he scored in an hour and a half 137 runs out of 181.

Yorkshire: 203 (Mr F. Mitchell 68; J. T. Hearne 5–79, A. E. Trott 5–98) and 283 (J. Tunnicliffe 85, J. T. Brown 80; Trott 4–130, W. Roche 5–93).

Middlesex: 488 (Mr P. F. Warner 150, Mr C. P. Foley 52, Trott 164; W. Rhodes 7–147).

v Lancashire

• August 19, 20, 21, 1901 •

R. N. DOUGLAS [of Middlesex] was placed in a false position by having to keep wicket, and in addition to making some mistakes he gave away 74 byes. His brother, James Douglas, and Warner batted superbly and scored 218 together.

v Somerset

• May 23, 24, 25, 1904 •

MIDDLESEX certainly showed brilliant all-round cricket in beating Somerset by an innings and 119 runs, but it must be said that the home side in winning the toss gained an advantage which practically ensured their success. To begin with, the wicket had not recovered from the effect of Saturday's rain and the west countrymen, thanks to some splendid bowling by J. T. Hearne, were dismissed in two hours. Middlesex had four wickets down for 89, but then the two Beldams obtained such a complete mastery over the bowling that they put on 201 in just over two hours and were still together at the drawing of stumps. No play was possible on Tuesday owing to rain, and on Wednesday George Beldam (right) was out second ball. He had played remarkably sound and skilful cricket for more than three hours. His cousin Ernest Beldam, in making his first [and only] hundred in county cricket, batted very carefully at first, but when the Somerset bowling had become loose he hit out with splendid vigour. After lunch, with batsmen again at a great disadvantage, Hearne and Trott disposed of Somerset cheaply, Hearne varying his pace well and breaking back just enough to beat the bat.

Somerset: 126 (Mr P. R. Johnson 43; J. T. Hearne 8–49) and 125 (Johnson 36; Hearne 7–44, A. E. Trott 3–73).

Middlesex: 370–8 dec. (Mr G. W. Beldam 140, Mr E. A. Beldam 105; B. Cranfield 5–100).

Two men who made Middlesex tick in the years up to the First World War. Australian all-rounder Frank Tarrant (left) did the double each season from 1907 to 1914. Pelham "Plum" Warner captained the county from 1908 to 1920.

v Sussex

• May 25, 26, 27, 1905 •

PLAYED JUST BEFORE the first of the Test games [against Australia], this was emphatically Bosanquet's match. Thanks chiefly to his superb batting and highly effective bowling, Middlesex, after declaring their second innings closed with a lead of 426, won by 324 runs. For the second time in his life Bosanquet made two separate hundreds in one match, and in all he took eleven wickets, carrying everything before him in

the last innings [8–53 in 13.2 overs]. He hit up his 103 in an hour and three-quarters, and his 100 not out in 75 minutes. Field (107 not out) played fine cricket of a far more careful kind, and Warner (86) and George Beldam (94) were seen at their best in the second innings. Fry was kept out of the Sussex team by a damaged finger and his absence clearly dispirited them.

v Lancashire

• July 22, 23, 1907 •

THIS MATCH proved an altogether unfortunate affair. So much rain fell during the early hours of Monday that no cricket could be attempted until after lunch. Later on there came a delay of 70 minutes owing to bad light, and at five o'clock further rain put an end to play with the Lancashire score at 57 for one wicket. That evening the pitch was practically under water and, with a wet night, the prospects of play next day were always remote. Unhappily, there came neither sun nor wind to improve the condition of the ground. The spectators, numbering about 600, waited patiently until half-past three, but then began to clamour for the game to be resumed, demonstrating two or three times in front of the Pavilion. After several visits to the wicket, the umpires made a final inspection at a quarter to five and, finding the ground still unplayable, pulled up the stumps. Thereupon, some section of the spectators walked right across the pitch and inflicted some damage, noticeably at one end. The crowd having dispersed, a prolonged discussion ensued between the captains [MacGregor of Middlesex and Lancashire's MacLaren] and some of their players and the umpires, and eventually MacLaren handed the

R. D. "Russie" Walker, sixth of the seven brothers integral to Middlesex in their early years, succeeded his brother V. E. as club president. Having batted against fast bowling without pads or gloves, he soon had the measure of Archie MacLaren (below).

As the relationship between the MCC and the Middlesex County Cricket Club has been misunderstood, a statement has been prepared and circulated amongst the counties, clearly showing what its nature is and pointing out that the arrangement has been carried out on lines which are for the mutual benefit of both clubs. It has recently been decided that the MCC shall take over the whole control of Middlesex matches at Lord's, and shall discharge the executive duties connected therewith, and an extra rent of £100 per annum is to be paid in respect of the work that this will entail. [1909]

following statement to the press: "Owing to the pitch having been deliberately torn up by the public, I, as captain of the Lancashire eleven, cannot see my way to continue the game, the groundman bearing me out that the wicket could not be again put right. – A. C. MacLaren." The match was accordingly abandoned. Rolled next morning for the regulation ten minutes, the pitch showed little trace of the treatment to which it had been subjected.

Opinion was very much divided as to the action MacLaren took, a letter of indignant protest being addressed to the *Field* by Mr R. D. Walker, the Middlesex president. The actual damage to the pitch did not, it was stated, amount to more than one rather deep heel mark.

v Gloucestershire

• June 27, 28, 1910 •

DISASTROUS RESULTS attended Jessop's policy in sending Middlesex in to bat. Heavy rains having left the ground somewhat soft, the course taken by the Gloucestershire captain would probably have been justified had the sun shone. The weather, however, remained gloomy except for one brief spell and, although after lunch the ball for a time turned quickly, all chance of disposing of Middlesex cheaply had then disappeared. To complete the visitors' discomfiture, a good deal of rain fell on Monday evening and, bright sunshine prevailing on Tuesday, the defeat of Gloucestershire in face of the Middlesex total of 279 was a foregone conclusion. On the treacherous pitch the Gloucestershire batsmen found

themselves practically helpless against J. T. Hearne and Tarrant and were twice dismissed in less than three hours and a half for an aggregate of 155. Hearne and Tarrant bowled unchanged, the former taking twelve wickets for 70 runs – a notable achievement for a man who, 43 years of age, had had more than twenty seasons of first-class cricket.

v Lancashire

• May 25, 26, 27, 1911 •

IN THIS match A. R. Litteljohn followed up his fine work against Kent with bowling of quite a sensational description. Lancashire had 170 on the board with only one man out, but Litteljohn wrought tremendous havoc, dismissing eight batsmen in ten overs and four balls for 19 runs. He brought about another startling change on Saturday, Lancashire at lunch time having scored 154 for the loss of four wickets and the match being finished off in three-quarters of an hour afterwards. Taking in all fifteen wickets in the match, Litteljohn made his aggregate 36 for six consecutive innings. After seven Middlesex wickets had fallen for 302, his brother, E. S. Litteljohn, and Anson completely mastered the Lancashire bowling, adding 120 in an hour and a half. Middlesex won by an innings and 11 runs.

Lancashire: 212 (H. Makepeace 77, W. Tyldesley 65; Mr A. R. Litteljohn 8–69) and 233 (Makepeace 60; A. R. Litteljohn 7–120).

Middlesex: 456 (Mr P. F. Warner 81, J. W. Hearne 77, Mr E. S. Litteljohn 105, Hon. R. Anson 70; Mr W. Brearley 6–162).

ARTHUR RIEUSETT LITTELJOHN As regards the Middlesex bowling in 1911, A. R. Litteljohn took the honours so long as he could spare time to play, his medical work leaving him little time for three-day matches. Practically unknown as a bowler in first-class cricket he had developed his skill by hard and assiduous practice. His success said much for the virtue of old-fashioned methods. His leg-break was slight, but with a good amount of spin he combined such extreme accuracy of length that even the most daring batsman had to treat him with respect. Whether his success would have continued had he played all through such a dry season it is impossible to say, but so long as he stayed in the eleven he was invaluable. A famous old Surrey cricketer, after watching him one day at Lord's, said that even Alfred Shaw could not have kept a better pitch. [1912]

Sir Pelham Warner

MIDDLESEX SECOND ELEVEN
v KENT SECOND ELEVEN
• July 27, 28, 1894 •

A beautiful wicket had been prepared for this match at Lord's, and so heavy was the scoring that in the course of the two days no fewer than 1,017 runs were obtained for the loss of 30 wickets. The bowling on both sides was rather weak, and the batsmen were not slow to avail themselves of the opportunity. There were three individual scores of over 100, and in the whole match the old Rugby boy, P. F. Warner, made 233 runs for once out [163 and 70 not out]. The match was drawn.

• • •

There could certainly be no more appropriate time to give Mr Warner's portrait in *Wisden*, the MCC having conferred upon the Middlesex batsman the great distinction of captaining their team in Australia. Apart, of course, from the Australian trip, Mr Warner has high claims to consideration, having during the last few seasons fairly won his place among the representative batsmen of his day. A more enthusiastic player it would be impossible to find anywhere. Cricket, if one may be permitted the expression, is the very breath of his nostrils. From the time of his school days at Rugby, Mr Warner was a batsman of great promise, but he made no sudden jump into fame, his position having been gradually won by strenuous and persistent effort. That he should have been rather slow to get to his best is not surprising, as he did not start with the physical advantages that have made easy the path of many of his contemporaries. Of medium height, small-boned and light of frame, he does not by any means fill the eye as a great batsman, but having once seen him get a hundred runs, one is no longer left in doubt as to his qualities. Lord's has always been his favourite ground, and nowhere else

... affectionately known as "Plum".

perhaps, despite his varied experiences, is he seen to quite such advantage. When the sun shines and the ground is hard, he is one of the best of batsmen to look at, combining a most attractive style with a great variety of strokes. His driving on both sides of the wicket is, for a man of his weight and stature, surprisingly hard, and he commands a very pretty and effective cut.

Personally, Mr Warner is one of the most popular of cricketers, and apart from his skill as a batsman he has, by reason of his contagious enthusiasm, done good for cricket wherever he has played. He has lately taken to writing about the game and, when cricket is the topic, he can make a capital after-dinner speech. [1904]

MCC AND GROUND v SUSSEX
• May 8, 9, 10, 1905 •

The outstanding feature of this match, despite Warner's wonderful innings, was the establishment by C. B. Fry of a new record in first-class cricket. By making 156 and 106, the famous batsman scored two separate hundreds in one match for the fourth time in his career, thus beating the performances of W. G. Grace and R. E. Foster, who previously shared the record with him. In the first innings Fry was batting three hours and twenty minutes and made his runs out of 304, hitting a five and sixteen fours, while in the second he was two hours and three-quarters making 106 out of 154. The captain's magnificent achievement notwithstanding, Sussex were defeated by seven wickets, thanks largely to Warner who, in the course of three hours and 50 minutes, contributed 204 out of 346. Batting almost perfectly he hit a five and 26 fours.

Sussex: 339 (Mr C. B. Fry 156, A. E. Relf 64; F. A. Tarrant 4–75) and 266 (Fry 106, J. Vine 51; G. J. Thompson 5–72).

MCC and Ground: 503–9 dec. (Mr P. F. Warner 204, Tarrant 56 not out, extras 52; F. W. Tate 3–90) and 104–3 (Mr C. H. M. Ebden 47 not out).

v Hampshire

• June 9, 10, 1919 •

IN WINNING the Whit Monday match with twenty minutes to spare, by an innings and 74 runs, Middlesex did something rather astonishing. Such a result did not seem within the range of possibility when, just before five o'clock on the Bank Holiday, Hampshire finished their first innings for 347. Hearne and Hendren were not out with 53 and 62 to their credit at the drawing of stumps, and on the second morning they put on runs at a tremendous pace, adding a hundred in the first hour and another hundred in still quicker time. Altogether, against fielding which never became in the slightest degree slack, they scored 325 together in rather less than three hours. Hendren in his great innings of 201 – his second of over 200 at Lord's within a fortnight – included four sixes, all on the on side. Though he scored at such a pace, he did not, so far as could be seen, give a chance. Hearne's innings, though not so perfect, was also a splendid display. G. T. S. Stevens bowled admirably in his first county

match, doing great things on the first day and managing to beat the clock at the finish. Brown, in scoring his 90 and 54 for Hampshire, showed that he could touch the extremes of brilliancy and caution.

Hampshire: 347 (Capt. B. G. Melle 78, G. Brown 90, Mr S. G. A. Maartensz 60; G. T. S. Stevens 7–104) and 187 (Brown 54; Capt. N. E. Haig 6–52, Stevens 3–32).

Middlesex: 608–7 dec. (J. W. Hearne 218 not out, E. Hendren 201; A. Kennedy 7–202).

County matches in 1919 were of two days' duration. The experiment "was doomed before the season had run half its course," editor Sydney Pardon wrote in Wisden 1920, *"and in August the Advisory Committee decided unanimously to go back to three-day matches in 1920."*

---

v Sussex

• May 22, 24, 1920 •

IN BEATING SUSSEX by an innings and 130 runs Middlesex did, to the best of one's knowledge, something without precedent in first-class cricket, their first four batsmen all scoring

Left: "Patsy" Hendren – double-hundred against Hampshire.
Above: Men of the centuries – "Plum" Warner, Harry Lee, J. W. Hearne and Nigel Haig.

over a hundred. Though 956 runs were obtained, the match was finished off in two days, play being prolonged on Whit Monday till a quarter to seven. There was a huge crowd on the Bank Holiday, 14,129 people paying for admission. Lee had a great match, as in addition to playing an innings of 119 he took eleven wickets at a cost of only 68 runs. His bowling was the more remarkable as the ground did not give him the least assistance. The match was played for the benefit of Whiteside, of the MCC groundstaff.

Sussex: 232 (G. Stannard 53; H. W. Lee 5–21) and 181 (G. Cox 38; Lee 6–47).

Middlesex: 543–4 dec. (Mr P. F. Warner 139, H. W. Lee 119, J. W. Hearne 116 not out, Mr N. E. Haig 131).

Three years later the first Middlesex four, H. L. Dales 103, Lee 107, Hearne 232 and Hendren 177 not out, hit hundreds against Hampshire at Southampton.

---

v Surrey

• August 28, 30, 31, 1920 •

THIS WAS THE MATCH of the season. Middlesex and Lancashire were running neck and neck for the Championship, and as Lancashire on the same days had the simplest of tasks against Worcestershire, Middlesex knew that nothing less than an actual victory would be of real value to them. Never before has a county match proved such an attraction at Lord's. On the Saturday there must have been nearly 25,000 people on the ground, 20,700 paying for admission at the gates. A great fight was looked forward to, and as it happened all expectations were exceeded. It was a game never to be forgotten, Middlesex in the end winning by 55 runs and so securing the Championship. Winning the toss Middlesex had the advantage of batting first on a hard wicket, but nothing could have been less promising than their start. For once Lee and Hearne failed them, and in less than an hour three wickets were down for 35 runs. After these disasters nothing was risked, and at the end of the afternoon the Middlesex score with eight men out had reached only 253. Warner was blamed in some quarters for over-caution, but he saved his side. In getting 79 he was batting for nearly four hours and a half. On the Monday there was again an enormous attendance, the number paying at the gates this time being 20,021. Owing nearly everything to Sandham, Surrey had the best of the day's cricket and, with the object of getting Middlesex in before the end of the afternoon, Fender declared with nine wickets down. But his policy met with no reward, Skeet and Lee batting for 40 minutes and taking the score to 27. For sustained excitement, the third day beat everything seen in London last season. Skeet and Lee made victory for Middlesex possible, staying in until after lunch and sending up 208 for the first wicket. Lee was splendid, and Skeet, though not so certain in timing the ball, played better than he had

Elias Hendren, the Middlesex batsman, will always have the pleasantest memories of the season of 1919. He was a first-rate cricketer before the war – a very dangerous bat and about the best outfield in the kingdom – but last summer he left all his previous form far behind and took rank as an England batsman. He began to play cricket as a child, with the nearest tree for a wicket, and at the age of fifteen he appeared for Turnham Green, a club that has a history going back 60 years. His first chance came when he played for a local eighteen at Chiswick Park against a team of England players got together by J. T. Hearne. Then through the influence of Mr George Beldam and Mr MacGregor he went to Lord's and in due course began his connection with Middlesex cricket by playing in colts and second eleven matches. Before long Mr C. B. Fry was predicting that he might become the Tyldesley of Middlesex.

. . .

Hendren cannot be described as quite a classic batsman. As Mr Warner has pointed out, his bat in back play is not perfectly straight, but this criticism would have applied in times past to many men short in stature. Hendren has abundant gifts, combining with his fine hitting great patience and self-control. He is very modern in his methods, using the pull and the hook at every opportunity. So sure is his eye, however, that he is not often at fault. An ardent footballer, he is one of the most prominent members of the Brentford team. [1920]

ever played before in a first-class match. Warner declared at twenty minutes to four, leaving Surrey to get 244 in a trifle over three hours. The downfall of Hobbs – caught in the slips at 22 – was discouraging, but Surrey went for the runs and, with Sandham playing even more finely than on the previous day, the

hundred was up in an hour and a quarter for two wickets. However, Hendren got rid of Shepherd by means of a wonderful catch in the deep field – just in front of the screen with his hands above his head – this being really the turning-point of the game. Surrey's great hope departed when Sandham – the sixth man out – was caught and bowled by Hearne from a full pitch. In the end Middlesex won with ten minutes to spare. Warner was carried off the field shoulder high, and before the crowd dispersed he and Fender had to make speeches.

Middlesex: 268 (Mr P. F. Warner 79, Mr G. T. S. Stevens 53; Mr P. G. H. Fender 4–76) and 316–7 dec. (Mr C. H. L. Skeet 106, H. W. Lee 108; T. Rushby 3–73).

Surrey: 341–9 dec. (A. Sandham 167 not out; T. J. Durston 4–97) and 188 (Sandham 68; Stevens 5–61, J. W. Hearne 3–37).

v Nottinghamshire

• June 1, 2, 3, 1921 •

MIDDLESEX BEAT NOTTS by the overwhelming margin of an innings and 197 runs. They practically won the match on the first day, getting rid of Notts on a perfect pitch for 132 and winding up with their own score at 247 for two wickets. Crutchley hit with astonishing brilliancy on the off side. His partnership with Lee for the first wicket produced 231 runs in two hours and a quarter, his 145 including 22 fours. On Thursday, Middlesex beat the record, their total of 612 for eight declared being the highest ever obtained at Lord's in a first-class match. Lee enjoyed the biggest success of his career. Getting, as usual, most of his runs on the on side, he hit in his 243 not out one six (four for an overthrow), 21 fours, fourteen threes and nineteen twos. Mann punished the worn-out bowling in tremendous style. Receiving only twenty balls he scored his 53 in fourteen hits, four of them sixes. Notts had a hopeless task.

v Surrey

• August 27, 29, 30, 1921 •

AS IN 1920, the Championship hinged on the return match with Surrey. Middlesex entered upon the all-important fixture with a good deal in their favour, as nothing short of an actual victory would have given Surrey the honours in the competition. As things turned out Middlesex, after more than once looking to be a beaten side, gained a wonderful victory to retain the Championship, going in to get 322 in the last innings and actually hitting off the runs for the loss of four wickets. The great point in their favour was that they were free from anxiety as to the clock. Lee was out at 48, and then came the batting that won the match. Hearne joined Twining at five minutes past twelve, and not until twenty minutes past five did the second wicket fall, 277 runs being added in four hours and ten minutes of actual play. Surrey fielded untiringly, trying their hardest until at five minutes past six Hendren made the winning hit. The match excited enormous interest, 15,945 people paying for admission on the first day, 17,663 on the second and 14,311 on the third.

Surrey: 269 (T. Shepherd 128 not out, Mr D. R. Jardine 55; T. J. Durston 4–47) and 184 (Mr D. J. Knight 74; Mr N. E. Haig 5–62).

Middlesex: 132 (Mr F. T. Mann 29; Mr G. M. Reay 4–44) and 322–4 (Mr R. H. Twining 135, J. W. Hearne 106).

v Yorkshire

• May 28, 29, 30, 1924 •

CLASHING WITH the Test Trial game at Nottingham, this proved a very disappointing match. Middlesex had to go into the field without Hearne and Hendren, and Yorkshire, suffering to a still greater extent, were without Holmes, Sutcliffe, Roy Kilner and Macaulay. As things

Frank Mann – Championship captain in 1921.

turned out, a win for Middlesex shortly before three o'clock on the last day by an innings and 152 runs was quite a fitting result. The cream of the cricket was Mann's superb driving. Four times he hit Rhodes for sixes, the first two – from successive balls – landing on the roof of the Pavilion. While G. T. S. Stevens (114) and Mann (79) stayed together, 151 runs were scored in 95 minutes.

v Yorkshire

• June 6, 8, 9, 1925 •

BRILLIANTLY as they performed on many occasions last summer, the Yorkshiremen excelled themselves in this match, dismissing Middlesex on a good wicket for 118, hitting up 538 for the loss of six batsmen, and gaining a glorious victory by an innings and 149 runs. The game was rendered especially memorable by the batting of Holmes who, in putting together an innings of 315 not out, beat the famous 278 by William Ward which had stood as the record score at Lord's for 105 years. Holmes' batting was superb. On Saturday, when he left off with 121 runs to his credit, he depended mainly upon cuts and skilful strokes on the leg side, but on Monday he drove splendidly on both sides of the wicket, displaying his varied resources as a batsman in a manner that compelled general admiration. Altogether he was at the wickets for six hours and 50 minutes, giving no chance, making very few faulty strokes and hitting 38 fours, 12 threes and 21 twos. The collapse of Middlesex was due primarily to Robinson, who made the ball swing a lot and come fast off the pitch. Macaulay, too, although handicapped by an injury, did fine work. Stevens and Hearne played admirably in the Middlesex second innings.

v Surrey

• August 28, 30, 31, 1926 •

HOBBS seized upon this occasion to make what was at once the highest score of his wonderful career and the highest ever made at Lord's, beating his own 266 not out, for Players against Gentlemen at Scarborough in 1925, and Holmes' 315 not out for Yorkshire against Middlesex – also put together in the previous summer. The great batsman, who obtained his runs mainly on the on side, placed the ball with marvellous skill and did not appear to give a chance. He was at the wickets six hours and 55 minutes, scoring 41 fours, 6 threes, 20 twos and 94 singles. Sandham helped to raise the total to 115 – the two Surrey men's 36th three-figure first-wicket stand. Ducat shared in a partnership of 101, and Jardine in one of 270. The home side had to follow on 304 in arrear and Surrey, fielding brilliantly, won the match by an innings and 63 runs.

v Lancashire

• June 22, 23, 24, 1927 •

RAIN PREVENTING any cricket on the third day, progress was restricted to the completion of an innings on each side. Lancashire led by 94 runs, but the outstanding feature of the game proved to be a display of batting by Enthoven. Middlesex, facing a total of 413, fared so badly that at the tea interval on the second day they had six men out for 150, and when the eighth wicket fell, 55 runs were still wanted to avert a follow-on. Then came the wonderful play by Enthoven who – given when 43 a life at long-off – had taken two hours and 25 minutes to bring his score to 50. Rising to the occasion in a manner worthy of Gilbert Jessop, he hit away with marvellous power and freedom. Time and again he jumped in to McDonald, and such brilliant success attended his enterprising methods that not only did he save the follow-on but went on at a tremendous pace to complete his hundred. Nothing latterly caused him any trouble, and getting nearly all the bowling he actually obtained the last 89 runs in 55 minutes. In his 139 – a really memorable achievement – were seventeen fours, four threes and sixteen twos.

v Surrey

• August 27, 29, 30, 1927 •

WONDERFUL BOWLING by Fender was the big factor in a Surrey victory by five wickets. Hitting the stumps six times and getting J. A. Powell leg-before, he took seven wickets for 10 runs. He obtained the last six in the course of eleven balls, with only 1 run scored off

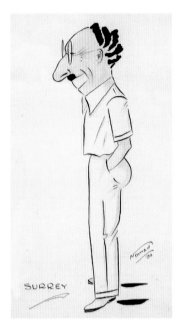

Crosstown traffic from The Oval in the 1920s included Andy Sandham (left), selfless in his support of Jack Hobbs at the top of the Surrey order, and Percy Fender, an inspirational captain and leg-breaking all-rounder.

him meanwhile, and the first five of these six in seven balls without a run. Twice in his fifth over he secured two wickets with following balls. On the same day Hearne took eight Surrey wickets for 39 runs, but Sandham defended skilfully for two hours for 39 and Fender hit with fine judgment in scoring 42.

v Yorkshire

• June 2, 4, 5, 1928 •

SHOWING SPLENDID CRICKET on Tuesday when they secured fifteen wickets for an aggregate of 171, Yorkshire beat Middlesex by an innings and 88 runs, and in so doing registered their first victory of the season. In finishing

off the game in this brilliant fashion, Yorkshire owed nearly everything to the 50-year-old Rhodes who, on a pitch slightly worn, secured in the second innings of Middlesex seven wickets for 39. The few spectators not only applauded Rhodes enthusiastically but gave three cheers for him. Holmes and Sutcliffe on Saturday opened Yorkshire's innings with a splendid stand which, lasting two hours and a quarter, produced 158 runs, this being their 50th three-figure first-wicket partnership – their 45th for Yorkshire. Holmes registered his sixth hundred at Lord's. In the Middlesex first innings, Yorkshire after the tea interval actually missed six possible chances in three-quarters of an hour, Hendren being let off five times.

v Lancashire

• June 15, 17, 18, 1929 •

ALTHOUGH LEFT DRAWN with Middlesex wanting 154 runs for victory and having five wickets to fall, this game produced several noteworthy performances. In the first place Allen, bowling at a fine pace, took all ten wickets in Lancashire's first innings, hitting the stumps eight times. Ernest Tyldesley, nevertheless, played a masterly innings of 102. Furthermore, although Middlesex had six men out for 71, Lee was in great form, batting for three hours and a half without a serious mistake in making 124. Hopwood in Lancashire's second innings played with excellent judgment – cautiously at first and afterwards freely in scoring 106 not out. When Middlesex went in with the game to save, Lee withstood the Lancashire attack for two hours and a half and was still unbeaten with a second hundred to his credit when the match ended.

v Sussex

• June 7, 9, 10, 1930 •

A MATCH, rendered memorable through a batsman on each side scoring two separate hundreds, was left drawn, Sussex, after Middlesex had declared, being within 72 of victory when 35 minutes before time the game, owing to bad light, was abandoned. Duleepsinhji not only played delightful cricket for 116 but with his second-innings 102 not out, after two wickets had fallen for 17 runs, helped to add 169 in two hours. Enthoven on Saturday batted 80 minutes for 21 and then, with the last Middlesex man in, hit up 102 out of 107 in 75 minutes. His 115 in the second innings, if not marked by such contrasts, was a faultless display.

"Gubby" Allen (left) and Walter Robins – Middlesex men with a finger on cricket's pulse. From Eton opener to MCC life vice-president, Allen's time at Lord's spanned 70 years.

consisting of deliveries tossed high or wide of the wicket, yielded 24 runs from byes and wides, while a fieldsman in the deep made no effort to prevent the ball from reaching the boundary. Protests came from the crowd, but before the new ball could be brought into use, a successful appeal against the light ended the unhappy proceedings. As the sun shone, it was ridiculous to suggest that the light was unfit for cricket, but a farcical situation was ended by this pretence.

The Middlesex batsmen when the appeal was made were R. W. V. Robins, the captain, and G. O. Allen.

v Yorkshire

• June 15, 17, 18, 1935 •

A GREAT PIECE of bowling by Smailes, followed by an opening partnership of 207 between Mitchell and Barber, might well have brought Yorkshire victory had not cricket been restricted to one day. Nothing could be done on Saturday, and though play went on without interruption on Monday, rain afterwards prevented another ball being bowled. Going in to bat upon winning the toss, Middlesex were dismissed before lunch, Smailes, who made the ball swing a lot, bowling in well-nigh irresistible form. When the seventh batsman left at 24, Smailes' figures read: five wickets for 13 runs. He hit the off stump each time. Smith retrieved the situation to some extent with an enterprising display and scored 57 in half an hour.

v Surrey

• August 28, 30, 31, 1937 •

D RAWN. Surrey made the highest total of the season from bowling which, after early successes, presented little difficulty. Middlesex lost two wickets for 4 runs, but Hendren, accorded a wonderful reception by 17,000 spectators upon the occasion of his last appearance in a Championship game, hit finely all-round in an innings of 103. He and Edrich put on 182 together. Edrich, not so free against the slow bowlers, made some capital strokes in front of the wicket. Surrey led by 90 and forced the rate of run-getting before declaring. Middlesex required 295 to win and, despite confident batting by Compton and Allen, looked like suffering defeat. With the score at 178 for eight wickets, Holmes, with a view to gaining the use of the new ball after 200 runs, bowled an over that,

A FTER BEING runners-up on five successive occasions, Middlesex in 1947 deservedly won the Championship. This was worthy reward for R. W. V. Robins in his final year as captain and a happy start for the new president, Mr F. T. Mann, who led Middlesex the last time they finished first, in 1921. His pleasure was shared by the former president, Sir Pelham Warner, who in 1920 crowned his captaincy in similar fashion to Robins.

The season will be remembered for the feats of Denis Compton and Bill Edrich. Yet magnificently as they performed for Middlesex as well as England, the Championship came to Middlesex not through any individual brilliance but by the combined efforts and team spirit of a particularly harmonious eleven, intelligently captained and backed by good reserves.

In all ways Middlesex provided the best illustration of the "dynamic attitude" ideal of the MCC Select Committee. From the first ball in every match they pursued one object only – victory. They studied closely the strong and weak points of opponents, their batting possessed a sense of urgency, the bowling was full of purpose, and the fielding rarely fell from a high standard. By their remarkably rapid scoring, the batsmen usually gave the bowlers maximum time to dismiss a side twice, and frequently Middlesex finished the first day with over 400 runs made and three or four wickets taken cheaply. [1948]

v Somerset

• May 10, 12, 13, 1947 •

SOMERSET WON by one wicket. Fortune frequently changed in a very interesting struggle. Edrich, when first playing as an amateur, revealed the best attributes in batting, going to 102 in a faultless display lasting three hours and a quarter. By taking four wickets for 5 runs in six overs on the second morning, he then helped materially in Middlesex leading by 97. Tremlett, on his first appearance for Somerset, surpassed this bowling effort in the second innings. Tall, fairly fast, with good action, he bowled at the stumps with some off-break and began by sending back five men in five overs for 8 runs. This startling work, supported by Wellard, left Somerset the task of getting only 176, but they lost five wickets for 101 on Monday, and next morning the pitch, slightly affected by rain, made run-getting difficult. However, Tremlett showed confidence without rashness, and lunch was taken with 16 wanted. Despite a close-set field, defence still prevailed until Tremlett lifted an almost straight drive into the members' stand and, with two threes to the on, won the match. The Middlesex team lined up and cheered as their opponents went to the Pavilion.

v Nottinghamshire

• May 7, 9, 10, 1949 •

DRAWN. Middlesex wanted 222 in two hours 35 minutes, and their efforts to hit off the runs nearly ended in defeat. Leslie Compton, who had developed a painful

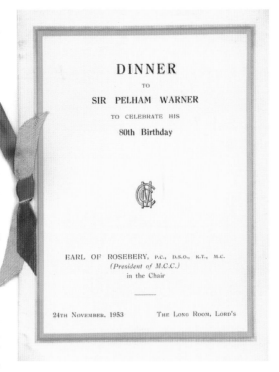

DINNER

TO

SIR PELHAM WARNER

TO CELEBRATE HIS

80th Birthday

EARL OF ROSEBERY, P.C., D.S.O., K.T., M.C.
(President of M.C.C.)
in the Chair

24TH NOVEMBER, 1953　　THE LONG ROOM, LORD'S

Lord's honours one of its own.

ankle when keeping wicket, went to hospital and was sent back on crutches. With five minutes left he hobbled to the crease with Mann as runner and played out the final over, a maiden, with nine of the Nottingham team within five yards of the bat.

v Hampshire

• May 14, 16, 17, 1955 •

MIDDLESEX WON by 55 runs. The faster bowlers, especially Moss, made best use of the rain-affected pitch. The game began so sensationally that the first five Middlesex wickets fell for 11, but Titmus, despite several painful blows, stood his ground and saw the total reach 100.

Hampshire offset the splendid bowling of Shackleton and Cannings by their unsound batting, and Middlesex possessed a match-winner in Moss. Consistently fast and accurate, he achieved his best analysis with seven wickets for 34, and when the game finished in the extra half-hour his full figures were twelve for 61 – a truly fine performance.

v Surrey

• August 12, 14, 15, 1961 •

SURREY WON by 29 runs on a worn and dusty pitch which developed a bad patch. Hooker, with medium-fast variations, brought about Surrey's first-day downfall, including the dismissal of May for a duck. At one stage Hooker sent back four men for 6 runs in fourteen balls. Eric Bedser, with accurately pitched off-breaks, showed his power for Surrey on the second day when Middlesex fared little better. Then Titmus upset Surrey after Barrington and Willett had shared a stand of 135. Once more May was out for a duck – the first time he had been dismissed for a pair – and Middlesex were left to make 231 in just under five hours. May depended on the experience of his spinners – they bowled for the last two hours – and was fully justified, Lock backing his guileful bowling with brilliant fielding. Such was the state of the pitch that six times in the last innings the ball beat the bat and wicket-keeper for four byes.

v Hampshire

• May 30, June 1, 2, 1964 •

DRAWN. After an innings apiece on the first day, no play was possible. The match hours had been lengthened from 11.00 until 6.45 on the first two days to permit an early finish on the third day so that preparations could be made for a cocktail party for the Middlesex lady members in the Pavilion on Tuesday evening. As it happened, the game was officially called off at one o'clock that day!

Bill and Denis – the boys of summer.

Compton & Edrich

They go together in English cricket, as Gilbert and Sullivan go together in English opera. Nor is the analogy so careless as you might suppose. It may be allowable that each or any of these four has been surpassed as executant in his own sphere; that would develop an argument to make any Paper Controller clutch his scanty reserves. But it should not be doubted that, in the art of giving pleasure to an English audience, both pairs lack rival.

In cricket of the first class, both D. C. S. Compton and W. J. Edrich have, Providence favouring, at least ten years to go of play and struggle and alliance. As a pair they have yet, at the hour of writing, to quell the fiercest Test attack, in the sense that Hobbs and Sutcliffe quelled it; or as Bradman and Ponsford lorded it over English bowlers here in 1934. In summer 1947, they scored between them over 2,000 runs against South Africa. To Tuckett and his fellow-bowlers, Compton and Edrich became the daily task and, maybe, the nightly vision. In the matter of Australia, fulfilment is awaited.

But, in that territory which lies outside the microcosm of numerals, already they are kings; benevolent kings appointed and acclaimed by like-minded subjects; champions in the fight against dullness and the commercial standard. In their cricket, it is what they are that matters far more than what they have done. They stand, in these eyes at least, for something which has no place prepared in the books of score and record. They are the mirror of hope and freedom and gaiety; heroic in the manner of the heroes of school stories; the inspiration, and quarry, of the young because, in a game that threatens to become old in the saddest sense, they do not outgrow the habit, the ideals, the very mistakes of youth. [*R. C. Robertson-Glasgow, 1948*]

Denis Charles Scott Compton, of Middlesex, one of the youngest cricketers ever to play for England against Australia, was born at Hendon on May 23, 1918. His activities in sport date back almost as far as he can remember. His outstanding ability did not long escape recognition. He was selected to play for the London Elementary Schools against Mr C. F. Tufnell's XI at Lord's, and his brilliant batting in scoring 112 so impressed those who saw it, among them Sir Pelham Warner, that Compton was induced to join the Lord's staff as soon as he left school. His achievements were not solely confined to cricket, for in the same year (1932) he joined Arsenal Football Club.

Compton made rapid progress and in 1936 he gained a place in the Middlesex side against Sussex in the Whitsuntide match at Lord's. As No. 11, he went in when Middlesex required 24 runs to secure first-innings lead and held out with G. O. Allen until his side was in front. His display on that occasion earned general admiration, he was immediately given a regular place in the eleven and, promoted in the batting order, Compton amply justified the faith shown in him by completing a thousand runs before the season ended.

An adaptable player with a touch of genius, Compton possesses a sound defence, a wonderful eye and the right stroke for every ball. Among the young batsmen of the day, there is no one better worth watching. He is particularly strong on the leg side and his confidence, coolness and resource are remarkable for so young a player. He has never concentrated upon bowling but he often secures valuable wickets with his slow left-arm deliveries. Leslie Compton, an elder brother of Denis, is also a member of the Lord's staff. [1939]

MIDDLESEX v AUSTRALIANS

• May 28, 30, 31, 1938 •

Drawn. After continuous rain on Saturday and Sunday, the Australians did not show to advantage under strange conditions. Bad light and showers interfered with the cricket on both remaining days, attempts to force the game met with disastrous results, and the Australians were outplayed until a draw became inevitable. Several good catches were made. Compton, running

Those were the days, my friend. "Compo" and Bill Edrich do their party piece, to the amusement of Sir Leonard Hutton and Keith Miller.

from slip to short leg, held a skier from Bradman; Fingleton, wide and deep mid-off, stopped a hard drive from Smith with both hands above his head and secured the dropping ball; best of all, Edrich, at second slip, took a fast-travelling ball close to the ground with his left hand wide, so helping Smith dismiss Fingleton for the second time. After Australian arrears of 56 had been turned into a lead of 58, Bradman declared in order to give Edrich an opportunity to complete 1,000 runs before the end of May.

———

Edrich's 20 not out took his aggregate in May to 1,010 runs, all of which were scored at Lord's.

ENGLAND v WEST INDIES

• June 24, 26, 27, 1939 •

Monday's cricket was memorable for the glorious batting of England's two youngsters, Hutton and Compton, who in a feast of run-making put on 248 for the fourth wicket in two hours twenty minutes. With only a single to his credit Compton offered a hard chance off Martindale to second slip, and from the next ball the Middlesex man gave one on the leg side to the wicket-keeper, who threw himself to the left but could not hold the ball. In the following over from Cameron, Hutton, too, might have been taken at slip but,

like the two chances given by Compton, this catch was very difficult. In this way the initiative passed to England, for Compton, appreciating his luck, immediately proceeded to attack the bowling. He refused to be curbed and delighted everyone with his easy strokeplay. Meanwhile, Hutton completed his first Test century at Lord's and then he followed Compton's example, so that from a sedate pace the score leapt ahead at 100 runs an hour. The new ball soon lost its shine. Compton claimed sixteen fours before a well-judged catch near the boundary brought his spirited innings of 120 to a close; Hutton, his defence absolutely sound, had one five and 21 fours in his 196.

MIDDLESEX v SOMERSET

• May 19, 20, 21, 1948 •

Middlesex won by ten wickets. The match was memorable for a stand of 424 between W. J. Edrich and Denis Compton, which beat all third-wicket records in first-class cricket except the 445 by W. N. Carson and P. E. Whitelaw for Auckland v Otago at Dunedin, New Zealand, in January 1937. They stayed together four hours until Mann declared at 478 for two with 50 minutes of the first day still to be played. In his highest first-class innings to date, 252 not out, Compton hit three sixes and 37 fours; Edrich hit one six and 18 fours in his unbeaten 168.

v Kent

• May 7, 9, 10, 1966 •

KENT WON by 117 runs. In their first encounter with the 65-over limitation, Middlesex displayed little idea of how to build an innings in this type of cricket. They could never shake off the burden of having spent twenty overs over their first 27 runs on the first evening. Wickets had to be sacrificed against accurate bowling on the second day in the vain attempt to match Kent's carefully compiled 170 for five. Middlesex finished 58 behind, and were denied the breakthrough they urgently needed in Kent's second innings when the opening batsmen, Luckhurst and Denness, put on 93.

In an effort to produce more entertaining cricket on the first day and to ensure, weather permitting, that first-day spectators could see both sides bat, the counties in 1966 played twelve matches with each first innings limited to 65 overs. After a season's trial, they voted 10–7 to abandon the experiment.

v Hampshire

• July 1, 2, 3, 1967 •

DRAWN, no decision, an extraordinary result for only twelve minutes were lost during the three days, which began with an exciting innings from Marshall. He hit one six and eighteen fours in his 153 out of 210 in only three hours 23 minutes. On his dismissal Hampshire tossed away a winning position, their laboured batting on a perfect pitch showing a lack of awareness of their mastery, and they toiled into the second day. Facing an imposing total of 421 for seven, Middlesex, too, proved cautious, and when they lost both opening batsmen for only 29 this attitude became deeply rooted. Thus

Comeback kid

MIDDLESEX v NORFOLK
• April 25, 27, 28, 1970 •

Rain prevented play until the third day of this Gillette Cup first-round match. Middlesex, who won by 147 runs, set a typical Cup pace, 190 in the second half of the innings to reach 264 for five in 60 overs. Norfolk never matched the required rate, opener Batteley struggling for 33 overs to score 29. Bill Edrich, returning to Lord's at the age of 54, 33 years after first playing there, ended his hour's batting with a flourish of 21 in six balls – 2,4,5,4,0,6 – before the next ball bowled him.

they failed to provide entertaining batting to mark the first Sunday of county cricket at Lord's and, beginning the last day, still required 148 to save the follow-on. This was achieved shortly before tea, after seven hours ten minutes' struggling. More assertive batting threatened briefly to take them in front, but when the seventh wicket fell Titmus deemed it strategic to deny Hampshire points, though this course also rendered the match fruitless for Middlesex. To the argument that Middlesex could have discarded their last three wickets, their secretary replied: "Having been set to score 272 to avoid a follow-on, or 422 for first-innings lead, and having lost four men for 123, Middlesex were not prepared to throw away wickets for the sake of gaining two points." The match received deserved and universal condemnation.

v Surrey

• August 6, 8, 9, 1977 •

MIDDLESEX WON by nine wickets. There was no play on the first day and only five overs on the second, so the stage was set for a remarkable last day. On a rain-damaged pitch the Surrey batsmen lacked both technique and resolution, and the innings folded for 49 at 12.15. But they were back twenty minutes later, Brearley having declared after one ball. This master-stroke brought Middlesex the chance of twelve extra points – the best they could have realistically hoped for by orthodox means would have been two batting points – but both batsmen and bowlers had to produce supreme efforts to bring in the prize. One advantage of the declaration was that Surrey again batted on a damp pitch, the unfortunate Lynch recording a pair before lunch. Middlesex, wanting 139 in 88 minutes, received a start of 47 in the first seven overs – Arnold was unable to bowl – and the task of 92 in the last twenty overs proved to be easy, victory coming with eleven balls to spare.

v Essex

· May 6, 7, 8, 1981 ·

DRAWN. For the first time in Championship history a full team of Test players took the field; yet all the illustrious names in the Middlesex side could not raise their collective game above the mediocre. Rain cut play to less than two hours on the first day, when Phillip took four Middlesex wickets for 8 runs in 50 deliveries after tea. Thomson, on his county debut, lifted his team with belligerent batting on the second morning and then formed a devastatingly fast new-ball partnership with Daniel. A feature of the last day, as the game moved sedately to a draw, was Edmonds' nightmare spell during which length and line deserted him.

Middlesex Test XI: J. M. Brearley, P. R. Downton, C. T. Radley, M. W. Gatting, R. O. Butcher, G. D. Barlow, J. E. Emburey, P. H. Edmonds, M. W. W. Selvey (*all England*), J. R. Thomson (*Australia*) and W. W. Daniel (*West Indies*).

v Worcestershire

· July 18, 20, 21, 1981 ·

DRAWN. Worcestershire's Alleyne produced the performance of a lifetime before being carried off with a twisted ankle, and Slack achieved a career-best 248 not out, surpassing his unbeaten 181 made on the same ground four days previously against Kent. On a fast pitch, Alleyne (14–1–43–8) was lightning quick and much too hostile and accurate for all but Butcher, who hooked him for one six and several fours. Having dismissed Emburey and Merry with the final two deliveries of the Middlesex first innings, Alleyne flattened Barlow's middle stump first ball of the second to complete a hat-trick; four deliveries later he had Radley lbw and Middlesex looked beaten. But his injury removed the pressure and, after Butcher had scored 50 of his 66 in boundaries, Slack on 110 not

The 1977 Middlesex team that successfully defended the Championship title won in 1976, and also won the Gillette Cup. Back (l-r): Harry Sharp (scorer), M. W. Gatting, N. P. D. Ross, T. M. Lamb, W. W. Daniel, J. E. Emburey, W. N. Slack, I. J. Gould, R. O. Butcher, Don Bennett (coach). Front: G. D. Barlow, A. A. Jones, M. W. W. Selvey, J. M. Brearley, M. J. Smith, C. T. Radley, N. G. Featherstone, P. H. Edmonds.

out saw Middlesex end the second day at 209 for three. He continued to bat forcefully and at the declaration (444 for seven) had hit 32 fours and one five in the highest score at Lord's since Denis Compton's 252 not out against Somerset in 1948.

v Surrey

· August 25, 26, 27, 1982 ·

MIDDLESEX WON by 58 runs. The match began and ended with little dramas involving Titmus. His arrival at Lord's was a chance matter and, as Brearley believed that the pitch would help spin, the 49-year-old player was recalled to action. Brearley's assessment was justified, though not at first. Middlesex intentions of compiling a large score at whatever pace – Slack batted five hours for 79 – were set back when Mackintosh took three wickets in four balls, the intervening delivery being a no-ball. In their second innings they hurried to set a target, which, with tea abandoned, set Surrey a generous 161 in 135 minutes. Now the pitch and circumstances vindicated Brearley, and his final appearance at Lord's was marked by a triumph he did much to engineer. Edmonds took three of the first four wickets, and when he withdrew with an injured back Middlesex had Titmus to step in with three timely wickets. Clarke hit three sixes and one four in scoring all 35 of the runs made while he was there, but Titmus (10–1–43–3) removed him with one of three catches in the deep by Cowans and Middlesex won with 7.3 overs in hand.

LORD'S DAY OBSERVANCES

• July 2, 1972 •

Middlesex lost to Leicestershire by 19 runs. Tolchard ensured Leicestershire's recovery from an early crisis with powerful back-foot play and the county's first hundred in the four years of the John Player League. His rare form of dismissal – obstructing the field – occurred off the last ball of the innings when, with his bat, he prevented a stroke by Haywood from reaching the bowler, Jones, who might have been able to achieve a run-out. In reply, Radley (88) batted magnificently, striking the ball with immense power and running swiftly, before Tolchard again made his presence felt with a stumping that turned the match.

. . .

• May 30, 1976 •

Middlesex beat Nottinghamshire by six wickets. This Sunday League match featured magnificent, hard-hitting batsmanship by three young players, with Randall leading the way. He struck two sixes and fourteen fours in his unbeaten 107, and none of the bowlers could contain his powerful, deftly placed strokes. Middlesex, needing 202, were badly placed at 25 for three, but Gatting and Featherstone settled in sensibly before pacing their assault perfectly in a stand of 173. At 198 Gatting was run out when he walked to the Pavilion believing that he had hit the winning stroke. In fact, the ball had been fielded just inside the boundary by Stead, whose return found the batsmen nowhere near the wickets.

. . .

• August 11, 1991 •

Middlesex beat Derbyshire on faster scoring-rate after rain revised Derbyshire's target from 242 to 211 from 34 overs, and then ended play four overs early. The Middlesex captain, Gatting, had planned to wear a microphone in order to join in television commentary while in the field, but he was forbidden to do so by the TCCB.

v Kent

• May 31, June 1, 3, 1991 •

DRAWN. Marsh dominated the game in a way that would have been a highlight even for his distinguished predecessors as Kent's wicket-keeper, first equalling the world record of eight catches in an innings – jointly held by A. T. W. Grout and D. E. East – and then hitting the fourth century of his career. He took one more catch in Middlesex's second innings before Ellison began hitting the stumps, instead of finding the edge. Marsh took six of his catches on the first day, and after his name had entered the record books he was only one yard away from heading the list. The last catch went to the substitute fielder, M. V. Fleming, at first slip. Kent were poorly placed at 137 for five in their second innings, a lead of 140, but Marsh and Ellison combined to add 145. Marsh batted for five hours and hit thirteen fours in his not out 108 before Kent set an unrealistic target of 343 in 62 overs.

v Warwickshire

• May 26, 27, 28, 30, 1994 •

DRAWN. After a blank first day Gatting put Warwickshire in, to the delight of those hoping to see Lara's sixth successive first-class century. But, when he had 26, Johnson induced an edge and Brown took the catch. Even in his short stay, Lara looked in a different class; his team-mates were less than inspired and gained only a single batting point. Middlesex fared little better and led by just 38. Lara then made amends with a scintillating 140 off 147 balls, his sixth hundred in seven innings and his tenth in 1994. Emburey dismissed him, though not before one ball had been lifted on to the south turret of the Pavilion, to go with his 22 fours.

On the second day a small fire forced the evacuation of the Warner Stand. The previous night MCC members had voted to ban smoking in the Long Room. [*Middlesex v Sussex, May 1997*]

Run-man on a roll. Brian Lara's century against Middlesex in May 1994 was immediately followed by his world-record 501 not out against Durham at Edgbaston.

v Gloucestershire

• May 31, June 1, 2, 3, 2000 •

GLOUCESTERSHIRE WON by 85 runs. Chris Taylor became the first batsman to hit a Championship hundred at Lord's on his first-class debut. The only two debutants who had scored centuries at Lord's previously were both playing for MCC, before the First World War: Cecil Payne against Derbyshire in 1905, and the Hon. Lionel Tennyson against Oxford in 1913. Coming to the wicket in the twelfth over, with Gloucestershire already 29 for four, Taylor demonstrated sound technique and mature temperament in his 184-ball 104, out of 191 runs added. He hit fourteen boundaries, as well as two all-run fours, and in his second innings, when Gloucestershire strengthened their position, he swept Tufnell for six. As for Middlesex, all the old failings returned. Catches were dropped and, when they batted, only Langer reached 40 in either innings, their last six wickets falling for 39 in thirteen overs. Alleyne led his side off the field with his career-best return of six for 49 and Gloucestershire's first Championship win of the season to celebrate.

v Durham

• May 31, June 1, 2, 3, 2002 •

DRAWN. Durham took full advantage of first use of an easy-paced pitch to make their highest-ever total, and the best in a Championship match at Lord's. In the fifth over, Gough ducked into a lifter from Abdul Razzaq and was knocked out, but after that neither the pitch nor the Middlesex attack showed much menace. Love led the way with a career-best 251 – Durham's highest individual score – which came from 335 balls, lasted nearly seven hours and included 39 fours. Muchall

kept pace to hit a maiden first-class hundred, and together they added 251. Strauss and Koenig replied with their fourth century partnership of the season before Shah showed a determination so often lacking, batting six hours for 112. However, Middlesex could not avert the follow-on and were soon in trouble at 29 for three. Shah and Joyce stayed together for 32 overs and Durham had to settle for a draw.

v Surrey

• June 27, 28, 29, 30, 2003 •

DRAWN. Once again Middlesex could thank Strauss and Koenig, who had another big second-innings opening partnership, and the weather, which washed out half the last

Middlesex "would sorely miss him if he were to become an England regular," pronounced *Wisden 2004*. Andrew Strauss soon put that prediction to the test.

day. A first-innings lead of 198 had given Surrey high hopes of a win, and they might have come much closer but for a strange performance by Stewart, who spent nearly four hours making 87 when fast scoring was required. He ran a single off the first ball in eight of the last ten overs. Ramprakash, spurred on by a hostile reception from his old club's supporters, batted determinedly to become the first man to complete centuries against all eighteen counties – but he also took his time: five and a half hours.

v Nottinghamshire

• September 10, 11, 12, 13, 2003 •

DRAWN. With rain culling 101 overs, a positive result always looked elusive, but Nottinghamshire, already relegated, might have made a game of it. They decided against and, with Middlesex not wanting to risk defeat in the quest for survival, the final day's cricket was possibly the most pointless either county has played. A scoreboard operator added a touch of humour. When wicket-keeper Nash became the tenth Middlesex bowler (it would have been eleven, but Bloomfield was injured) his figures were omitted on the board, with a note at the top reading: "Sorry Nashy – no more room." Nottinghamshire started the day 83 ahead, and batted on and on, apparently with two objectives: a second century of the match for Warren, and the season's fastest hundred for Pietersen. Strauss's first-ever wicket stopped Pietersen at 68 in 57 balls, but Warren achieved his target, assisted by some very occasional bowling. The ultimate nonsense came when he scored his last 2 runs off Keegan, a right-arm quickie bowling slow left-arm.

Lord's in Wartime

"Up at Lord's during the war we have been delighted with one-day matches. We have had some wonderful finishes, but you cannot imagine great Surrey, Middlesex and Yorkshire matches without a morrow."

[Wisden 1943]

THROUGH THE LONG and anxious years during the Great War, Lord Hawke was President of MCC. The ground was being used for military purposes, training and recreation. Problems frequently arose, and he was the greatest help in giving wise counsel towards their solution. After the war he followed Lord Harris as Treasurer of MCC and resigned only shortly before his death [in 1938]. Like Lord Harris, he was devoted to the MCC and believed that the well-being of cricket depended on the allegiance given to the club by its members, by the county clubs, and by the judicial and impartial administration of its Committee. [*Sir Francis Lacey, 1939*]

ONLY MILITARY cricket matches were played at Lord's last season. Wounded soldiers were entertained at tea while some of the matches were being played. Facilities for playing and practising cricket will again be offered to soldiers training in or near London.

At the request of the Canadian contingent, a baseball match was played at Lord's, in September,

King George V at Lord's in 1918, accompanied by Lord Hawke (left) and Walter Long, MCC President in 1906 and soon to be First Lord of the Admiralty.

between Canadians and London Americans for the benefit of a fund raised for the widows and orphans of Canadians who fall in battle. HRH Princess Louise

(Duchess of Argyll) graciously gave her patronage to the undertaking and watched the game from the Pavilion. The proceeds exceeded £100. [*1917*]

England Army XI v Australian Army XI

• July 14, 1917 •

IT WAS an excellent idea to arrange two charity matches during the height of the summer, in which well-known players could be seen in the field, and from every point of view the result more than realised expectation. [Navy & Army v Australian & South African Forces was played on August 18.] In the bright July sunshine, Lord's ground looked quite its old self. The public mustered in surprisingly large numbers, the pleasure felt in seeing even a one-day match of some general interest being very keen. So good was the attendance and the sale of tickets beforehand that St Dunstan's Hostel for blinded soldiers and sailors benefited to the extent of about £620. An auction sale during the afternoon of cricket bats, balls and pictures proved disappointing.

Two capital sides were got together, the English team being composed entirely of men who before the war had taken part in first-class cricket. Some good cricket was seen, but the play was too sedate in character to be exciting. The wicket, though in excellent condition, was a trifle slow and the batsmen were perhaps rendered cautious by lack of practice.

England Army won by five wickets and batted on.

Australian Army XI: Lt C. Kelleway, WO C. G. Macartney, Sgt W. J. Munday, Capt. E. P. Barbour, Pte P. W. Docker, St/Sgt W. S. Stirling, Cpl T. J. Matthews, Lt C. T. Docker, Cpl N. G. Dean, Cpl G. B. Inkster and Pte W. McAndrews. *Score*: 130 (Kelleway 53; Lee 5–23).

England Army XI: Cpl H. Makepeace, Pte H. W. Lee, Cpl E. Tyldesley, Capt. P. F. Warner, Lt-Col J. W. H. T. Douglas, Pte E. Hendren, Cpl D. W. Jennings, Lt P. G. H. Fender, Lt N. A. Knox, Sgt C. Blythe and Capt. W. B. Franklin. *Score*: 162 (Tyldesley 38; C. T. Docker 3–16, Macartney 3–33).

England XI v Dominions XI

• July 13, 1918 •

THE SECOND of the charity matches at Lord's was honoured by the presence of The King, but conditions were not so favourable as they had been a fortnight before, rain restricting play to rather less than four hours and a half. No definite result could be arrived at, but with a few more minutes at their disposal the Englishmen would have taken a handsome revenge for their previous defeat, the Dominions at the drawing of stumps being 123 runs behind with only two wickets to fall. Hendren surpassed himself at short leg, and Fender, after bringing off a fine catch in the slips, caught and bowled Moyes in wonderful fashion with the right hand from a very hot return. Seldom has one seen such a brilliant series of catches.

England XI: 157 (L/Cpl G. Gunn 36; Major A. G. Moyes 3–19).

Dominions XI: 34–8 (Moyes 10; Sgt-Instr E. C. Kirk 4–10).

Jany 21

Any further communication on this
subject should be addressed to—

The Secretary,
    War Office,
        London, S.W.,

and the following number quoted.

LONDON.8/792(S.D.3.c.)

War Office,
London, S.W.

January, 1919.

Sir,

    I am commanded by the Army Council to ask you to convey to the Members of your Committee their deep appreciation of the patriotic action of the Marylebone Cricket Club in so promptly placing their ground and premises at Lords at the disposal of the Military Authorities in August 1914.

    The Army Council consider that the use of your historic grounds for training purposes has been invaluable, especially in the case of those candidates for the Kings Commission who have received their training in the very home of the great game which has done so much in producing that spirit of sportsmanship which is a tradition of the British Officer.

    The Army Council also desire to thank you and your Staff for the assistance which has been so readily given on every occasion.

        I am,

           Sir,

             Your obedient Servant,

F.E.Lacey Esq

    Secretary M.C.C.,

        Lords Cricket Ground.

The work done by the staff and others in supplying hay-nets for horses for the Army was discontinued at the request of the War Office. Subsequently this labour was employed in netting bed stretchers. This, however, was of intermittent character owing to a difficulty in obtaining string. [1919]

. . .

The RA Cadet School vacated Lord's Cricket Ground in January. A letter of thanks, now hanging in the Pavilion, has been received from the War Office. [1920]

. . .

I must not forget to mention the dinner given by Messrs Wisden to the Australian Imperial Forces Team. Not since the MCC dinner in 1914, to celebrate the centenary of the present Lord's ground, had so many famous cricketers gathered together under one roof. Lord Harris took the chair and in all the speeches the one note was confidence in the future of cricket. [*Notes by the Editor, 1920*]

THE OUTBREAK of the European War of 1914–18 will always be associated in my mind with Lord's. I was up there watching the Lord's Schools v The Rest match and can remember buying an evening paper on the ground and reading in the stop-press column the opening sentences of the speech which Lord Grey was then making in the Commons, and subsequently travelling down from Waterloo to Esher, where I was staying with the Howell brothers, and seeing in the blood-red sunset over the Thames an omen of the years to come. The younger Howell, whose batting had dominated the match and for whom no honours in the game seemed unobtainable, fell in the Salient less than a year afterwards.

Today the horizon is again dark, and it is idle to try to look far ahead, but I believe there is a general feeling that the game can and should be kept going wherever possible. With the military service act in operation, and the nation mobilised as never before for its war effort, there is no room for the charge of scrimshanking, and where cricket can be played without interfering with the national effort it can only be good for the national morale. Of course anything like county cricket is out of the question, but the MCC have arranged one or two big charity matches at Lord's with a number of minor games, and undertaken a long programme against the schools, with the Lord's Schools and The Rest match to end the season at Lord's. The Club Cricket Conference have decided that, with the obvious reservations, the clubs should keep going as much as possible.

A visit to Lord's on a dark December day was a sobering experience; there were sandbags everywhere, and the Long Room was stripped and bare, with its treasures safely stored beneath ground, but the turf was a wondrous green, old Time on the Grand Stand was gazing serenely at the nearest balloon, and one felt that somehow it would take more than totalitarian war to put an end to cricket. *Merses profundo, pulchrior evenit.* [*Major H. S. Altham, 1940*]

Denis Compton and Middlesex wicket-keeper Fred Price on duty as auxiliary policemen in 1939.

Buccaneers v British Empire XI

• August 31, 1940 •

DRAWN. The "Battle of Britain" interfered with the match, causing late arrivals, which necessitated an altered batting order, and bringing about an early cessation when the Buccaneers seemed within sight of victory. F. R. Brown accepted the unaccustomed honour of opening batsman so successfully that he hit two sixes and eight fours in scoring 77 out of 114 for the Buccaneers in 65 minutes. He drove superbly. Brown then took all the six Empire wickets that fell. Pitching well up, with his customary varied spin, he lured unwary batsmen to attempt big hits that often brought disaster. Mr Stanley Christopherson, MCC President, Sir Stanley Jackson, Lord Lucan and Mr H. D. G. Leveson Gower,

after a night in command of the local Home Guard, were among the company of about 3,000 who supported the Red Cross Fund.

WAR DAMAGE IN 1941

Considerable damage has been done to Lord's by enemy action. Two bombs have fallen in the playing area, luckily off the centre of the ground, and incendiary bombs have hit the top of the Pavilion and the NE corner of the Grand Stand. Thanks to the efforts of MCC's fire-fighter squad, helped by the military and fire services, the fires caused by the incendiaries were quickly got under control. The Secretary's house was also set on fire by incendiaries, and here again the fire squad did fine work. Happily there have been no casualties to any of the staff. [*1942*]

Army v A Lord's XI

• September 6, 1941 •

DRAWN. Over 10,000 people watched a splendid day's cricket and the Army Comforts Fund received the gate money paid by 7,166. Denis Compton provided the chief feature of the cricket when Major G. O. Allen gave the Army first innings, being seen at his best in a stay of two and a half hours. Edrich, just honoured with the DFC, aroused enthusiasm by dismissing the first Army batsman with a smart catch in the slips, and later he was cheered all the way to the wicket when going in to bat. He fell to a brilliant catch in front of the Pavilion, Compton covering a lot of ground before reaching the ball.

Army: 235–9 dec. (Sgt-Instr D. C. S. Compton 114, Sgt M. Leyland 42; Sgt L. J. Todd 4–39).

A Lord's XI: 186–6 (Todd 57, R. E. S. Wyatt 48; Lt T. P. B. Smith 4–40).

August 1940, and life during wartime finds the President's Box accommodating officers of the Scots Guards and 903 Squadron Balloon Barrage. Nine men down, the Guards held on for a draw.

By war's end the "Middlesex twins" were Squadron Leader Edrich DFC and Sergeant-Major Compton.

Surrey Home Guard v Sussex Home Guard

• July 23, 1942 •

ABANDONED. This match was given up in tragic circumstances after Andrew Ducat, the Surrey and England cricketer and international footballer, collapsed and died at the wicket. Ducat had begun his innings before lunch and was 17 at the interval. On resuming he scored steadily, carrying his score to 29. Then he hit a ball from Eaton to mid-on. The ball was returned to the bowler, who was about to send down the next delivery when Ducat fell forward and apparently died immediately, though he was moved to the Pavilion and quickly taken by ambulance to a nearby hospital.

England v Australia

• May 29, 1944 •

ENGLAND WON by six wickets. Captained by G. O. Allen, the side composed of Test players, except Evans, the young Kent wicket-keeper, Trevor Bailey and Mallett, the two old Dulwich College boys, won even more decisively than the score suggests, for, whereas Australia occupied 235 minutes in getting 243 runs, victory was gained in 146 minutes in a race against the clock with fourteen minutes to spare. The admirable performance deserves this exact statement as to the time occupied by each team at the wicket. England proved their superiority to a degree expected when reading the names of the players. Australia to some extent made up for the difference in reputations by being in better match practice in Australian Air Force engagements; while their determination in facing adversity, keenness and safety in the field helped to put them more on equality with opponents mostly of recent familiarity in meeting a fast-moving ball – a noteworthy condition in the Whitsuntide cricket at Lord's.

Australia: Flt/Sgt J. Workman, Flt/Sgt W. A. Roach, Flt/Lt S. G. Sismey, F/O D. K. Carmody, Flt/Sgt K. R. Miller, Sgt C. P. Calvert, F/O R. Stanford, P/O R. Cristofani, F/O A. D. McDonald, P/O R. E. Ellis and Flt/Lt A. W. Roper. *Score*: 243 (Calvert 62, Stanford 51; Wright 4–61).

England: Flt/Lt C. J. Barnett, L. Hutton, Sqdn/Ldr W. J. Edrich, Flt/Lt W. R. Hammond, Sqdn/Ldr L. E. G. Ames, Sqdn/Ldr R. W. V. Robins, Lt-Col G. O. Allen, Lt T. E. Bailey, 2nd Lt A. W. H. Mallett, Sgt T. G. Evans and Lt D. V. P. Wright. *Score*: 244–4 (Hutton 84, Ames 60 not out).

West of England v Lord's XI

• July 8, 1944 •

LORD'S XI WON by five wickets. For their first appearance at Lord's, West of England were originally matched against AA Command, but, owing to the gunners being engaged with the flying bombs, the opposition was changed to a Lord's XI. The brothers Lyon were the rival captains.

HAMMOND THE SPORTSMAN

Lord's continued to stage the best cricket and some of the closest struggles in 1944. As a tense finish, nothing could have excelled the victory at Whitsuntide of Australia over The Rest by one wicket a few seconds before seven o'clock off the fourth ball of the last over – begun when 5 runs were wanted. W. R. Hammond captained The Rest, and I must mention here his decision to decline a tea interval for which the umpires were preparing. This sporting action, after his declaration with eight wickets down, increased the likelihood of a definite result and made the day memorable for a crowd of 28,000.

[*Notes by the Editor, 1945*]

A Lord's XI v Canada

• July 20, 1944 •

A LORD'S XI won by 213 runs. Americans were to have appeared at Lord's on this date, but their team, chosen entirely from bomber crews, were too busily engaged in the initial stages of the liberation of Europe campaign. Consequently Canada found themselves against stronger opposition.

"Flying bomb stops play," ran *Wisden 1945*. **On the deck are the Army's Captain Jack Robertson, RAF keeper Pilot Officer Andy Wilson, Squadron Leader Edrich (slip) and Flight Lieutenant Austin Matthews. Robertson celebrated this near miss in July 1944 by hitting a six.**

Lord's XI v Public Schools

• August 11, 12, 1944 •

LORD'S XI WON by 72 runs. Although his opponents lacked experience of first-class cricket, Robins accomplished a remarkable feat in scoring 170 runs and taking seventeen wickets for just under 8 runs apiece. His quick-footed moves when going out to drive gave an object lesson in playing spin bowling, but few of the boys when batting were capable of timing his varied deliveries which often broke the width of the wicket. White of Eton, who proved an exception, played a splendid innings. His century was full of sound strokes made without hurry; during a stay of two hours he showed equal dexterity in scoring to the off or to leg, and his 102 included fifteen fours. During the first innings a flying bomb exploded less than 200 yards from Lord's. Pieces of soil fell on the pitch, but the players, particularly the boys, most of whom had never experienced such an attack, stopped only while the bomb was seen hurtling down. The break in the game lasted little more than half a minute, and the spectators, some of whom had thrown themselves flat under seats for protection, showed their appreciation of the boys' pluck with hearty hand-claps.

England v Dominions

• August 25, 27, 28, 1945 •

DOMINIONS WON by 45 runs with eight minutes to spare. One of the finest games ever seen produced 1,241 runs, including sixteen sixes, a century in each England innings by Hammond, and grand hundreds for the Dominions by Donnelly, the New Zealand left-hander, and Miller, of Australia. In addition, the result was a triumph for Constantine, who was chosen captain by the Dominions players just before the match began.

Big-hitting Australians Cec Pepper (left) and Keith Miller
"emulated the giants of the past in the carry
of their long drives".

individual record. After he left there followed some daring batting by Davies and Griffith, but England for victory needed to get 74 in three-quarters of an hour when Phillipson joined Davies. Brilliant fielding by Constantine ran out Phillipson, and next Pepper bowled Davies. Only fifteen minutes remained when the last man, Hollies, joined Wright. In tense excitement Ellis and Pepper each delivered a maiden with the fielders round the batsmen. Constantine then brought back Cristofani, who bowled Wright, and the Dominions gained a grand victory.

Dominions: 307 (H. S. Craig 56, M. P. Donnelly 133, C. G. Pepper 51; D. V. P. Wright 5–90) and 336 (K. R. Miller 185, L. N. Constantine 40; Wright 5–105, E. Hollies 3–115).

England: 287 (W. R. Hammond 121, W. J. Edrich 78; Pepper 4–57, D. R. Cristofani 3–82) and 311 (Hammond 102, J. G. W. Davies 56; Pepper 3–67).

MCC President Stanley Christopherson with Field-Marshal Lord Alanbrooke (left), Chief of the Imperial General Staff, and General Sir Miles Dempsey at Lord's in August 1945.

The final stage will be remembered chiefly for the glorious driving of Miller. He outshone everyone by his dazzling hitting. In 90 minutes he raised his overnight 61 to 185, and in three-quarters of an hour of superb cricket he and Constantine put on 117. Though travelling at such a pace, Miller played faultlessly. One of his seven sixes set the whole crowd talking. It was a terrific on-drive off Hollies, and the ball lodged in the small roof of the broadcasting box above the England players' dressing-room. Besides his sixes, Miller hit thirteen fours, his 185 taking him only two and three-quarter hours. This was a wonderful finish to his season at Lord's, where in four first-class matches he scored 568 runs in eight innings, twice not out, with three centuries and an average of 94.68.

England wanted 357 in four and a half hours and, thanks to Hammond, they made a worthy challenge. Always seeking runs, the England captain was twice missed in the deep before completing 50, but, though tiring, he carried on freely, getting 102 out of 152 in two hours. By hitting two separate hundreds in a match for the seventh time, Hammond set up an

Fay Speed

Favell May (Fay) Ashmore worked for MCC for 40 years up to 1986, first as personal assistant to the Secretary, Colonel R. S. Rait Kerr, then in the museum. Her late husband, Bill, played twice for Middlesex. As Corporal Fay Speed, she is believed to have been the first woman to act as scorer at Lord's, in 1944. [1998]

MR STANLEY CHRISTOPHERSON, President of MCC from 1939 throughout the war years, surpassed the record established by Lord Hawke during the 1914–18 war. Kindly answering an enquiry from me, he wrote that he was the only survivor of the ten sons who, captained by their father, played as an eleven for several seasons from 1877 on Blackheath. The youngest brother, the Rev. Derman Christopherson, received his colours at Rugby from Sir Pelham Warner.

When finishing these notes during the marvellous spell of summer weather that marked the start of spring, a visit to Lord's revealed everything in preparation for a resumption of first-class cricket under the best possible conditions. The turf looked superb – a real green carpet without a blemish, in as good order as ever could be wished – encircled by the stands receiving a new coat of white paint, with "Old Father Time" in position once more – a resplendent golden figure looking down with benign expectancy. [Notes by the Editor, 1946]

ALL-INDIA CRICKET TEAM, 1932

Top row left to right—Lall Singh, P. E. Palia, Jahangir Khan, Mahomed Nisar, Amar Singh, B. E. Kapadia, S. R. Godambe, Ghulam Mahomed, J. G. Navle
Centre—Syed Wazir Ali, Capt. C. K. Nayudu, H.H. Maharaja Porbandar (*Capt.*), K. S. C. Limdi (*Vice-Capt.*), Syed Nazir Ali, Capt. Joginder Singh
Bottom—Naoomal Jeoomal, S. H. M. Colah, N. D. Marshall

On the 1932 team's showing at Lord's in India's first official Test, *Wisden* noted that "It can be said at once that
the Indian cricketers, and especially Amar Singh and Nissar, bowled splendidly, while from start to finish their fielding reached a very high level indeed.
The team did not enjoy the best of luck, for Nayudu, who in the absence of the Maharaja of Porbandar and Ganshyamsinhji captained the eleven with no little skill,
damaged his hand so badly when trying to catch Ames in the gully that he batted under a severe handicap in each innings, while Nazir Ali, on the first day, and Palia,
later on, each strained a leg muscle when fielding and had their value as bowlers completely ruined and their usefulness as batsmen very considerably diminished."
The Maharaja, having begun with scores of 0, 2, 0, 2, 2, did not play on tour after that. According to Mihir Bose's *History of Indian Cricket*,
"He was said to be the only first-class cricketer in England to have more Rolls-Royces than runs."

Kiwis, Calypsos and Subcontinentals

"Pakistan achieved a feat without parallel in winning a Test in England during their first tour.
West Indies took part in their first Test in England in 1928, but success did not attend their efforts until 1950.
New Zealand, 1931, and India, 1932, still seek a first victory in the home of cricket."

[Wisden 1955]

New Zealanders at Lord's

v MCC

• May 16, 18, 19, 1931 •

BEATING AN MCC eleven which, although including only one professional, was undoubtedly a powerful combination, by an innings and 122 runs, the New Zealanders accomplished nearly their best performance of the tour. Rain prevented any cricket after lunch on the first day, and at the end of Monday's play the New Zealanders had made 302 for the loss of nine men. Lowry, on a slow pitch and with the outfield very dead, completed a splendid hundred; he batted two hours and a half but hit only five fours. All the excitement came on the last day when, after Lowry had declared, Cromb, Merritt and Blunt bowled so effectively that the MCC were twice dismissed. Cromb, making the ball swerve and occasionally straighten itself, took five of the first six wickets for 15 runs, and in the second innings Merritt and Blunt bowled leg-breaks with an occasional googly so extraordinarily well that scarcely a bad ball was sent down by either man. In both innings the fielding – especially Page's slip catching – was magnificent. Only Jardine faced the bowling with any success, and after the MCC followed on he alone reached double figures.

New Zealanders: 302–9 dec. (R. O. Talbot 66, T. C. Lowry 101 not out; Mr V. W. C. Jupp 3–106, Mr J. C. White 3–66).

MCC: 132 (Mr D. R. Jardine 62 not out; I. B. Cromb 6–46) and 48 (Jardine 19; W. E. Merritt 7–28, R. C. Blunt 3–13).

Leg-spinner Bill Merritt had just left school and had played only twice for Canterbury when chosen for New Zealand's first tour of England, in 1927.

v MCC

• May 12, 13, 14, 1937 •

DRAWN. The first appearance of the touring team at Lord's was ruined by the weather. The start, intended for half-past two in order that the New Zealanders could see the Coronation, was delayed owing to the soft state of the wicket, and play in the whole match was limited to 75 minutes during the first afternoon.

v England

• June 25, 27, 28, 1949 •

DRAWN. On a pitch which seemed to improve the longer the match progressed, there appeared little hope of a definite result, but the game was made memorable by an incorrect declaration on the part of F. G. Mann, the England captain, and a brilliant innings of 206 by M. P. Donnelly, the New Zealand left-hander. Shortly after six o'clock on Saturday, with England's total 313 for nine wickets, Mann closed the innings and New Zealand in fifteen minutes scored 20 without loss. At the time he did not realise his mistake, but on Sunday he issued the following statement:

"When I declared the England innings closed on Saturday evening I thought that the experimental rule which allows a declaration to be made on the first day of a three-day match applied to the present series of Test matches. I regret very much that I was wrong in this respect, but I am very glad indeed that we did not in fact gain any advantage from the declaration." An official announcement from Lord's stated that as no protest was made at the time, the match would carry on as if no breach of regulations occurred.

So lively was the pitch for the first three hours that it began to look as if Mann was not so fortunate in winning the toss as was at first considered. England lost their first five wickets for 112 runs, but a change in fortune came when Bailey joined Compton. Fortunate to receive two loose balls down the leg side which he turned for four apiece immediately he went in, Bailey showed complete confidence and for a long time he overshadowed Compton. He continued to punish anything loose, mainly by going down on one knee and sweeping the ball hard to the square-leg boundary. Ten fours came in his first fifty, made in 67 minutes. Bailey was unlucky to miss his first Test hundred, for with only 7 wanted he cut a ball on to wicket-keeper Mooney's foot, whence it rebounded into the hands of Sutcliffe at second slip.

Far left: Trevor Bailey in full flow.

Left: England captain Douglas Jardine.

England. The Surrey spinners, Lock, nine wickets for 29, and Laker, five for 37, proved almost unplayable. It was Lock's first Test at Lord's.

The match began in sad circumstances with the announcement that news had just been received of the death of Douglas Jardine in a Swiss nursing home. Jardine had captained England at Lord's in 1931 when New Zealand played their first Test match. The MCC and New Zealand flags were lowered to half-mast.

grimly in the gloom, England were relieved to escape with a draw.

The Test was a fascinating contest and, for the unfancied tourists, an enormously encouraging match. Just as England had dominated at Trent Bridge, so New Zealand were always in command here, but without quite getting the reward they deserved – their first ever Lord's Test victory. Their young and talented team came of age and suggested the future of New Zealand cricket was not in such bad hands after all. None of the bright lights shone more brilliantly than Dion Nash, a boyish, enthusiastic pace bowler who was overcome with emotion by the ovation he received from the Lord's crowd. Bowling at a vigorous fast-medium from the Pavilion end, he got extra bounce from a slow wicket; he disconcerted even the best England batsmen and made the ball move sharply, especially away from the bat. In only his fifth Test, Nash finished with figures of eleven for 169, the best bowling return by a New Zealander against England; and with a half-century too – a double no player had achieved in a Lord's Test before – he was named Man of the Match.

v England

• June 19, 20, 21, 1958 •

ENGLAND WON by an innings and 148 runs with more than two days to spare, the match being completed by half-past three on Saturday. New Zealand had the ill luck to be trapped twice on a wet pitch after England, with May winning the toss, had batted on a true surface, and they were dismissed for 47, the lowest total in the long history of Tests at Lord's and the fourth-lowest in

v England

• June 16, 17, 18, 19, 20, 1994 •

DRAWN. Their innings victory at Trent Bridge brought a bullish response from the England camp when they turned up in London for the Second Test, with Atherton talking about his team "developing a ruthless streak, kicking opponents while they are down and wrapping up the series". By Monday evening, with their tailenders hanging on

v England

• July 22, 23, 24, 25, 1999 •

NEW ZEALAND WON by nine wickets. England arrived at Lord's promising to debunk the theory that they are never more vulnerable than at the home of cricket. They departed in something approaching disarray, having

Above: Dion Nash in a bubbly mood after his first Test at Lord's. Sadly, injuries would stymie *Wisden's* forecast that in Nash "New Zealand discovered a champion for the future".
Right: Nasser Hussain has one of those digital days.

BACK ON BOARD
On the second day of the 1986 New Zealand Test, former England wicket-keeper Bob Taylor was called away from his duties as host for the match sponsor, Cornhill, to deputise for the injured Bruce French. Despite having retired from first-class cricket two years earlier, Taylor, at the age of 45, kept almost without blemish. His stint lasted until just before lunch next day.

done nothing but support the legend that had built up around their performances at Lord's during the 1990s. In just under four days, New Zealand had levelled the series, wiped out the psychological edge England had gained from the First Test and abruptly brought to an end the honeymoon that Hussain had enjoyed since succeeding Stewart.

To make matters worse, Hussain had to spend most of the second part of the match watching from the balcony, after breaking a finger while trying to stop a ball at gully early on Saturday. His humour could not have been helped by the knowledge that his decision to bat first had contributed to the team's downfall, handing his batsmen the worst of the conditions. He himself had battled through for 61 and got a close-up view of an all-too-familiar lack of application from his team-mates. For most of the first afternoon, at least three scoreboard lights were showing in murk that a few years earlier would have seen a suspension long before it came – shortly after the tea interval. The ball moved considerably and, with some moisture in the pitch, did more off the seam than expected, but there was still huge disappointment among the full house, which saw 102 for two eventually translate itself to 186 all out.

England's second innings was very much the same as the first, and this time they could not blame the conditions. Butcher, Stewart and Ramprakash were all guilty, for the second time running, of playing one-day shots in a five-day game. New Zealand needed just 58, and shortly after 5 p.m. on the fourth day they were celebrating their first-ever victory at Lord's, having struck lucky at their thirteenth attempt. It took England's record there since 1992 to six defeats, three draws and just one win: against West Indies in 1995.

WEST INDIES CRICKET TEAM, ENGLAND, 1939

Standing :- W. Ferguson, G. Gomez, J. B. Stollmeyer, L. G. Hylton, T. Johnson, C. B. Clarke, H. P. Bayley, E. A. V. Williams

Sitting :- G. Headley, I. Barrow, R. S. Grant, J. M. Kidney, J. H. Cameron, L. N. Constantine, E. A. Martindale

Front :- K. H. Weekes, J. E. D. Sealey, V. H. Stollmeyer

West Indians at Lord's

v Middlesex

• June 9, 11, 12, 1928 •

A SPLENDID all-round performance on the part of Constantine enabled West Indies to gain a memorable victory by three wickets. When that player went in on Monday, the tourists, as the result of more than two hours' laborious batting, had lost half their wickets for 79 and stood in no small danger of having to follow on. In

such a brilliant manner did he deal with the situation that, driving with great power and pulling in daring fashion, he made 86 out of 107 in less than an hour. Despite this fine effort, the visitors fell 122 short of the total at which Middlesex had declared, but in the county's second innings Constantine, hitting the stumps five times, proceeded to take seven wickets for little more than 8 runs apiece. On going on to bowl for the second time, he sent down six overs and three balls for 11 runs and six wickets. Even after this deadly piece of bowling, West Indies – set 259 to win and losing five batsmen for 121 – looked sure to be beaten.

Coming once again to the rescue of his side, however, Constantine crowned a wonderful display by hitting up 103 out of 133 in an hour, with two sixes and twelve fours as his chief strokes. In stopping a drive from Constantine, Hearne had a finger so badly damaged that he could play no more cricket last season.

Middlesex: 352–6 dec. (Mr N. E. Haig 119, J. W. Hearne 75, E. Hendren 100 not out) and 136 (Hendren 52; L. N. Constantine 7–57).

West Indies: 230 (Constantine 86; T. J. Durston 4–16) and 259–7 (M. P. Fernandes 54, Constantine 103).

v MCC

• May 20, 22, 23, 1933 •

WEST INDIES BEAT a fairly strong MCC side by 152 runs. The match brought distinction to Headley, who hit up 129 in his first innings at Lord's. He showed delightful footwork, ability to cut crisply with power, and he drove splendidly. Inniss helped in a third partnership of 149, but when Headley left, the batting broke down. Leading by 63, West Indies batted consistently in their second innings and Constantine, in 27 minutes, scored 51 out of 66. MCC broke down badly after tea on Tuesday when, against Achong and Da Costa, their last seven wickets fell for 37. Hit on the chest by a ball from Bowes, Headley was kept out of the next three matches.

v Middlesex

• June 3, 5, 6, 1939 •

WEST INDIES WON by an innings and 228 runs. Below full strength, Middlesex were outplayed. J. Stollmeyer distinguished himself by scoring a century when first batting at Lord's, and Sealy gave a good display of sound hitting that lasted three hours and a half. Both these batsmen helped Headley in splendid stands in his progress to 227: the second wicket put on 216, and the third 218. Headley batted five hours ten minutes with easy freedom and, like his partners, did not give a chance. On Saturday 491 runs were scored for three wickets and the total was raised to 665, the second-best ever hit at Lord's.

v England

• June 24, 26, 27, 1939 •

ENGLAND WON by eight wickets. While England were unquestionably the better side, the match provided a personal triumph for Headley, who had the distinction of being the first cricketer to make two separate hundreds in a Test at headquarters. Moreover he became the first player to hit two hundreds against England twice, for besides his 106 and 107 at Lord's in 1939 he made 114 and 112 at Georgetown in 1930. The West Indies bowled and fielded keenly, but in batting, too much responsibility devolved upon Headley. While he stayed the resistance was stubborn, but the side collapsed twice. In the first innings the last five wickets fell for 32 runs, and when the side batted again the last five fell for 35.

"George Headley's scoring feats led to his being dubbed 'the black Bradman'. His devoted admirers responded by calling Bradman 'the white Headley' – a pardonable exaggeration."

v England

• June 24, 26, 27, 28, 29, 1950 •

WEST INDIES WON by 326 runs. They fully merited their first Test victory in England, which, to their undisguised delight, was gained at the headquarters of cricket. In batting, bowling and fielding they were clearly the superior side, with Ramadhin this time the more successful of the two twenty-year-old spin bowlers who during the 1950 summer wrought such destruction among English batsmen. In the match Ramadhin took eleven and Valentine seven wickets. No blame could be attached to the pitch. It gave slow bowlers a little help, but only to those who used real finger-spin as did Ramadhin and Valentine.

Ramadhin bowled with the guile of a veteran. He pitched a tantalising length, bowled straight at the wicket and spun enough to beat the bat. No English batsman showed evidence of having mastered the problems of deciding which way Ramadhin would spin, and he was too quick through the air for any but the most nimble-footed to go down to meet him on the half-volley with any consistency. Valentine lent able support, but the English batsmen might, with profit, have tackled him more boldly. England's 151 in the first innings was their lowest for a completed innings in a home Test against West Indies.

v England

• June 20, 21, 22, 1957 •

ENGLAND WON by an innings and 36 runs with over two days to spare. They were vastly superior in the field and possessed a much better-balanced side for the occasion. The Lord's pitches throughout the season had shown themselves to be eminently suited to fast and fast-medium bowling, but whereas the England selectors

West Indies' supporters make a song and dance out of
"Those little pals of mine, Ramadhin and Valentine"
having spun their team to a historic victory in 1950.

hours and a quarter, but after tea eight wickets fell for
53, no attempt being made to save the game.
Substitutes were required for Worrell, Allan and
Gibbs. Gibbs was prevented from bowling for a time
when he returned to the field and Hunte wanted to
put him on immediately. The umpires considered this
came under "fair and unfair play", as he came "warm"
from the Pavilion and all the other players were "cold".
When he bowled half an hour later he soon finished
the innings.

v England

• June 20, 21, 22, 24, 25, 1963 •

DRAWN. One of the most dramatic Test
matches ever to be played in England
attracted large crowds and aroused
tremendous interest throughout the country.
All through, the cricket had been keen and thrilling,
but the climax was remarkable, Cowdrey having to go
in with a broken bone in his arm after being hit above
the left wrist by Hall earlier in the innings. About 300
people rushed the ground at the end of the match
seeking souvenirs and patting the players on the back.
The West Indies supporters called for Worrell and
Hall, who appeared on the balcony, sending them
home happy.

When the final over arrived, any one of four
results could have occurred – a win for England,
victory for West Indies, a tie or a draw. The match was
drawn with England 6 runs short of success and West
Indies needing one more wicket. Most people felt
happy about the result, for it would have been a pity if
either side had lost after playing so well.

West Indies: 301 (R. B. Kanhai 73, J. S. Solomon 56;
F. S. Trueman 6–100, D. Shackleton 3–93) and 229
(B. F. Butcher 133; Trueman 5–52, Shackleton 4–72).

England: 297 (E. R. Dexter 70, K. F. Barrington 80,
F. J. Titmus 52 not out; C. C. Griffith 5–91) and 228–9
(Barrington 60, D. B. Close 70; W. W. Hall 4–93,
Griffith 3–59).

realised this, West Indies' did not, or at least chose to
ignore the facts. They went into the match with only
one bowler of real pace and preferred to recall
Valentine, who was given only three overs in
England's total of 424.

West Indies won the toss, but broke down so badly
on a lively pitch that all the advantage they gained
from batting first was lost. Trueman struck an early
blow, but the real trouble for West Indies began when
Bailey appeared. In his 50th Test match, Bailey had
rarely bowled better. Moving the ball either way off the
seam and making an occasional ball lift, he completely
demoralised the batsmen and West Indies were
dismissed in under four hours. Bailey's seven for 44
was the best performance by any bowler against West

Indies in a Test in England. In the match, he took
eleven wickets, equalling C. S. Marriott and W. Voce
for the highest number of wickets obtained in any Test
against West Indies.

v MCC

• May 18, 20, 21, 1963 •

WEST INDIES WON by 93 runs with half
an hour to spare after a contrived finish
on the last day. A crowd of 20,000 saw
West Indies bat brightly on the Saturday,
but the last seven wickets fell for 97. On the second
day, when the weather was dull and cold, two hours
were lost. MCC batted cautiously and slowly, reaching
120 for five. On the last morning Cowdrey declared
first thing and Hunte, acting-captain because of injury
to Worrell, did not enforce the follow-on although 186
ahead. When he declared, MCC needed 266 in four

England expects – or "a man got to do what he got to do". As it happened Colin Cowdrey, going in at the fall of the ninth wicket with two balls of the 1963 Test remaining, didn't have to face either of them.

Wisden at Lord's

Ken Medlock, chairman of John Wisden & Co Ltd, presents the Wisden Trophy to MCC President Lord Nugent "to be competed for between England and West Indies... to commemorate the publication in 1963 of the 100th edition of *Wisden Cricketers' Almanack*." *Wisden* editor Norman Preston stands alongside his chairman.

For victorious captain Garry Sobers, the 1966 Tests "were one triumph after another with bat and ball, as well as in the field as a master tactician and fantastic catcher close to the bat".

v England

• J U N E 16, 17, 18, 20, 21, 1966 •

DRAWN. Despite losing the toss again, England, who had a different captain in Cowdrey, gave a much better account of themselves than in the First Test. Again Sobers was a key figure for West Indies, and he thwarted England on the fourth day when victory seemed just round the corner for the old country. Having gained a lead of 86, England took the first five

West Indies second-innings wickets for 95 and looked to be romping home. Then Sobers was joined by his young cousin, Holford, and they remained together for five hours and twenty minutes until Sobers declared at ten minutes to one on Tuesday, leaving England to get 284 to win in four hours. This unbroken stand of 274 was a record for the fifth wicket for West Indies against England. Sobers, who batted ten minutes longer, hit thirteen fours in his excellent 163 and Holford showed six boundaries in his 105. He gained the distinction of hitting his maiden Test century on only his second Test

appearance. Later in the day Milburn, three sixes and seventeen fours, wound up this grand struggle by emulating Holford's feat and taking out his bat for 126, made in three hours.

The return of Graveney to Test cricket after an interval of three years, during which England played 38 Tests, proved a wise move by the selectors. In the first innings he batted almost without blemish for four hours and twenty minutes as Sobers attacked persistently and Hall and Griffith kept more in line with the stumps. He wanted only 4 for his hundred when he cut at a rising ball from Hall and was taken

Far left: David Holford is the man in 1966.
Left: Roy Fredericks and Charlie Davis look on as Prince Charles is introduced to Vanburn Holder in 1969. Davis's maiden hundred in West Indies' first innings was trumped by John Hampshire's 107 on debut (below).

by wicket-keeper Allan. It had not been intended that he should bat in the second innings, owing to a badly bruised right thumb, but he came to the rescue, averted a hat-trick after Hall had removed Cowdrey and Parks, and stayed with Milburn for the last hour and 50 minutes while they added 130 in England's highest fifth-wicket stand against West Indies. Graveney batted almost one-handed, continually drawing away the other, and while he defended Milburn followed up his 94 at Manchester with another amazing display of powerful hitting. This was a much better effort. He hoisted Holford, Gibbs and Hall in turn for six and made very few false strokes.

England, who did not claim the extra half-hour, fell 87 short of their target. The receipts of £58,000 were a record for a cricket match in any part of the world. The full attendance was estimated to be 125,000, of whom 104,000 paid the six shillings outer gate admission fee.

v England

• June 26, 27, 28, 30, July 1, 1969 •

DRAWN. This Test took two days to get properly moving, but the cricket was always keen and the last three days found the teams locked in a tremendous struggle for supremacy. The sun shone gloriously all the time, and

altogether 100,500 people attended. On Saturday, the gates were closed with 27,000 spectators inside the ground. On Monday, when 19,000 were present, The Queen, accompanied by Prince Philip and Prince Charles, met the officials and players of both teams, who were presented to her in front of the Pavilion.

Batsmen generally held sway, except when England broke down at the beginning of their first innings. The match brought distinction to John Hampshire, who became the first Englishman to hit a century on his Test debut at Lord's. Back in 1893, H. Graham did likewise for Australia. It seemed strange that until that day Hampshire, in eight years of first-class cricket, had hit only ten hundreds. He had shown no decent form even this season and only got his place in the absence of Cowdrey, Barrington, Milburn, Graveney and Dexter – all of whom played against Australia the previous year. Now he produced the courage and ability to match the occasion which most Yorkshiremen knew that he possessed. For once his concentration did not falter; he excelled in forcing the ball off his legs and driving straight and to the off side off his back foot. As Illingworth and Boycott also reached three figures, we had three Yorkshiremen making centuries in the same Test.

v MCC

• May 22, 24, 25, 1976 •

WEST INDIES WON by 219 runs, and gave notice of the strength of their fast bowling. Roberts, Holding and Holder took nineteen of the twenty wickets and ran through MCC in 35 overs when dismissing them for 83 runs on the last day. Honours were even in the first innings. West Indies were restricted to 251 for nine before they declared, and some stout batting by Brearley, in two and three-quarter hours for 36, and the captain, Gilliat (66), enabled MCC to approach within 54 of that total. The main incident to this point was perhaps an injury to Amiss five minutes from the close on Saturday. He ducked without keeping his eye on the ball and was struck on the back of the head by a delivery from Holding, short but by no means a bouncer. Amiss batted again on the Monday, his wound containing four stitches and his suitability for a return to Test cricket once more in doubt. The match swung quickly in West Indies' way once they batted a second time. Richards (113) took the lead with his eighth century since the turn of the year, and Gomes (101 not out) gave him excellent support with his first hundred in England. Then it was the turn of the three pace bowlers to wreak havoc and produce a feeling of contentment in the minds of their colleagues for the Test series.

v Middlesex

• July 31, August 2, 3, 1976 •

MIDDLESEX WON by four wickets, inflicting on West Indies the first defeat of their tour. The badly under-strength Middlesex team performed wonders to hustle West Indies out cheaply for 222. Middlesex were 160 for three at the close of the first day, Edmonds hit powerfully on the second morning, and Clark, making his first appearance for the county since 1968, provided a glimpse of past glories. The West Indies batsmen again surged away with fierce,

There was drama on the Saturday afternoon [of the 1973 Test] when 28,000 people were ordered to leave the ground following a telephone warning that a bomb had been planted. The call proved to be a hoax, but no chances could be taken because an IRA bomb campaign was in full swing at the time.

reckless strokeplay, 146 coming in the opening 25 overs, but eventually Middlesex wanted 274 and had almost all the last day to make them. Smith and Brearley recorded their third century partnership in the last four innings and they were halfway there before a wicket fell. Butcher followed the openers' methodical example, but Smith's departure at 240 introduced an abrupt collapse as Middlesex stuttered at the gates of victory. When it came, it was their first over a touring team since the 1936 Indians. A strange feature of the match was that five wicket-keepers were used, Brearley and then Butcher replacing the injured Kinkead-Weekes, and Findlay relieving Murray.

West Indies: 222 (C. G. Greenidge 123; M. W. W. Selvey 4–58, F. J. Titmus 5–41) and 308 (Greenidge 67, I. V. A. Richards 53, A. M. E. Roberts 56 not out; N. G. Featherstone 4–50).

Middlesex: 257 (M. J. Smith 95, P. H. Edmonds 53; A. L. Padmore 6–69) and 275–6 (Smith 108, J. M. Brearley 62; Padmore 4–78).

v England

• June 28, 29, 30, July 2, 3, 1984 •

WEST INDIES WON by nine wickets. England were either level or on top until the last four hours of the match. West Indies then strolled nonchalantly to victory, making the fifth-highest score to win a Test. Only Bradman and Hammond have made higher scores in a Lord's Test than Greenidge's 214 in West Indies' second innings. Yet despite their overwhelming defeat, England managed several skilful and brave performances. Gower, however, might not have relished the occasion. It was his second defeat as captain at headquarters and he became the first England captain since Yardley in 1948 to declare in the second innings and lose.

Fowler (106) mustered all his technical ability and much fortitude in an admirable hundred, but Gower, on the first evening, and Lamb and Gatting on the second morning became the first three of a record twelve lbw victims in the match, equalling the number in Dunedin in 1979-80 (New Zealand v West Indies). Miller was run out in spectacular fashion when Baptiste uprooted the middle stump at the Nursery end with an 80-yard throw from the long-leg boundary in front of the Warner Stand.

Botham bowled very well to unseat the first three West Indies batsmen. He was equally bouncy and effective on the third morning, a real reminder of his old self as he bowled unchanged and productively to take eight for 103 and gain England a 41-run lead. It was generally expected that Richards would crown a sunny Saturday with a century; but, after a fascinating duel, he was lbw to a ball from Botham that did a lot. Umpire Meyer later stated that he "may have made a mistake" and that he had considered recalling

Richards. The consensus was that such post-mortems should not involve directly the players and umpires. Donald Topley, a groundstaff boy, came within inches of cricketing immortality during the afternoon when, fielding as substitute, he caught Marshall brilliantly on the deep square-leg boundary, one-handed but with one foot over the rope.

When West Indies set out to chase 342 to win in five and a half hours, the swing and movement that had been there all match seemed to have vanished. England's change bowlers looked second-rate and nobody but Willis bowled the right line or set the right field to the powerful and phlegmatic Greenidge, whose ruthless batting probably made the bowling look worse than it was. Although England finally blocked his square cut, the mid-wicket and long-on boundaries saw plenty of Greenidge's 29 fours. He was dropped by an inattentive Botham, the sole slip, off Willis when he was 110, but by then a West Indies win was certain. Gomes was missed as soon as he arrived, but these were the only real hints that the two great batsmen padded up, Richards and Lloyd, might be required. The unbroken stand of 287 between Greenidge and Gomes was a second-wicket record for West Indies against England, and West Indies won with 11.5 of the last twenty overs to spare.

Gordon Greenidge in 1984. "Seldom can he have played on such a high plane of inspired brilliance."

v England

• May 27, 1991 •

ENGLAND WON by seven wickets. A third-wicket stand of 213 in 31 overs between Fairbrother and Hick, a record for any wicket in one-day internationals in England, made light of a substantial target and gave the home side a clean sweep in the three-match series. Both might have gone before they settled, but Hick (86 not out) went on to his first fifty and Fairbrother to his maiden hundred (113) for England. They also won the hearts of a full house, including the Compton and Edrich stands, officially opened by D. C. S. Compton during lunch, by refusing an offer of bad light.

v England

• June 22, 23, 24, 25, 26, 1995 •

ENGLAND WON by 72 runs. A match of startling fluctuations and compelling cricket was finally settled by a historic bowling performance. Dominic Cork, the 23-year-old Derbyshire bowler, returned an analysis of seven for 43, the best by an England player on Test debut and fifth on the list for any country. His virtues were old-fashioned – wicket-to-wicket line, length and movement – coupled with a fierce and demonstrable will. Indeed, England levelled the series with the sort of aggression, determination and plain good sense that were so woefully lacking in the First Test. For West Indies, it was their third defeat in six Tests – a sequence of failures unknown during their two decades of world dominance – and their first at Lord's since 1957. After the second day, West Indies coach Andy Roberts claimed the pitch had been "deliberately under-prepared" in England's favour, and he was later repri-manded for his comments by match referee John Reid. In the event, the parched and cracked surface became easier and offered less sideways movement as the match progressed.

It had begun with an undercurrent of disharmony between Ray Illingworth, England's overlord, and Mike Atherton, his captain. The full selection panel decided at its regular Saturday meeting that Steve Rhodes would keep wicket, Stewart return to his favoured place at the head of the order and Smith bat at No. 5 after opening at Headingley. Then, on the eve of the match, Illingworth unilaterally overturned this central plank of team strategy and inflicted on Atherton a line-up he strongly opposed. To cram in five specialist bowlers, Illingworth coerced Stewart into the all-rounder's role of wicket-keeper/opening batsman, with Smith on standby to go in first if Stewart was too tired after a stint in the field. Rhodes was omitted from the thirteen, as was DeFreitas. It was an unprecedented display of autocracy by Illingworth and the manner in which he did it outraged many. Yet he was appointed to make such decisions and his vindication came with victory – which also, as if by magic, brought public unity with Atherton.

v England

• June 29, 30, July 1, 2000 •

ENGLAND WON by two wickets. The 100th Test match played at Lord's also proved to be one of the most exciting, with England winning a low-scoring encounter to level the series 1–1. Many talk about the Lord's Test of 1963 as being the apogee between these two sides: for sheer drama and sustained excitement, this one may have usurped it. The uncertainty was contagious and, right up until Cork struck the winning boundary just after 7 p.m. on Saturday, it was a match that defied prediction. Momentum in Test cricket is usually a gradual, shifting force, but here it changed hands quicker than a spare ticket among the touts, who, sensing something special, thronged the pavements surrounding the ground. Whether or not the innovation of live music during the lunch break played a part – on the first day it was Third World and the Jools Holland Big Band – business was brisk. On Friday, when 21 wickets fell in 75 overs, including West Indies' second innings for just 54, value for money was given ten times over. In fact, the day saw at least one ball of all four innings, an instance unique in more than 1,500 Tests.

After losing heavily at Edgbaston, England turned up at Lord's – not somewhere recently associated with home victories – without the services of their captain,

It's him again. In 1995 Dominic Cork was
Man of the Match with the ball. Five years later he was
England's man of the hour with the bat.

Hussain, who had cracked a thumb playing for Essex the previous weekend. It created an irony in which English cricket seems to specialise: Stewart, almost a year to the day after being sacked as captain, was once more asked to lead the side. In the event, it proved something of a masterstroke: Stewart's terse dressing-room speech – following England's first-innings collapse to 134 all out – was later cited as a contributory factor to West Indies' capitulation immediately afterwards.

England's response was emphatic, bold and, given the evidence of the first day, when West Indies scored their 267, entirely unexpected. It also required some early fortune to start the process, which happened in the fourth over when Campbell was caught, cutting Caddick to third man. The wicket turned Caddick, with his curious tendency to be more effective in the second innings, into an assassin. Eschewing the theory that West Indies batsmen are vulnerable to the ball of full length, he banged it in short and literally went for the jugular. Only Jacobs, with a couple of fortuitous boundaries, made double figures; West Indies' 54 was their third-lowest total, their lowest-ever against England. Just over two hours of incredible drama had transformed a match with only one conceivable outcome into an endgame where both teams had a chance of victory.

Chasing 188 did not sound much, but on a bouncy seaming pitch, against two of the world's best new-ball bowlers, Ambrose and Walsh, the task was stern. If most realists made West Indies favourites, they hadn't reckoned on Atherton and his heir apparent, Vaughan (playing only because of Hussain's injury). Coming together in the sixth over, they added 92 painstaking runs, each one cheered to the echo by a full house now reaching the point of emotional saturation – itself a rarity at Lord's. Both fell in the forties to Walsh, who took the first six wickets to fall and improved his best figures against England for the second Test running, completing ten in the match for the first time against them. At 140 for six the pendulum, having creaked England's way, was back in West Indies' territory.

However, Cork, dripping adrenalin and with a decisive glint in his eye, had entered the fray at the fall of the sixth wicket. Unfazed by the tension, he set about getting the runs. A lofted drive for four off the tiring Walsh, a pull for six off Rose and sundry stolen singles were all executed with his usual sense of theatre. As Gough kept him company with an admirably straight bat, Cork chipped away at both the total and the heartstrings of the public. Only when he had forced Walsh through the covers for the winning runs was the tension finally released, amid euphoria and ecstasy.

and could not bat, was hardly felt. MCC began their innings after lunch on the second day, with hot sun quickly drying the wicket. Though Yardley batted well, Amarnath and Hazare were almost unplayable with the new ball. When MCC followed on, Mankad took three wickets cheaply overnight and, after delay till quarter-past four on Tuesday, he and Amarnath dismissed the last seven batsmen for 45 runs on turf which made the batsman's task most unenviable.

v Middlesex

• June 23, 24, 25, 1971 •

INDIA WON by two wickets. On the same pitch which had been used a week earlier for the rain-marred Test against Pakistan, spin bowlers received considerable assistance and the Indians fielded three, whereas Middlesex were without Titmus. Though Middlesex made the highest score of

Orthodox left-arm spinner Bishan Bedi
"must rank amongst the finest bowlers of his type to have toured this country," *Wisden 1972* concluded.

Indians at Lord's

MCC and Ground v Parsees

• May 27, 28, 1886 •

FOR THIS MATCH the Marylebone Club put an altogether unnecessarily strong team into the field, and there was really no serious interest in the game. From the first it was seen that the Parsees (above) were utterly overmatched and had not the smallest chance of success. Their notions of bowling and fielding were at that time of the most elementary description. It should be stated, however, that Mr W. G. Grace played at the request of the Parsees, who were anxious to have the champion on the opposing side once during their tour. Lord Harris

was also asked to play as a compliment, but was prevented from doing so by his parliamentary engagements.

v MCC

• May 25, 27, 28, 1946 •

INDIA WON by an innings and 194 runs. A wicket that played easily on the first day turned difficult after weekend rain, and India took full advantage of the opportunities given them in batting first. Merchant, with his second century in successive first-class matches, Hazare, Hindlekar and Modi ensured a big score, so that the absence of the Nawab of Pataudi, who slipped on the Pavilion stairs

BOWLED OVER

Soon after the start of the Indian second innings, when the game was crucially balanced, Gavaskar, racing to complete a quick single, was barged to the ground by Snow as the pair ran up the pitch together – an incident for which the England fast bowler was requested to apologise by the chairman of selectors, Mr A. V. Bedser, and Mr S. C. Griffith, secretary of the TCCB. The England selectors omitted Snow from the Second Test as a disciplinary measure. [1972]

the game in the first innings (233), it should have been much lower for catches were dropped wantonly. Bedi gave a memorable exhibition of classic left-arm slow bowling, his teasing flight and perfect length confusing all the batsmen. A remarkable feature of the game was that on all three days Price took two wickets in two balls after also achieving this feat on the Tuesday of the Pakistan Test.

v England

• June 5, 6, 7, 9, 10, 1986 •

INDIA WON by five wickets, their first Test victory at Lord's and only their second in 33 Tests in England. It was, in addition, England's sixth successive defeat since regaining the Ashes so comprehensively the previous season, and at the end of the match Gower was informed by the chairman of selectors, Mr P. B. H. May, that he had been relieved

of the captaincy. Gatting, the vice-captain, was promoted to lead England in the next two Tests.

Gower's tenure began to look insecure on the third afternoon when, with Vengsarkar suffering from cramp in his left arm, India's last two wickets put on 77 runs in 25 overs. Yet the collapse that followed Azharuddin's dismissal might have stranded Vengsarkar short of his hundred. He was 81 when Pringle knocked over Chetan Sharma's off stump. Instead, More announced himself as a batsman of higher ranking than ten, Maninder Singh (coming in when Vengsarkar was 95) proved equal to the occasion, and Vengsarkar, with a push for a single, became the first overseas batsman to score three hundreds in Test matches at Lord's. G. Boycott, D. C. S. Compton, J. H. Edrich, J. B. Hobbs and L. Hutton had done so for England. Of the sixteen fours in his unbeaten 126, his tenth century and one of classical elegance, charm and responsibility, many came from handsome drives.

So ebbed England's prospects of victory. When India's bowlers, Kapil Dev and Maninder especially, exposed all manner of deficiencies in England's batting on the fourth day, Gower's fate was sealed. England could not even rely on the weather: when they batted, the cloud came down to encourage movement through the air and off the seam; when India batted , the cloud was high and the sun shone in approval of their batsmen's technique. On the final afternoon Kapil Dev set the seal on a momentous match for his country by hitting Edmonds for 18 in one over: three fours and the six over mid-wicket with which the game was won. There were other candidates for the Man of the Match award but it was appropriate that it went to Kapil Dev, for whom it was his first victory in 21 Tests as captain. There was no way, given India's performance at Lord's, that it would be his last.

The third of Kapil Dev's four successive sixes to save India from the follow-on in the 1990 Test.

v England

• July 26, 27, 28, 30, 31, 1990 •

ENGLAND WON by 247 runs. The Indians, and especially their captain, Azharuddin, had small reason to think so by the end, but the First Test was as brilliant a match as the players could hope to take part in, or spectators to watch. England's winning margin made it look one-sided; and no one would dispute that, from lunch on the first day, England after being put in were in control. Certainly their win, inspired by Gooch's historic innings of 333 and 123, which broke all kinds of records, was the result of a powerful performance by his team.

Yet it would not have been the match it was without the vibrant batting of the tourists. Shastri and Azharuddin made splendid hundreds of contrasting styles, and Kapil Dev struck a high-velocity 77 not out, jauntily rounded off with four successive sixes, to limit England's lead to 199 and thus save the follow-on. Each was straight driven off Hemmings' off-spin into the building works that throughout the season masqueraded as the Nursery end. By using Shastri to open the batting, India made room to play the seventeen-year-old Bombay student, Tendulkar, who in England's second innings brought off as wonderful an outfield catch as Lord's has seen, holding Lamb's straight drive one-handed at knee height after hurtling more than 30 yards from wide long-off to a point behind the bowler.

When India were challenged by Gooch's second declaration to make 472 to win, or bat seven hours on a crusting pitch to draw, they were fighting a losing battle once Fraser and Malcolm dismissed their openers on the fourth evening. The 6ft 5in Fraser, recovered at last from a rib injury suffered while in the

Caribbean, played a leading part. Figures of five for 104 and three for 39 were due reward for his accuracy, bounce and movement at a lively pace.

This match report appears on page 333 of Wisden 1991.

Mongia and Tendulkar followed cheaply, before Ganguly fell victim to one of the greatest catches ever held at Lord's. Launching Giles towards wide long-on, he watched in horror as Kirtley hared round the boundary, dived at full stretch and clung on with his left hand an inch above the turf. [2003]

v England

• July 13, 2002 •

INDIA WON by two wickets. This NatWest Series final wasn't merely a case of saving the best until last: it was one of the most thrillingly topsy-turvy limited-overs internationals ever played. At 146 for five in pursuit of 326 – more than they had ever scored batting second – India were down and out. Only Yuvraj Singh, aged 20, and Mohammad Kaif, 21, stood between England's bowlers and the tail. But Yuvraj played some punishing strokes off the back foot, Kaif was all wrists through mid-wicket, and the pair added 121 in less than eighteen overs. Harbhajan Singh helped add a quick 47 with Kaif to take India to the brink, but Flintoff tilted the balance with two wickets in the 48th over. Even so, India needed just 11 runs off twelve balls. Kaif thick-edged Gough to the third-man boundary to reduce the target to 2 off six, and Zaheer Khan stole the winning runs with three balls remaining, courtesy of an overthrow. In an echo of Flintoff's antics at Mumbai five months earlier, Ganguly whipped off his shirt and whirled it round his head on the players' balcony, before running through the Long Room to kiss the Lord's turf and embrace Kaif. After nine consecutive defeats in one-day finals, India had made it tenth time lucky.

England's innings of 325 for five, their fourth-highest in this form of the game, had inspired drama of its own. In his 72nd innings, Hussain reached his first one-day international century, a dogged but scratchy innings, full of miscues and failed reverse sweeps. When he reached three figures, from 118 balls, he embarked on an impassioned series of gestures to the press box, where several commentators – "ex-players",

Mohammad Kaif a gogo.

Hussain later said – had questioned his position in the batting order. Hussain held up three fingers and gesticulated angrily to the No. 3 on the back of his shirt. It was pure theatre, and almost overshadowed an outstanding display from Trescothick, who added 185 for the second wicket with Hussain in just 177 balls. Trescothick motored to his third one-day century in 89 balls with some hammer-on-anvil cover drives.

Needing six and a half an over, India came racing out of the blocks too. Ganguly pummelled fifty in 35 deliveries, and his opening partnership with the dashing Sehwag had reached 106 in the fifteenth over when he was bowled – the first of five wickets to fall for 40 runs in less than ten overs. The game seemed over. But England had reckoned without the youthful daring and verve of Yuvraj and Man of the Match Kaif.

Pakistanis at Lord's

v England

• August 8, 9, 10, 12, 13, 1974 •

DRAWN. Rain and leaky covers spoilt this match, but when cricket was possible Underwood excelled in exploiting damp patches. Taking five wickets for 20 and eight for 51, he was the first Englishman to capture eight wickets in an innings in a Lord's Test since 1934 when, following a storm on the Saturday night and sunshine throughout Sunday, Hedley Verity – the pitch was never wholly covered in those days – took fourteen Australian wickets on the Monday. If England were unfortunate that no play took place on the last day, when they wanted only 60 to win with all wickets intact, at least justice was done considering that previously all the bad luck had fallen on Pakistan.

After rain on the first day and showers on Saturday, much rain fell on Sunday and on Monday morning, and again the covering did not contain the water down the slope which soaked the pitch. The Pakistan manager, Omar Kureishi, accused MCC, in an official protest, of "an appalling show of negligence and incompetence in not covering the wicket adequately". MCC replied through their secretary, Jack Bailey: "It is deeply regretted that the covering did on this occasion prove inadequate. Even more comprehensive precautions than those which had previously kept the pitch and surrounds dry throughout three days and nights of heavy intermittent rain were taken, but the deluge overnight and this morning meant that some water escaped on to the wicket.

"MCC have experimented continuously, and have spent many thousands of pounds over the past few years in trying to devise a means of overcoming a covering problem which is made extremely difficult by the slope at Lord's, and by the necessity of having at the same time to allow air to circulate under those covers which are on the pitch. I am certain that the head groundsman and his staff have done everything that could humanly be asked of them in order to provide a good wicket and keep it that way."

v England

• June 15, 16, 17, 19, 1978 •

ENGLAND WON by an innings and 120 runs, seven minutes before lunch on the fourth day following a blank first day. The victory was a triumph for Botham, who hit a dazzling century – his second in successive Test innings – and finished the match by taking eight wickets for 34 runs. These were the best figures by an England bowler in an innings since Jim Laker's nine for 37 and ten for 53 against Australia at Old Trafford in 1956. There had never been an all-round performance like Botham's in a Test match. In his seven Test matches to date, he now claimed three hundreds besides five wickets or more in an innings five times. Moreover, England's performance could be attributed to the success of their young men, Gooch (24), Gower (21) and Botham (22). Gooch and Gower put on 101 in 97 minutes for the third wicket after two wickets had fallen for 19, but England were soon 134 for five. Up to this point the Pakistan attack had performed exceedingly well. However, Botham's second scoring stroke was a magnificent pull for six into the Mound Stand, and he completed his spectacular hundred in the last over of the day in two hours 40 minutes, with eleven boundaries in addition to his six.

On Saturday Willis wrought destruction on the Pakistan batsmen, taking five for 47 on a hard pitch. Edmonds completed the devastation with four victims for only 6 runs from six overs, and Pakistan followed on 259 behind England's 364. The openers went quickly but again Mohsin Khan played well and raised the score to 96 without further loss before the close.

**Left: Wasim Bari looks, Javed Miandad leaps and
Ian Botham lashes another four towards his 1978 century.
Right: Mohsin Khan's double-hundred in 1982 raised him
"to the top rank of Pakistani batsmen".**

The fall of the last eight wickets for 43 on Monday morning came as a complete surprise when, on a cloudless day, Botham swung the ball in astounding fashion. He beat the bat with three or four out-swingers an over. The ball was a substitute for one that went out of shape on Saturday evening, after which the spinners, Edmonds and Miller, had gone into action. Brearley expected to have to rely on them on this Monday morning. Instead, Botham seized his opportunity when he went on at the Nursery end so that Willis, with the wind having veered, could change ends. Miandad alone showed ability to cope with the situation before being last out, caught in the gully.

v England

• August 12, 13, 14, 15, 16, 1982 •

PAKISTAN WON by ten wickets, a margin which reflected their superiority but failed to record the tension of the closing stages as the Pakistanis sought only their second-ever

victory over England. The first had been in 1954, at The Oval, in the Fourth Test of Pakistan's first series in England. It in no way detracts from Pakistan's win to say that England were handicapped by the limitations of their attack once Willis, the captain, pronounced himself unfit, ironically as a result of a neck injury incurred avoiding Imran Khan's bouncers at Birmingham. Gower, with little experience at the job, assumed the captaincy.

The quality of England's bowling and the pitch were both shown in true perspective when Mohsin Khan drove Botham's first ball for four. Before lunch the batsmen had disdained wearing helmets and these did not reappear until Pringle took the new ball and, with his third delivery, had Zaheer Abbas dropped by Tavaré at second slip. Had England held their catches,

the day might have ended differently. Mohsin was let off twice, once when 72 at first slip and again shortly after reaching his second Test hundred when he gave Jackman the hardest of caught-and-bowled chances. On Friday, a brief stoppage for showers in the morning, a four-hour delay after lunch, and Gower's strengthening of his on-side field meant it took Mohsin, 159 overnight, until six o'clock to become the second post-war batsman to score 200 in a Lord's Test. M. P. Donnelly, 206 in 1949, was the other – though he did not have to wait for four hours on 199.

v England

• August 22, 23, 1992 •

PAKISTAN WON by 3 runs. An enthralling Texaco Trophy match, spread across two days, was decided in Pakistan's favour when Waqar Younis bowled last man Illingworth with the second delivery of the final over. Unhappily, the match

Waqar Younis – reverse swinger.

will be remembered primarily for what followed off the field. Within minutes of the close, it was revealed that umpires Palmer and Hampshire had found it necessary, during the second-day lunch interval, to change the ball being used by Pakistan's bowlers. They had consulted with match referee Deryck Murray, who refused to make public comment. The implication was "ball-tampering", though Pakistan argued the ball was merely out of shape. Five days later – with allegations, counter-claims and threats to sue for libel still coming thick and fast – the International Cricket Council ruled the matter closed without either clearing or convicting Pakistan. What was undeniable was that the tourists had bowled brilliantly to win against the odds and end England's hopes of a clean sweep in the one-day series.

Pakistan: 204–5 (50 overs) (Javed Miandad 50 not out).

England: 201 (49.2 overs) (A. J. Lamb 55; Waqar Younis 3–36).

Sidath Wettimuny

Had cricket followers known in advance that the record for the longest Test innings ever played at Lord's was to be broken last summer by an opening batsman, most would have assumed that Gordon Greenidge would be the man to take that honour, or conceivably Desmond Haynes. Few, surely, would have backed a 28-year-old Sri Lankan Buddhist, and a vegetarian at that, to demonstrate his stamina for 637 minutes, or 642 minutes if the two hold-ups by Tamil protesters are included. But Sidath Wettimuny did so, and thereby converted sceptics who had previously doubted Sri Lanka's right to Test status.

His innings of 190 was enhanced by some of the finest cover driving seen in England all summer, which was all the more creditable for someone who had never played at Lord's before. His experience of the ground was limited to the nets at the Nursery end, where he and several team-mates had practised for a fortnight before the tour (rain in Colombo having limited the Sri Lankans to a couple of outdoor practices in the previous four months). So he had to overcome his own nervousness, along with the apprehension that all the Sri Lankans felt at playing their inaugural Test in England, before completing his historic achievement.

The background to that innings was a stern lecture by their coach, Don Smith, formerly of Sussex, on the morning of the match. He told the Sri Lankans that everyone, during their warm-up county games, had remarked how they looked the part: but where was the substance, where were the victories? Wettimuny went out to bat full of the determination which Sri Lankans had

hitherto been accused of lacking.

His first runs, and boundary, came from cuts backward of square. He reached 50 in the over before lunch, and 100 out of 154 in 219 minutes, whereupon he slowed down, partly because of cramp. His last 90 runs took 418 minutes, but to the end he remained neat and effective on the off side: of his twenty boundaries, sixteen came from cuts and cover drives to the area around the Tavern. As if his stamina had not been taxed enough, he was then subject to a series of telephone calls from official dignitaries, congratulating him on putting Sri Lanka on the cricket map. [*Scyld Berry, 1985*]

Benson and Hedges gold for the boys from Foster's-shire: Alec Stewart, captain Adam Hollioake and brother Ben celebrate Surrey's victory over Kent in the 1997 final.

Up for the Cup

"So smoothly did Gillette's knockout cup overcome the objections to one-day cricket that one of their reasons for giving it up was that it had come to be associated not with anything they made but almost exclusively with cricket."

[Wisden 1981]

The Knockout Competition

• September 7, 1963 •

SUSSEX beat Worcestershire by 14 runs. The weather, cold and cloudy with periods of light rain, in no way doused the spirits of the 25,000 spectators or the cricketers. Indeed, the match ended in twilight and a heavy drizzle and it was this, coupled with Dexter's superior tactics, which almost certainly cost Worcestershire the match. Sussex, having won the toss, decided to bat on a soft pitch, and it soon became evident that their normally free-scoring batsmen would find the going difficult. Spin bowlers, normally so despised in this type of cricket, caused most trouble. The left-arm Gifford took four wickets for 33 in his fifteen overs – a spell which earned him the Man of the Match award – and Slade, possessing a similar action, was almost as deadly.

Sussex totalled 168 and Worcestershire had to score at 2.5 runs per over to win. Buss made an early breakthrough and then Oakman, keeping his off-spin an impeccable length, prevented any attempt to score

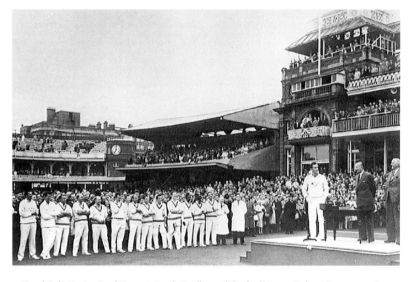

"Lord Ted" Dexter, Lord Nugent, Frank Woolley and the finalists await the 1963 presentation.

quickly. As the light deteriorated, so did Worcestershire's chance. Dexter brought back his fastest bowlers and captured the ninth wicket at 133. The Sussex supporters were ready to cheer their side home, but Booth kept them waiting, striking some telling blows and forcing Dexter to place every available fielder on the boundary. Amidst tremendous excitement, the last pair took the Worcestershire score

to 154 before Carter was run out in the penultimate over.

Gillette Cup

• September 4, 1965 •

YORKSHIRE beat Surrey by 175 runs. They deservedly became the new holders of the trophy in a surprisingly one-sided match. Despite this, the 25,000 spectators received six hours of capital entertainment. Yorkshire, spearheaded by an aggressive Boycott, broke most of the competition's records. Boycott made the highest individual score (146), shared in the biggest partnership with Close, his captain (192 for the second wicket), and Yorkshire reached a new total (317 for four). The previous highest total – 314 for seven by Sussex against Kent in 1963 – was scored off 65 overs as opposed to 60. Yorkshire, sent in, began slowly but gradually Boycott completely mastered Surrey's attack. After an indifferent season and without a first-class century, he cast aside his troubles and played forcing shots all round the wicket. He struck three sixes and fifteen fours; Close hit one six and seven fours in his 79. Surrey's batsmen never got into their stride and the writing was on the wall when Trueman sent back Edrich, Smith and Barrington in four deliveries. Illingworth also captured three wickets in one over.

The scorer

• May 27, 1964 •

Middlesex beat Yorkshire by 61 runs. They knocked out the county champions and favourites for the Gillette Cup after Close had sent them in. Yorkshire were handicapped through John Hampshire being taken ill with serum fever following an anti-tetanus injection necessitated by a cut eye when fielding a fortnight earlier. They had no twelfth man and Ted Lester, their scorer, who had not held a bat for three years nor played for the first team for nine years, was pressed into service. He was bowled by Price before scoring.

Mike Selvey – a razor-sharp start to the 1977 final. Of Jack Bond (far left) *Wisden* said, "The dynamic little cricketer from Bolton proved himself the ideal leader of a Lancashire side determined to enjoy and succeed in one-day cricket."

Gillette Cup

• September 2, 1972 •

Lancashire beat Warwickshire by four wickets and so lifted the trophy for the third consecutive year under Jackie Bond's inspiring leadership. No one quarrelled with Basil D'Oliveira when he named Clive Lloyd the Man of the Match. Not only did the talented West Indies cricketer subdue Warwickshire when M. J. K. Smith decided to bat first – Lloyd bowled his twelve overs on the trot – but he played one of the finest innings imaginable, hitting his 126 off 42 overs after making only 6 runs in his first eight overs. Among Lloyd's many wonderful strokes were three sixes and fourteen fours, and few of the 25,000 onlookers, plus the untold number who were glued to their TV sets, will forget his sparkling straight drives which passed the fielders before they could move. Lancashire wanted 235, a target never previously accomplished by the victors batting second in a Gillette Cup final, and they succeeded with more than three overs to spare.

Gillette Cup

• September 3, 1977 •

Middlesex beat Glamorgan by five wickets after Brearley had put Glamorgan in to bat. Following many hours of rain the ground was only just fit for play, and Glamorgan did not get the full value for powerful strokes as the ball travelled slowly over the wet outfield. On the other hand the pitch lacked the pace which would have suited Daniel, whereas Selvey (12–4–22–2) bowled splendidly from the start. The tall left-handed Llewellyn gave the best batting display of a rather dreary day's cricket. His first three strokes were 4,6,4 off Gatting. Later he hoisted a ball from Emburey over mid-on which dropped into the guttering beside the broadcasting box near the top tier of the Pavilion – a colossal carry. Middlesex did not face a tall task (178), but they lost Brearley, caught behind, to the first ball of their innings. Radley, who was fortunate to be missed when 2 at second slip and had other escapes while Glamorgan paid dearly for poor fielding, took out his bat for 85.

B&H Cup

• July 21, 1979 •

ESSEX beat Surrey by 35 runs, and carried off their first trophy since the present county club was formed 103 years earlier. They achieved it in a great match and with the highest total ever made in a Benson and Hedges final. The main hero was Gooch. His 120 was the first century scored in eight Benson and Hedges finals, an innings of high quality and memorable strokes including three mighty sixes and eleven fours. When he was fifth to leave, he had seen Essex amass 273 runs following Knight's decision to take the field. Praise must also be given to Surrey for a stout-hearted performance. Whereas Essex were at full strength, Surrey were without their key fast bowler, Sylvester Clarke, and Robin Jackman was not really fit to play, although he made a brave and valuable contribution.

Gillette Cup

• September 8, 1979 •

SOMERSET beat Northamptonshire by 45 runs before a capacity crowd of 25,000 who saw them gain their first victory in any competition since they were formed 104 years previously. Next day they completed a memorable double by heading the John Player League. While their triumph was a team effort, two of their West Indies players

achieved outstanding performances. Vivian Richards gave of his best in scoring 117 and, when Northamptonshire faced the enormous task of getting 270, Joel Garner took six wickets for 29. Richards, whom Cyril Washbrook named Man of the Match, batted superbly from the seventh to the last over; he did not offer a chance. Most of his eleven boundaries came from powerful leg hits and straight drives during an innings which lasted three hours and nine minutes. Botham, in his most belligerent mood, struck five hearty fours while putting on 41 in seven overs with Richards.

With three world-class competitors in Joel Garner, Ian Botham and Vivian Richards, Somerset marched to five Lord's finals between 1978 and 1983, winning all but the first of them. Superb centuries brought Richards the match award in 1979 and 1981.

Smoking guns

• June 11, 1980 •

Middlesex beat Sussex by 29 runs. This Benson and Hedges Cup quarter-final had an extraordinary start and an even more unusual finish. Imran Khan was involved both times. In the morning he swung the ball so extravagantly that he bowled eight wides in his first five overs, and eleven of the final count of nineteen. The extras conceded by Sussex (38) were higher than their margin of defeat. Eight hours later, as Daniel produced some characteristically explosive bowling to clinch Middlesex's win, there was plenty of stuff whistling round the batsmen's heads and Imran protested to umpire van Geloven when Pigott was hit on the arm. (Daniel had broken Wessels' hand with an earlier lifter.) Immediately Brearley came in to give his view and, almost incredibly, he and Imran appeared on the point of grappling. The intervention of van Geloven prevented an unsavoury incident from degenerating. Imran said: "When I bowl bumpers at tailenders, I am warned. Daniel bowled five, so I objected." In his report van Geloven stated that he had never heard such bad language, on or off the field, as Imran's. The TCCB asked each county to enquire and to take action. Over a month later the Board's disciplinary committee stated that the matter was ended, as they were satisfied with the reprimand Sussex delivered to Imran and with Middlesex's expression of regret that Brearley had become involved. Otherwise the sides produced excellent cricket.

B&H Cup

• July 25, 1981 •

SOMERSET beat Surrey by seven wickets to claim the Benson and Hedges Cup for the first time. On the day they were much the better side, restricting Surrey to 194 for eight, a total they passed with 10.3 overs to spare. As he makes a habit of doing, Vivian Richards, Somerset's great West Indian batsman, carried off the main honours, including the Gold Award, with a brilliant innings of 132 not out. When Somerset lost Denning and Rose in their first three overs, he was obliged to play himself in with some care. Having done so, he finished by treating the bowling much as he pleased. By the time the match ended, Botham was trading strokes with Richards in a way that suggested 275 might not have been out of Somerset's reach. It was a handicap to Surrey that Clarke was not fully fit, and his appearance in the final delayed his recovery from the back injury which kept him out for most of the rest of the season.

NatWest Trophy

• September 7, 1985 •

ESSEX beat Nottinghamshire by 1 run, their first success in the 60-overs competition and their seventh title in as many years. It was a marvellous match, in which Randall (66) all but conjured up an improbable victory for Nottinghamshire, who had seen Essex openers Gooch and Hardie put on 202, the highest partnership in any Lord's final, after Essex had been put in. Hardie's innings of 110, made from 149 balls, outshone Gooch's 91 in its vigorous strokeplay, though he needed some luck when the ball moved about early on. Robinson and Broad, in turn, encountered few problems in putting on 143 for Nottinghamshire's first wicket, but the innings faltered from the moment

The Botham factor

• August 17, 1983 •

Somerset won their NatWest Bank semi-final against Middlesex by virtue of losing fewer wickets with the scores level. A captain's innings lasting 205 minutes by Botham inched Somerset into their first 60-overs final for four years from an almost irretrievable position. Middlesex's 222 for nine looked well within reach in conditions which by afternoon had turned in favour of the bat. But Somerset were in trouble when Cowans dismissed Lloyds and Denning with successive balls in his second over. Worse followed. A disdainful Richards saw Daniel at mid-off reach behind him with a desperate left hand to clutch a checked on-drive, and when Roebuck edged a cut to second slip they were 52 for five. But Botham, communicating vast assurance and an unfamiliar air of calculation, inspired Popplewell and Marks in saving stands of 104 (in 33 overs) and 62 (in thirteen). The crowd was close to 20,000 and nobody who did not have to do so left before the end.

Broad was run out, underestimating the power of Pont's throw from the mid-wicket boundary. By the time Randall was joined by Martindale, appearing in his first one-day match, Nottinghamshire still required 37 with only three overs left; Essex seemed clear-cut winners. Randall, however, at last began to negotiate most of the strike, improvising to find the gaps, and Pringle bowled the last over to him with 18 needed. To defeat Pringle's leg-stump attack, Randall made room to play on the off side, taking 16 from the first five deliveries so that, remarkably, Nottinghamshire were now only one stroke away from winning. With the last ball, however, Pringle tucked Randall up as he again tried to move inside the line, and Prichard plucked down the resulting catch at short mid-wicket.

NatWest Trophy

• September 5, 1992 •

NORTHAMPTONSHIRE beat Leicestershire by eight wickets. The county used to being criticised for fouling up promising situations won with such uncompromising efficiency that it could be remembered as the most boring of all the Lord's finals, if anyone outside Northamptonshire bothers to remember it. From the start, the atmosphere had been lifeless: for the first time in many years the final was not a sell-out. Most people put this down to the presence of two of the smaller counties. More relevant were the weeks of bad weather before the event, the high prices (£35 for a half-decent view) at a time of recession and a certain loss of novelty value: for Northamptonshire this was their eighth Lord's final in seventeen years. Those who did pay were able to watch skydivers in the lunch interval; they might have been more entertained had they been privy to events behind the scenes, especially when Allan Lamb, the Northamptonshire captain, received a writ for libel from his former team-mate Sarfraz Nawaz because of allegations about ball-tampering. When he went out to bat, Lamb was accompanied through the Long Room by two county officials to prevent anyone choosing that moment to hand over another writ. [He scored 24 not out.]

NatWest Trophy

• September 3, 4, 1994 •

WORCESTERSHIRE beat Warwickshire by eight wickets, with ten overs and five balls to spare. So Warwickshire's wonderful adventure, in which they went so close to winning all four domestic titles, ended at Lord's, two days after they had secured the Championship. Instead, in what became a one-sided final through

luck, keen bowling and magnificent batting, Worcestershire completed a quadruple of their own; victory meant they had won all four trophies in seven years.

Warwickshire feared that their epic ambition would perish here, especially if they lost the toss and were asked to bat in damp conditions. It was worse than that. In a match carried over to the second day, after rain washed out all play after 12.25 p.m., they were required to bat on two successive moist mornings. The ball moved around so much on Saturday morning, especially when Newport was bowling, that even Lara (81) needed 26 balls to get off the mark. When Worcestershire replied to Warwickshire's 223 for nine, Hick and Moody shared a magnificent stand of 198 off just 212 balls – the second-highest for any wicket in 32 finals. Hick, his confidence restored by his recent Test successes, hit twelve fours and a six in his 93 from 101 balls. It was Moody, however, who won the Man of the Match award: earlier, he had bowled twelve overs off the reel

Tom Moody, Worcestershire's top-scorer in their 1994 B&H defeat by Warwickshire, turned the tables when the teams met again in September, adding 198 in an unbroken partnership with Graeme Hick.

for only 17 runs. There were ten fours and two sixes in his 88, and one six, off Paul Smith, went over the Grand Stand roof.

NatWest Trophy

• September 7, 1996 •

LANCASHIRE beat Essex by 129 runs. The toss of the coin before the final of the premier one-day competition has become a matter of such perceived importance that the successful captain is sometimes feted by team-mates as if he has actually won the game. In the ten previous finals, the

team batting second had won, hours after the morning dew had evaporated in the autumn sunshine. So when the toss was won by the Essex captain, Paul Prichard, and he invited the favourites Lancashire to bat, Ladbrokes adjusted their odds dramatically. The conditions did indeed favour the Essex seamers, in particular Ilott and Irani, but they continued to assist bowlers throughout. Chasing a modest target of 187, Essex were routed, cutting the record for the lowest total in the competition's 34 finals – 118 by Lancashire against Kent in 1974 – by more than half. They were all out for 57, not merely beaten but humiliated. Gooch, who had batted like an emperor throughout the season, was denied the valediction he craved in what was presumed to be his last major appearance at Lord's. Chapple and Martin had bowled even better than Ilott and Irani: Chapple's figures of six for 18 replaced Joel Garner's six for 29, for Somerset in 1979, as the best in a September final. The match was over a little after tea with more than a quarter of the scheduled 120 overs still to bowl, and the Sunday newspaperman who had started his mid-afternoon first-edition report by writing, "Ronnie Irani was the only happy Lancastrian at Lord's yesterday", turned pale, lit a cigarette, and rewrote frantically.

B&H Cup

• July 12, 1997 •

SURREY beat Kent by eight wickets. An innings of innocent near-genius from Ben Holioake – a reprise of his international debut on the same ground in May – created a one-sided victory for Surrey. This was a disappointment for most but a relief for some: the malfunctioning main scoreboard looked incapable of coping with a close finish. It was Kent's sixth consecutive defeat in a Lord's final, and if there was a pivotal moment, it came early in Holioake's innings. He had struck three carefree fours when he got a leading edge and the ball looped just short of Ealham at mid-on. Unsettled for the first and last time, he was immediately almost run out by McCague. But he survived, and so did Surrey. Upright and poised and driving the ball from the top of its bounce, he made 98 from 112 balls, with fifteen fours. When he was second out, at 161, Surrey were 51 short of Kent's 212 and Stewart, who made 75 not out, emerged from Holioake's long shadow to see his side home.

Surrey dedicated their victory to the memory of team-mate Graham Kersey, who had died in a car crash in Australia on New Year's Day. Five year's later they would dedicate their 2002 Championship title to Ben Holioake following his death in a car crash in Australia in March.

Glen Chapple had Essex in tears before teatime.

B&H Cup

• July 11, 12, 1998 •

ESSEX beat Leicestershire by 192 runs. Their crushing victory in the last Benson and Hedges final reflected the topsy-turvy nature of county cricket. Next to bottom in the Championship, but top of the Sunday League, Essex outplayed Leicestershire, second in the Championship. They were lucky with the weather: no sooner had they completed their innings on the first day than the rain came, and Leicestershire – who had won the toss – could not bat until late on Sunday afternoon. By then the pitch had become ideal for seam bowling. Leicestershire were dismissed inside 28 overs for 76, the lowest total in all 27 Benson and Hedges finals,

while Essex's margin of victory was the widest in terms of runs.

The Essex innings produced some compelling batting. Conditions should have favoured the bowlers early on, but Mullally and Lewis, pitching wide of the stumps, wasted the new ball. Prichard and Stuart Law opened with 40 in ten overs, then Hussain and Prichard played adventurous, high-class cricket in a decisive 134-run partnership spanning 25 overs. Prichard can seldom have looked so dominating, except perhaps in the previous Lord's final when he led his team to victory in the 1997 NatWest. As a square-cutter he looked as good as Steve Waugh, and he pulled and drove with power and fluency. Hussain capitalised on the width he was given, opening the face of the bat, as he prefers, and driving square on the off side. With the score on 174, Prichard was eventually caught driving at cover for 92, from 113 balls, containing eleven fours and two sixes.

Leicestershire's downfall the following afternoon was begun by two catches at second slip – one good, the other brilliant. First Sutcliffe flashed at Cowan, Stuart Law taking it two-handed up by his ear. Next ball, Smith pushed forward and edged, probably nearer to first slip than second, but Law saw it early and dived far and low to his left, pulling off a spectacular catch, again with both hands. The pitch helped the Essex bowlers more than it had their opponents but, once they had lost their first three wickets for 10 runs, the Leicestershire batsmen came and went like lambs to the slaughter.

This proved not to be the last Benson and Hedges Cup final. By demand of the counties, the league/knockout competition was resumed from 2000 until 2002.

NatWest Trophy

• August 26, 27, 2000 •

GLOUCESTERSHIRE beat Warwickshire by 22 runs (D/L method). Rain washed out the scheduled day, truncated the reserve one, and brought Duckworth/Lewis into play for the first time in a Lord's final. It may have made history – doubly so with Gloucestershire winning their fourth successive final – but it was an unsatisfactory and anticlimactic way for the curtain to fall on the NatWest Trophy after twenty years.

Warwickshire's scoring remained well below par until their captain, Neil Smith, struck a lusty 28 in 29 balls, with Piper helping him take 35 off the last four overs and get their side to 205. If only psychologically, Warwickshire then needed an inspirational opening burst from Donald. Instead, the Gloucestershire openers were not rattled until his arrival in the ninth over. Bursting with energy on his last big occasion for Warwickshire, roared in by an appreciative following, he unnerved Hancock in a ferocious first over before defeating him with a slower sixth delivery. His first spell of 4–1–4–1 earned rapturous applause but, while he rested, Harvey and Barnett, playing in his fifth consecutive Lord's final, registered the only fifty partnership of the match. Donald returned for two overs and, with his second ball, bowled Barnett middle stump. Harvey and Russell then added 29 untroubled runs under darkening skies, and as Harvey walked off, caught just inside the mid-wicket rope for 47, a downpour sent the other players hurrying after him.

Torrential rain and lightning made further play unlikely and at 5.45 p.m. the match was called off, with Gloucestershire safely ahead on the Duckworth/Lewis reckonings. The announcement sparked an incongruous outburst of rain-sodden joy as Gloucestershire supporters slid across the outfield, apparent despair from Donald, whose efforts earned him the match award, and a touch of the absurd as

Channel 4 staff belatedly rushed the NatWest Trophy from their television studio to the Pavilion so the winning captain could hold it aloft for the final time.

B&H Cup

IN PITTING SURREY, the reigning county champions, against Gloucestershire, triple one-day champions of 2000, the 2001 Benson and Hedges Cup final could have been one of the summer's highlights. Instead, it drew the smallest crowd for a one-day final at Lord's. Some uncertain early-morning weather might have been a contributing factor, as might ticket prices ranging from £22 to £45, although the latter did not stop Gloucestershire's supporters taking up more than their initial allocation. Not even the offer of half-price entry for children and pensioners could hide the gaps around the ground. The conclusion to be drawn was that the season's new format, with a one-day international final at this venue only three weeks earlier and a Test match starting there later in the week, had relegated this domestic occasion to the second division in the cricketing public's consciousness.

C&G Trophy

• August 31, 2002 •

YORKSHIRE beat Somerset by six wickets. A close encounter between two teams having a nightmare in the Championship was decided by the one man on the field who had not spent months worrying about relegation. When he strode out to bat in a mini-crisis, Matthew Elliott had been a Yorkshire player for two and a half weeks and had not even followed this year's C&G, let alone played in it. After a watchful start, he rediscovered the booming strokeplay that had rung out in the Lord's Test of 1997. He reminded a capacity crowd why the Australian selectors had once preferred him to

Matthew Hayden, and played out a trailer for the Ashes by singling out Caddick for rough treatment. Caddick went wicketless for the third time in four Lord's finals. Somerset, fielding the eleven that had won the competition the year before, were comfortably beaten, and Yorkshire lifted their first Lord's trophy in fifteen years. Elliott finished with 128 off 125 balls, while his English colleagues managed 108 off 164 between them. In Australia, Elliott had acquired a reputation as an awkward character; at Yorkshire, this meant he fitted in perfectly.

C&G Trophy

• August 30, 2003 •

GLOUCESTERSHIRE beat Worcestershire by seven wickets. Despite the window-dressing of a violent half-century by Harvey (61 from 36 balls) and Gloucestershire's latest triumph of teamwork over ego trips, another Lord's showpiece receded quickly into a one-horse race. Ever since Warwickshire scored 15 runs from the final over to scramble past Sussex's 321 for six back in 1993, English cricket's blue-riband cup final had been crying out for a cliff-hanger. But in a summer in which crowds had flocked to the gimmicks and gusto of twenty-over slogfests, the C&G Trophy final had the appearance of a neglected child. The 6,000 empty seats winked at the ECB's marketing gurus like lightbulbs on Blackpool Illuminations, and Worcestershire's feeble performance gave those who did turn up scant value for money. Within ten overs they slumped from 64 without loss to 99 for six; they were all out for 149 inside 47 overs. Weston gave the Gloucestershire reply irresistible impetus with eight fours in 50 balls, and Man of the Match Harvey brutalised Worcestershire by unfurling a series of withering off-side strokes. In all, Gloucestershire needed only 92 minutes and a little more than twenty overs to take the chequered flag. It was all over by 4.10 p.m.

The Reeve

NATWEST TROPHY
• September 6, 1986 •

Sussex beat Lancashire by seven wickets. No team batting second had previously scored 243 to win either of the two domestic one-day finals at Lord's, and yet so commonplace was Lancashire's bowling that Sussex never looked like falling short, achieving their target with ten balls to spare. Reeve, their medium-pace bowler, made their victory possible, taking four wickets for 12 runs in 45 balls after Fowler and Mendis had put on 50 in thirteen overs. The most important wicket was that of Lloyd, who was given a standing ovation, in which the Sussex players all joined, as he made his way to the wicket in what seemed likely to be his last appearance in a Lord's final. With the first ball of this over, his third, Reeve had trapped Mendis; with his fifth he dismissed Lloyd lbw for 0. Throughout his twelve overs, Man of the Match Reeve bowled commendably to a full length on a slowish pitch, obtaining movement both ways off the seam. Gould backed him by maintaining an attacking field, keeping two slips and having only two men outside the fielding circle.

NATWEST TROPHY
• September 4, 1993 •

Warwickshire beat Sussex by five wickets. The 53rd one-day final at Lord's was widely regarded as the greatest ever played. Off the last ball, Warwickshire overhauled the Sussex total of 321 for six, the highest score in a cup final. The result has to be judged in the context of poor Sussex fielding and some unimaginative captaincy by Wells, but the magnificence of the victory and the thrilling nature of the cricket were beyond dispute.

The eighth consecutive win in this final for the team batting second came after Warwickshire had chosen to bowl first in the hope that, even without their customary match-winner, Donald, their seamers would be able to make use of the morning dampness. This did not happen. Speight set the tone of the match. Pulling off the front foot and jumping down the wicket to the bemused Munton as if he were a spinner, Speight scored 50 off 51 deliveries and allowed David Smith, less pugilistic than normal, to provide the backbone of the innings. Smith, who averages over 50 in the competition after a career spanning twenty years and three counties, returned from injury to score 124, full of powerful drives. He shared stands of 103 with Speight, at a run a ball, and 119 in sixteen overs with Lenham, who played a depth charge of an innings: 58 from 51 balls. The fielders were demoralised and Sussex scored 83 from the final ten overs. Smith was run out off the final ball –

Roger Twose and Dermot Reeve scamper two off the last ball to win the 1993 NatWest final for Warwickshire.

which hours later attained far more significance than anyone imagined at the time.

Warwickshire's task looked hopeless, the more so when they lost both openers with the score on 18. Paul Smith, all long hair and long handle, then added 75 in sixteen overs with Ostler, but it was only after tea that Sussex first realised the awful possibility of defeat. Smith, with flowing drives, and Asif Din, with wristy improvisation, added 71 in fifteen overs. Smith was fourth out at 164 in the 36th over, and Asif Din and Reeve were required to score at more than a run a ball. They kept going, but with 20 needed from two twilit overs Sussex still held a slender advantage. They strengthened their position in the 59th when Giddins conceded just 5 runs and had Asif Din caught at deep cover. He had scored 104 from 106 balls and added 142 in 23 overs with his captain, Reeve. Fifteen were needed from the last over: Reeve, without Ian Botham's outrageous talent but with much of his competitive sense, scored 13 from the first five deliveries. Twose, facing his first and last ball, sliced it through the close off-side field for 2 to give Warwickshire their victory. Stumps were pulled at both ends before the completion of the second run, and Warwickshire should have been awarded the match through losing fewer wickets. However, it was a day for romance rather than technicalities.

B&H CUP

• July 9, 1994 •

Warwickshire beat Worcestershire by six wickets with more than ten overs to spare. The Al Fresco Marching Jazz Band, making its debut at Lord's, provided perhaps the brightest moments of a mundane cup final. Worcestershire were outgunned, outclassed and sunk virtually without trace, and many of their supporters were fleeing back up the M40 before the end.

Paul Smith and Dermot Reeve in 1994.

They did have the worst of the conditions, losing the toss and batting first in the morning haze on a pitch which had not fully dried out. The ball swung much more than it seamed and there was variation in the bounce, especially at the Pavilion end. That said, Small and Munton were a high-class double act, commanding the first seventeen overs. It was English fast-medium bowling on an English morning and enabled Warwickshire to put a stranglehold on the game in which their opponents barely wriggled. Hick managed only 11 runs off 46 deliveries and by 3.25 p.m. Warwickshire were embarking on the near formality of scoring 171 to win their first Benson and Hedges Cup. Paul Smith seized the Gold Award by adding an unbeaten run-a-ball 42 to his three wickets; as in the NatWest final ten months earlier, Reeve was there at the death, confirming that as a tactician, motivator and bits-and-pieces cricketer he is currently *sans pareil*.

NATWEST TROPHY

• September 2, 3, 1995 •

Warwickshire beat Northamptonshire by four wickets. Allan Lamb spat in the face of cricketing history when he chose to bat; history exacted the customary penalty. For the tenth year running, the NatWest final went to the team batting second, and for the second year out of three that team was Warwickshire. Lamb's decision was quite logical and legitimate: rain delayed the start until 3 p.m. on the Saturday, thus in effect reversing the normal sequence – the team batting second could expect to have to contend with any morning juice in the wicket. However, Sunday dawned bright and clear, with no sign of moisture in the air, and Lord's was only a third full for what most people presumed would be the formality of Warwickshire's victory. It did not work out like that. As on the previous afternoon, the batsmen were unable to establish any dominance. Kumble began to assert something of the mastery he had shown all season and the advantage began to shift. However, the more wickets the opposition take, the more dangerous Warwickshire become. And when Reeve strode to the wicket at 122 for five – the target was 201 – Northamptonshire's nemesis had arrived. Twose was dropped twice, arguably three times, as the batsmen applied pressure with which fielders less accustomed to major occasions could not cope. Even so, Northamptonshire would probably have won if umpire Bird had shared the majority opinion that Man of the Match Reeve was out lbw to Kumble in the 52nd over. Reeve survived and Warwickshire began an unstoppable surge towards victory.

Dermot Reeve was playing in his sixth Lord's final in ten seasons, and won the Man of the Match award for the third time.

Karen Smithies and her England team savour a triumph that England's men had yet to achieve – winning a World Cup final. Their 1993 defeat of favourites New Zealand brought England their first World Cup since they won the inaugural tournament in 1973.

Stage to the World
World Cup tournaments

*"The first World Cup tournament, officially called The Prudential Cup, proved an outstanding success.
The highlight came in the final at Lord's where Australia and West Indies were in combat from 11 a.m. until 8.45 p.m.
when HRH The Duke of Edinburgh presented the Cup to Clive Lloyd, the West Indies captain."*

[Wisden 1976]

England v India

• June 7, 1975 •

ENGLAND WON by 202 runs before a crowd of nearly 20,000, receipts £19,000. With Amiss in his best form and admirably supported by Fletcher (68), England ran up the highest score in this country for a 60-over match, although later in the summer it was beaten by Hampshire in the Gillette Cup. Both sides relied almost entirely on seam bowlers, which meant that India left out Bedi, a decision that caused much surprise. Timing the ball perfectly, Amiss raced to 98 out of England's 150 for one before lunch, and altogether he made his 137 out of 245 by the 51st over and struck eighteen fours. The runs flowed so freely that finally Old (two sixes and four fours) helped himself to 51 off 28 balls and England finished with 334 for four.

India, in turn, gave such a disappointing exhibition that even their own large contingent of supporters showed their disapproval. The culprit was Gavaskar, who sat on the splice throughout the 60 overs for 36 not out. Neither G. S. Ramchand, India's manager, nor the captain, Venkataraghavan, agreed with the way Gavaskar performed. It was said that the pitch was slow and he took the opportunity to have some practice.

Collis King dazzled from his arrival at the crease, and dashed England's hopes in the 1979 final.

England v West Indies

• June 23, 1979 •

WEST INDIES WON by 92 runs and so retained the Prudential Cup and the title of world champions which they first won in 1975. On another fine day the ground was completely filled by the all-ticket crowd of 25,000, and many would-be spectators were locked out. For a long time England put up a gallant fight after Brearley had won the toss and sent in the opposition to bat. The absence of Willis, injured in the semi-final, probably made the West Indies' task easier, although his replacement, Edmonds, delivered his left-arm slows with much skill. However, in preferring an extra batsman in Larkins, Brearley had to call on Boycott, Gooch and Larkins as his "fifth" bowler. Their twelve overs cost 86 runs – and brought no wickets.

England produced their highest standard of fielding, and a superb left-handed catch by Old, when Lloyd drove the ball back low, meant that England had taken the first four wickets for 99 and clearly held the initiative. Then came the partnership that turned the scales. Richards, the hero of the day and rightly named Man of the Match, was already installed, and he found the right ally in King, who virtually took charge from the moment he arrived and made 86 out of 139 for the fifth wicket in only 77 minutes. Many of these runs came from England's three "fill-in" bowlers as King struck three sixes and ten fours in an amazing display. He drove, hooked and pulled with astonishing power and accuracy. Richards, at first, was subdued by Edmonds, but he completed his hundred in the over (the 52nd) following King's dismissal and remained unbeaten, having hit his 138 in just under three and a half hours. It contained three sixes and eleven fours.

England had the better batting conditions in brilliant sunshine, and Brearley and Boycott gave them a sound start by staying together for two hours ten minutes, although they never managed to take the West Indies' pace bowlers apart. Boycott occupied seventeen overs to reach double figures, and when Brearley went England wanted 158 from the last 22 overs. This looked to be out of the question and so it proved when Garner and Croft swept through the remainder of the innings. The 6ft 8in Garner took five wickets for 4 runs in eleven balls and was twice on a hat-trick as the West Indian supporters made the evening a Caribbean carnival.

West Indies: 286–9 (60 overs) (I. V. A. Richards 138 not out, C. L. King 86).

England: 194 (51 overs) (J. M. Brearley 64, G. Boycott 57; C. E. H. Croft 3–42, J. Garner 5–38).

India v West Indies

• June 25, 1983 •

INDIA defeated on merit the firm favourites, winning a low-scoring match by 43 runs. It was an absorbing game of increasing drama and finally of much emotion. The result, as surprising as, on the day, it was convincing, had much to do with the mental pressures of containment in limited-overs cricket. Amarnath was named Man of the Match by Mike Brearley for a stabilising innings of 26 against hostile fast bowling after the early loss of Gavaskar, followed by his taking three late West Indian wickets,

Kapil Dev and the cup that cheered a nation.

Dujon's being especially important. Dujon and Marshall had lifted West Indies, needing 184 to win, from 76 for six to 119 for six, a recovery based on the calm application of sound batting principles and one which was threatening to achieve after all the result which everyone had expected.

The Lord's wicket often inclines to extravagant morning life; this day it never lost its capacity to allow movement off the seam, sufficient to be of much significance for the medium-pace of Madan Lal and Sandhu, who removed the cream of the West Indian batting, and for the seemingly inoffensive Binny, who accounted for the dangerous Lloyd. It remained for Amarnath to break the partnership between Dujon and Marshall which, just in time, he did. India were an entertaining and well-drilled team, learning and improving as they progressed towards the final.

England v New Zealand

• August 1, 1993 •

ENGLAND WON by 67 runs. New Zealand entered the women's World Cup final as favourites, having been unbeaten in the qualifying matches, including a notable victory over England. But the occasion proved too much for an inexperienced team; their earlier sure fielding and line-and-length bowling were rarely in evidence. Brittin and Hodges added 85, slowly but surely swinging the match England's way. Still, their final total of 195 was made possible only by Chamberlain scoring 38 from just 33 balls, complemented by intelligent running between the wickets from newcomer Daniels; England took 71 off the final ten overs. New Zealand's target did not look too formidable when they reached 50 with only one wicket down in the twentieth over. But two magical moments all but ensured it would be England's day. First, Kitson flung herself wide to her left in the gully to dismiss Bond with a spectacular catch off Chamberlain's bowling. Then Player of the Match Chamberlain ran out New Zealand's top bat, Hockley, with a fine pick-up and direct hit from extra cover. There proved to be no way back for New Zealand, who were bowled out for 128 with nearly five overs to spare.

Australia v Pakistan

• June 20, 1999 •

AUSTRALIA WON the seventh World Cup with such single-minded ruthlessness that even an eight-wicket victory failed to do them justice. Pakistan, the most exciting team in the tournament, were totally outplayed and outwitted at the crucial moment. There were barely four and a half hours of cricket, most of it one-sided. For all but the most fervent Australian, it was not a pretty sight.

Adam Gilchrist moved through the 1999 World Cup on a slow-burning fuse. Come the final, he caught fire. The boundaries blazed thick, fast and off the middle of the bat as he stormed to his half-century in 33 balls. Shoaib Akhtar was unlucky when his first ball was edged by Gilchrist and fell short of long leg – but this World Cup was memorable for "if only".

It was a sight, though, spared many Pakistanis by a controversial ticketing policy. This favoured not the fans of the competing teams but those who had ostensibly proved their loyalty to the game – and the depth of their pocket – by buying a package of tickets long before. So Lord's was awash with disinterested observers, while from outside came the klaxon, whistle and bugle of fanatical Pakistan support. About a hundred fans clambered up a building site overlooking the ground. As the police moved in, a game of cat and mouse ensued, providing an alternative spectacle for the Grand Stand opposite. Eventually the fans, like their team, were unceremoniously bundled out of St John's Wood.

On a pitch that Steve Waugh believed was good for 260 or so, Wasim Akram chose to bat. With Pakistan faltering at 69 for three after 21 overs, Waugh brought on Warne. It was, literally, the turning point of the match. He produced an outstanding delivery to dismiss Ijaz Ahmed; the ball pitched on or just outside leg and hit off. It was not quite the famous Gatting ball, but it sent shockwaves through the lower order. Pakistan tried to get out of trouble with all guns blazing. But for every ball that ricocheted off the boards, another landed in Australian hands. When Wasim holed out, Warne had claimed four wickets for the second game running, taking his tally to twenty, a World Cup record shared with Geoff Allott of New Zealand.

Australia's target was just 133. Wasim later claimed he could have defended 180 but, the way Gilchrist began, 300 would have been within reach. When he fell to the first ball of the eleventh over (75 for one), the broadcasters felt the end was close enough to remove the stump cameras. In fact, it took another ten overs.

Pride, passion and pitch invasions

The inaugural under-15 World Cup, staged in August 1996, culminated in a final at Lord's that will be remembered less for the cricket than for several pitch invasions, the inadequacy of MCC's stewarding and for the police frog-marching one so-called supporter to custody through the Long Room. He was not even wearing a tie. India were the winners. The fact that they were contesting the final against their traditional rivals, Pakistan, should have alerted MCC to the possibility of crowd trouble. They were warned by the organisers, English Schools' Cricket Association, that the attendance could be as big as 10,000, since admission would be free.

When 6 runs were required, the Indian batsmen, Ratinder Sodhi, the captain, who made a match-winning unbeaten 82, and his partner, Vivek Mahajan, sought refuge in the Pavilion. Men as well as boys were running on to the square; stumps were uprooted and cans thrown on to the outfield. The police were called by a schoolmaster and arrived through the Grace Gate with sirens at full blast. Seemingly concerned that the Pavilion would be stormed, they formed a protective barrier in front of aghast MCC members. But it is an indication of the problems faced by ground authorities all over the world that the first person arrested was not some over-enthusiastic teenager, but a man who had been led away during the England-Pakistan Test at Lord's earlier in the summer. Roger Knight, MCC's Secretary, admitted the following day that the club was simply not expecting such trouble at a match between schoolboys. Nobody was seriously injured and, once the presentations had been made amid the sanctuary of the balcony, the trouble-makers dispersed. The cricket itself had been enjoyable.

Abel, Bobby, 22, 30, 32
Aird, Ronald, 70
Akers-Douglas, I. S., 128
Al Fresco Jazz Band, 183
Allen, D. A., 40
Allen, Sir G. O. B., 36, 39, 49, 72, 84, 142, 145, 152, 154; all 10w, 141; last match at Lord's, 57
Alleyne, H. L., 8 for 43 incl. hat-trick, 147
Alleyne, M. W., 149
Altham, H. S., 41, 152
Amarnath, Mohinder, 186
Amarnath, N. (Lala), 169
Ambrose, C. E. L., 167
Ames, L. E. G., 100, 113, 154
Amiss, D. L., 165, 185
Anderson, J. M., 113
Armstrong, W. W., 98
Army v Aust. Army, 150–1; v Lord's XI, 152; v Public Schools, 128; v RAF, 121; v Royal Navy, 119
Ashmore, F. M., 155
Ashton, Sir Hubert, 35, 83–4
Asif Din, M., 183
Atfield, A. J., 120
Atherton, M. A., 105, 112, 129, 158, 166–7
Attewell, William, 11, 21, 28, 58, 60, 62, 63, 95, 133–4
Australians at Lord's, 80, 91–107, 132, 150–1, 153–5; World Cup, 186–7
Azharuddin, Mohammad, 169–70

. . .

Bailey, J. A., 87, 103, 171
Bailey, T. E., 71, 102, 121, 129, 153, 158, 162
Baldwin, J. L., 115, 118
Bannerman, A. C., 91–2, 95, 117
Bannerman, Charles, 91–3
Baptiste, E. A. E., 165
Barber, Wilfred, 142
Barclay, J. R. T., 129
Bardsley, Warren, 98, 100
Barlow, G. D., 71, 147
Barlow, R. G., 20, 25, 56, 59, 62, 93, 117
Barnes, S. F., 12, 66, 103, 119
Barnes, William, 20, 56, 58, 60–2, 79
Barnett, C. J., 101, 154

Barnett, K. J., 181
Barrie, J. M., 9
Barrington, K. F., 143, 162, 176
Bartlett, H. T., 39–40
Baseball at Lord's, 18, 150
Bates, Willie, 15, 20, 62
Bathurst, Lt-Col Sir F. T. A., 11, 16, 92
Bedi, B. S., 168–9, 185
Bedser, A. V., 69–70, 121, 169
Bedser, E. A., 143
Beldam, E. A., 107, 135
Beldam, G. W., 107, 135, 139
Bell, A. J., 109
Benaud, Richie, 102, 121
Biddulph, Samuel, 16, 54, 115
Binny, R. M. H., 186
Bird, H. D., 183
Blackham, J. M., 35, 91, 94, 116
Bland, C. H. G., 64, 134
Blofeld, H. C., 128
Bloomfield, R. B., 50
Blunt, R. C., 157
Bomb-scare Test, 165
Bomford, Sir Hugh, 65
Bond, J. D., 176
Bonnor, G. J., 93, 116–7
Booth, M. W., 66
Bosanquet, B. J. T., 32–3, 107, 135
Botham, I. T., 104, 113, 165–6, 172, 177–8; 108 & 8w v Pak., 171–2; hat-trick, 71
Bowes, W. E., 161
Box, Thomas, 10–11
Boycott, Geoffrey, 164, 169, 175–6, 185–6
Boyd-Moss, R. J., 88
Boyle, H. F., 91, 93–4
Boys, J. J., 56
Bradman, Sir D. G., 99, 101–2, 113, 145, 165
Bray, Sir E. H., 63
Brearley, J. M., 41, 71, 88, 122, 146–7, 165, 172, 176–7, 185–6
Brearley, Walter, 32–3, 35, 66, 98, 136
Briggs, John, 29, 62, 133
Brittin, J. A., 186
Broad, B. C., 73, 178
Brougham, Henry, 63
Brown, F. R., 25, 36, 39, 40, 102, 111, 152
Brown, George, 65, 138

Brown, J. T. (batsman), 30, 32, 64, 134
Brown, J. T. (bowler), 64
Brown, W. A., 100–1
Buller, C. F., 17, 19, 56, 92, 115
Burki, Javed, 87
Burton, H. G., 120, 132
Buss, Antony, 175
Butcher, M. A., 105, 113, 125, 159
Butcher, R. O., 147, 165
Butler, S. E., 44, 75–6; all 10w, 75
Byes (92) in match, 65; (74), 134

. . .

Caddick, A. R., 167, 181
Cambridge University, 609–8 dec. v MCC, 65; 507 to beat MCC, 30, 65; highest total v Oxford, 87; beat Australians, 92–3
Cameron, H. B., 109–10
Cameron, J. H., 145; all 10w, 128
Canadians v MCC, 57; v Middx, 57; v Lord's XI, 154
Cannon, James, 68
Cardus, Sir Neville 12–13, 101, 127
Carpenter, H. A., 64
Carpenter, R. P., 26, 115
Carr, A. W., 35
Carter, R. G., 175
Carrying bat, 17, 21, 34, 98, 100, 127, 134
Catches of note, 55, 82, 93, 104, 151, 170
Chanderpaul, Shivnarine, 73
Chapman, A. P. F., 35, 83–4, 99
Chappell, G. S., 104
Chapple, Glen, 179–80
Charlwood, H. R. J., 116
Chatterton, William, 29, 64
Christopherson, Stanley, 117, 152, 155
Clark, E. A., 165
Clarke, S. T., 147, 177–8
Clarke, William (Mx), 132
Clarke, William (Notts), 9–11
Clayton, R. O., 116
Close, D. B., 7, 121, 162, 176, 175–6
Cobden, F. C., 75–6
Collins, H. L., 98
Compton, D. C. S., 40, 51, 69, 102, 104, 121, 142, 144–5, 147, 152–3, 158, 166, 169
Compton, L. H., 143, 145

Compton, N. R. D., 51
Constantine, Lord (L. N.), 154–5, 160–1
Cooper, B. B., 17, 62
Cork, D. G., 166–7
Cosh, N. J., 88
Cowans, N. G., 147, 178
Cowdrey, Lord (M. C.), 41, 86, 121–2, 129, 162–4
Craig, E. J., 88
Crawley, J. P., 88, 105
Cristofani, D. R., 155
Crowd behaviour, 50, 96, 104, 116, 135, 187
Crutchley, Edward, 49
Crutchley, G. E. V., 139; measles, 83

. . .

Daft, Richard, 15, 20, 27, 53, 115–6
Daniel, W. W., 147, 176–8
Daniels, B. A., 186
Darling, Joe, 96–8
Darling, L. S., 99
Davies, J. G. W., 85, 155
DeFreitas, P. A. J., 113, 167
de Silva, P. A., 73
Dexter, E. R., 40–1, 122, 162, 175
D'Oliveira, B. D., 71, 121, 176
Donald, A. A., 73, 106, 181–2
Donnelly, M. P., 85–6, 154–5, 157, 172
Douglas, James, 29, 134
Douglas, J. W. H. T., 66, 98, 151
Douglas, Rev. R. N., 74 byes, 134
Dowson, E. M., 44, 65
Doyle, Dr Sir A. I. Conan, 9
Drake, Alonzo, 66
Ducat, Andrew, 140, 153
Dujon, P. J. L., 73, 186
Duleepsinhji, K. S., 25, 36, 99, 127, 142
Durston, T. J., 139–40, 160

. . .

Ealham, M. A., 180
Edmonds, P. H., 122, 146–7, 171–2
Edrich, J. H., 122, 169, 176
Edrich, W. J., 41, 69, 101, 142–6, 152–5
Elliott, M. T. G., 181
Ellis, R. G. P., 88
Ellis, R. S., 155

Ellison, R. M., 148
Emburey, J. E., 73, 122, 147–8
Emmett, Tom, 15, 17, 19–20, 27, 115–7
Enthoven, H. J., 84–5, 104, 141–2; hat-trick, 99
Evans, T. G., 102, 121, 153

. . .

Fairbrother, N. H., 166
Falcon, Michael, 98
Farnes, Kenneth, 39–40, 68
Farrands, F. H., 16, 54, 92
Fatalities, 53–4, 132, 153
Featherstone, N. G., 71, 122, 147–8, 165
Fender, P. G. H., 139, 141, 151
Field, Edwin, 135
Fielder, Arthur, 34; all 10w, 33
Fillery, Richard, 26, 56
Findlay, William, 45, 65–6, 71
Fingleton, J. H., 103, 145
Fishlock, L. B., 39
Fitzgerald, A. W., 16, 92
Fitzgerald, R. A., 19, 26, 55, 92
Five wicket-keepers, 165
Fleming, M. V., 51, 148
Flintoff, Andrew, 113, 170
Flowers, Wilfred, 29, 60, 62–3, 79, 91
Foley, C. P., 80, 134
Follow-on law, 81
Forbes, W. F., 46–7
Ford, F. G. J., 63, 134
Ford, W. J., 45, 63
Fosh, M. K., 51
Foster, H. K., 32–3, 67, 82
Foster, N. A., 129
Foster, R. E., 30–3, 35–6, 82, 137
Fowler, Graeme, 165, 182
Fowler, R. St L., 47–9; hat-trick, 49
Francis, C. K., 26, 75–6; all 10w, 126
Fraser, A. R. C., 170
French, B. N., 73, 159
Fry, C. B., 23, 30–3, 40, 66–7, 80, 98, 134–5, 137, 139

. . .

Gaby family, 68
Ganguly, S. C., 170–1
Garner, Joel, 177, 179, 186
Gatting, M. W., 73, 104, 147–8, 165, 169
Gavaskar, S. M., 73, 169, 185–6
Gibbs, L. R., 162, 164

Giffen, George, 93, 95, 117
Gifford, Norman, 175
Gilbert, W. R., 15, 20, 56
Gilchrist, A. C., 187
Gilliat, I. V. A., 84
Gilliat, R. M. C., 165
Gilligan, A. E. R., 35
Goldstein, F. S., 88–9
Gomes, H. A., 165–6
Gooch, G. A., 73, 104, 171, 177–9, 185; 333 & 123 v India, 170
Goonesena, Gamini, 87
Gough, Darren, 105, 112–3, 167, 170
Gough, M. A., 149
Gould, I. J., 147, 182
Gover, A. R., 69, 111
Gower, D. I., 73, 165, 169, 171–2
Grace, Dr E. M., 11, 16–17, 20, 117, 132
Grace, G. F., 15, 17, 20, 25–7, 56, 58, 131
Grace, Dr W. G., 9, 14–23, 25–9, 32, 36, 40, 53–6, 62–5, 67, 79, 91, 97, 107, 115–7, 121, 131–3, 137, 168; 1,000 in 1871, 15–16; carrying bat, 17, 21; 50th birthday, 22; testimonial, 20–1
Grace, W. G. jun., 23, 64
Graveney, T. W., 7, 102, 163–4
Green, C. E., 56, 67
Greenidge, C. G., 73, 165–6, 173
Greenwood, Andrew, 27, 55, 116
Gregory, S. E., 94–5
Gregg, Thomas, 59
Greig, A. W., 71
Grenfell, Capt. F. O., 45
Griffin, Geoff, 111–2
Griffith, C. C., 162–3
Griffith, M. G., 71
Griffith, S. C., 122, 155, 169
Griffiths, W. H., 85
Grimmett, C. V., 98–9
Grundy, James, 10, 17, 92
Gunn, William, 22, 29, 60–2, 94–5, 117, 134
Gupte, C. M., 89

. . .

Hadlee, Sir R. J., 73
Hadow, W. H., 19, 26–7, 92
Haig, N. E., 138, 140, 160
Haigh, Schofield, 22, 34
Hall, Louis, 62, 132
Hall, W. W., 121, 162–4

Hammond, W. R., 36, 39, 100–1, 154–5, 165
Hampshire, J. H., 164, 173, 176
Hardie, B. R., 178
Hardstaff, Joe sen., 25, 65
Harper, R. A., 73
Harris, Lord (G. R. C.), 15, 26–7, 43–4, 67, 74, 79, 94, 117, 150, 168
Harrison, G. P., 58
Harvey, I. J., 181
Hassett, A. L., 102
Hat-tricks, 40, 49, 57, 71, 99, 104, 111, 147
Hawke, Lord (M. B.), 62, 65, 67, 119, 150, 155
Hawkins, M. M. J., 51
Hayden, M. L., 104, 181
Hayman, H. B., 134
Haynes, D. L., 73, 173
Hayward, T. W., 30, 32–4, 119–20
Headley, D. W., 125
Headley, G. A., 125, 161
Hearn, William, 29, 58, 82
Hearne, Alec, 22, 37–8
Hearne, G. F., 37–8
Hearne, G. G., 20, 37–8, 59, 62
Hearne, J. T., 22–3, 29, 32, 37–8, 63, 64, 95–6, 133–6, 139
Hearne, J. W., 136, 138–41, 160
Hearne, Thomas, 17, 37–8, 53, 115, 117, 131
Hedley, Sir W. C., 29
Hemmings, E. E., 170
Hendren, E. H., 39, 49, 68, 99, 109, 138–42, 151, 160
Heyhoe Flint, Rachael, 123
Hick, G. A., 166, 179, 183
Hide, A. B. & J. B., 61, 63
High indiv. innings, 22, 32, 40, 46, 58, 98–100, 108, 113, 140, 165, 170
High partnerships, 58, 61, 108, 166, 175, 178–9
High totals, 22, 30, 61, 63, 65, 99, 139, 149, 161
Hill, Allen, 27, 116
Hill, Maurice, 71
Hinkly, Edmund, 9
Hirst, G. H., 32, 34, 65
Hits of note, 20, 40, 43, 55, 58, 70–1, 117, 121, 124, 132, 140, 148, 155, 170, 177, 179
Hobbs, Sir J. B., 35–6, 68, 108, 119–20, 139–40, 144, 169
Hockley, D. A., 186
Hodges, C. A., 186

Holder, V. A., 164
Holford, D. A. J., 163–4
Hollies, W. E., 40, 155
Hollioake, A. J. & B. C., 104–5, 174, 180
Holmes, E. R. T., 36, 39, 68, 127, 141
Holmes, Percy, 140–1
Hooker, R. W., 143
Hornby, A. N., 15, 20, 25–7, 29, 55–6, 62, 78–9, 91, 116, 133
Howell, W. P., 97–8
Howitt, George, 55, 115, 131
Howitt, R. W. J., 89
Hubble, J. C., 66, 107
Hughes, Q. J., 89
Humphrey, Richard, 26, 55
Hundred on debut, 149; on Test debut, 164
Hurst, R. G., 120–1
Hussain, Nasser, 105, 113, 159, 167, 171, 180
Hutton, Sir Leonard, 40, 69, 87, 101–2, 111, 145, 154, 169
Hutton, R. A., 87

. . .

Ikin, J. T., 111, 121
Illingworth, Raymond, 112, 121, 164, 166–7, 176
Ilott, M. C., 179
Imran Khan, 73, 172, 177
India at Lord's, 156, 168–71; Under-15s, 187; World Cup, 185–6
Ingleby-Mackenzie, A. C. D., 129
Insole, D. J., 69, 86, 121
Irani, R. C., 179–80
I Zingari, 115, 118

. . .

Jackman, R. D., 172, 177
Jackson, Sir F. S., 22, 29–30, 32–3, 64, 67, 81, 96, 152
Jameson Raid, 44
Jardine, D. R., 25, 83–4, 140, 157–8
Jardine, M. R., 64, 80
Jarvis, C. J. E. & L. K., 61, 77
Javed Miandad, 73, 172–3
Jessop, G. L., 30–1, 33–4, 65, 119, 136
Johnson, I. W., 101
Johnson, P. R., 82, 135
Johnston, Brian, 51
Jones, K. V., 148
Jorden, A. M., 88
Jupp, Harry, 15, 17, 26–7, 55, 115–6

Kallis, J. H., 113
Kapil Dev, 73, 169–70
Kendall, W. S., 89
Kerslake, R. C., 71
Key, Sir K. J., 82
King, C. L., 185–6
King, J. H., 32, 36
Kippax, A. F., 99
Kirtley, R. J., 170
Kitson, S. J., 186
Knight, A. E., 32
Knight, R. D. V., 177, 187
Knott, C. J., 70; hat-trick, 40
Knox, N. A., 33, 35, 151
Kortright, C. J., 22, 30, 32–3, 39

. . .

Lacey, Sir F. E., 65–6, 150
Laker, J. C., 70–1, 101, 103, 158
Lamb, A. J., 165, 170, 173, 178, 183
Lamb, T. M., 41, 147
Langley, G. R., 102
Langridge, J. G., 7, 112
Lara, B. C., 148, 179
Larwood, Harold, 109
Law, S. G., 180
Lawn tennis, 19
Leather-jackets, 110
Le Couteur, P. R., 83
Lee, H. W., 138–41, 151
Lester, E. I., 176
Leveson Gower, Sir H. D. G., 85, 152
Levett, H. W. V., 25, 39, 98
Lewis, C. C., 180
Leyland, Maurice, 39, 100, 152
Lillee, D. K., 103–4
Lillywhite, James jun., 15, 17, 115
Lillywhite, Fred, James sen. & John, 9–11
Lindwall, R. R., 102, 120
Lithgow, A. O. L., 49
Littlejohn, A. R. & E. R., 136
Llewellyn, M. J., 176–7
Lloyd, C. H., 166, 176, 182, 185–6
Lloyd, David & G. D., 129
Lock, G. A. R., 70, 111, 143, 158
Lockwood, Ephraim, 15, 27, 55–6, 116
Lockwood, W. H., 11, 22, 29
Lohmann, G. A., 62, 100
Long, R. P. & W. H., 118, 150
Longman, G. H., 26, 44, 76; & H. K. 45
Love, M. L., 149

Lowest Test totals, 158, 161, 167
Lowry, T. C., 157
Lucas, A. P., 15, 67, 77, 79, 84, 92
Lyons, J. J., 94–5
Lyttelton, Hon. Alfred, 20, 27, 46, 74, 77, 83, 92–3, 131
Lyttelton, Rev. the Hon. Edward, 67, 77, 81, 92, 131

. . .

MacGregor, Gregor, 22, 29, 31, 67, 80, 107, 135–6, 139
McIntyre, Martin, 26, 116
Mackintosh, K. S., 147
MacLaren, A. C., 22, 29, 32–3, 67, 135–6
Makepeace, J. W. H., 136, 151
Malcolm, D. E., 170
Mann, F. G., 143, 145, 157
Mann, F. T., 35, 139–40, 142
Marks, V. J., 178
Marlar, R. G., 86
Marriott, C. S., 25, 162
Marsh, J. F., 85
Marsh, S. A., 148
Marshall, M. D., 73, 166, 186
Martin, Frederick, 29, 63–4, 103
Martyn, Henry, 32, 35
Mason, J. R., 22, 29–31, 67
Massie, R. A. L., 103–4
May, P. B. H., 129, 143, 158, 169
Mead, Walter, 23, 63
Melville, Alan, 39, 85
Mendis, G. D., 182
Merchant, V. M., 168
Merritt, W. E., 157
Midwinter, William, 58, 91, 132
Milburn, Colin, 71, 121, 163–4
Miller, Geoff, 165, 172
Miller, K. R., 101–2, 121, 145, 154–5
Mitchell, Arthur, 142
Mitchell, Bruce, 109–10
Mitchell, Frank, 81, 107
Mitchell, R. A. H., 17, 45–6, 80
Mohammad Kaif, 170–1
Mohsin Khan, 171–2
Moody, T. M., 179
Morkel, D. P. B., 109
Morley, Fred, 15, 20, 27, 56, 58, 91, 116; hat-trick, 57
Mortlock, William, 10, 17, 131
Morton, P. H., 77, 92–3

Moss, A. E., 40, 143
Munton, T. A., 182–3
Murdoch, W. L., 23, 64, 91, 93–4, 108, 117
Murray, D. L., 165, 173
Murray, J. T., 41, 121
Mushtaq Mohammad, 71, 125
Mycroft, William, 20, 56, 61, 116
Mynn, Alfred, 9, 11

. . .

Nash, D. J., 158–9
Neame, A. R. B., 50
Nepean, E. A., 132–3
Nepean, Rev. C. E. B., 126
New Zealand at Lord's, 157–9
Nicholson, William, 11, 57
Noble, M. A., 96
Ntini, Makhaya, 113

. . .

O'Brien, Sir T. C., 67, 95, 117, 132–4
Obstructing the field, 148
Old, C. M., 185
Oscroft, William, 15, 20, 26–7, 53, 55–6, 116
Ottaway, C. J., 26–7, 44, 46, 75–6
Oxford University, highest inns v Camb., 89
Oxford v Camb., 74–89; highest inns, 76, 82, 85, 87; highest totals, 80, 85, 89; 100s by brothers, 82, 88; 100s by father & son, 87; consec. 100s, 84, 88

. . .

Pair before lunch, 146
Pakistan at Lord's, 171–3; Under-15s, 187; World Cup, 186–7
Palairet, L. C. H., 29, 80
Palmer, K. E., 121, 173
Pardon, S. H., 9, 11–13, 23, 29, 55, 96, 138
Pardon family, 9, 11, 13
Parfitt, P. H., 41, 121–2
Parks, J. M., 122, 164
Parr, George, 10, 27
Parris, Fred, 63–4
Parsees at Lord's, 168
Pataudi, Nawab of, jun., 87
Pataudi, Nawab of, sen., 25, 36, 68, 85, 87, 168
Patterson, W. H., 49, 80
Peel, Robert, 133
Penn, Frank, 20, 27, 56

Pepper, C. G., 155
Perkins, Henry, 55, 58, 97
Philadelphians, 59, 67
Pigott, A. C. S., 51, 177
Pilkington, C. C., 44
Pilling, Richard, 15, 35, 62, 117
Pinder, George, 56, 116
Pitches, 103, 112, 166, 171
Platts, J. T. B. D., 53–4
Ponsford, W. H., 98–9
Ponsonby Fane, Rt Hon. Sir S. C. B., 115, 118
Pooley, Edward, 15, 17, 20, 27, 54
Powys, W. N., 75–6
Preston, Hubert, 7, 9, 13
Preston, Norman, 13, 111, 163
Price, J. S. E., 104, 169, 176
Price, Walter, 16, 54, 60, 115
Prichard, P. J., 178–80
Pringle, D. R., 88, 169, 172, 178
Pyemont, J. P., 89

. . .

Quaife, Walter, 21

. . .

Radley, C. T., 71, 147–8, 177
RAF v Army & Royal Navy, 120–1
Rait Kerr, Col R. S., 70, 155
Ramadhin, Sonny, 161–2
Ramprakash, M. R., 105, 129, 149, 159
Randall, D. W., 148, 178
Ranjitsinhji, K. S., 22, 31–3, 64, 97
Ratcliffe, A. T., 85
Rawlin, J. T., 62, 133–4
Read, J. M., 62, 95
Read, W. W., 27, 62
Reeve, D. A., 182–3
Rhodes, Wilfred, 30, 32, 34, 64, 100, 108, 134, 140–1
Richards, B. A., 71
Richards, I. V. A., 165–6, 177–8, 185–6
Richardson, H. A., 17
Ridley, A. C., 89
Ridley, A. W., 19, 26–7, 44, 56, 67, 76
Roberts, A. M. E., 164–5, 166
Robertson, J. D., 69, 121, 154
Robertson-Glasgow, R. C., 84
Robins, R. W. V., 25, 69, 99, 142, 154
Roche, William, 134
Rothman World Cup, 122

THE OVER

With regard to the suggested increase from four to five balls an over, Lord Harris could see that there was some advantage in that, and that some little time would be gained. But there were also disadvantages, and one was that the best bowler on a side would be bowled more than he used to. Further, there was the value of the tradition attaching to the four balls an over, and if the alteration were made now they might in a year or two have a suggestion to increase the number to six. With regard to the proposals, he thought it would be wise to defer action. [1889]

. . .

In spite of his lordship's reservations, MCC adopted the five-ball over the following season, 1889, and in 1900 the six-ball over was adopted by a "virtually unanimous" vote.

Royal Navy v Army & RAF, 119–20
Royle, Rev. V. P. F. A., 20, 76
Rushby, Tom, 119, 139
Russel, J. S., 21, 56, 59, 62–3
Russell, R. C., 169, 181
Rylott, Arnold, 55, 58, 115–6

. . .

Sandham, Andrew, 139–41
Scott, Dr H. J. H., 93–4, 117
Sehwag, Virender, 171
Selby, John, 15, 20
Selvey, M. W. W., 122, 147, 165, 176
Shackleton, Derek, 143, 162
Shacklock, F. J., 63, 133
Sharp, H. P. H., 124, 147
Shastri, R. J., 73, 170
Shaw, Alfred, 15, 18–20, 26–7, 53, 55, 58, 91, 115–6, 136; all 10w, 55; hat-trick, 57

Shaw, J. C., 26, 53, 115–6
Shepherd, T. F., 139–40
Sheppard, Lord (D. S.), 41, 121, 129
Sherwin, Mordecai, 60, 62, 133
Shine, E. B., 64, 81
Shoaib Akhtar, 187
Shrewsbury, Arthur, 21–2, 27, 56, 62, 79, 116, 133
Shuter, John, 27, 67, 120
Silk, D. W. R., 86–7
Single-wicket competitions, 121
Slack, W. N., 147
Slatter, W. H., 120
Smaller ball, 70
Smith, Sir C. A., 27–8, 63
Smith, D. M., 182
Smith, G. C., 112–3
Smith, Harry, 36
Smith, John, 54–5, 115
Smith, M. J., 71, 122, 147, 165
Smith, M. J. K., 88, 111, 176
Smith, N. M. K., 181
Smith, P. A., 179, 183
Smith, R. A., 166–7
Smith, T. P. B., 40, 152
Smithies, Karen, 184
Snow, J. A., 169
Sobers, G. S., 121, 163
South Africans in England, 71, 106–13
Southerton, James, 9, 54, 116
Southerton, S. J., 9, 13, 64
Speight, M. P., 182
Spofforth, F. R., 79, 91, 93–4, 117
Spooner, R. H., 33, 67, 127
Spooner, A. H., 127
Sri Lanka at Lord's, 173
Steel, A. G., 15, 27–8, 67, 77, 79, 91–4
Stephenson, J. W. A., 39
Stevens, G. T. S., 35, 83–4, 138–40
Stewart, A. J., 105, 129, 149, 159, 166–7, 174, 180
Stoddart, A. E., 22, 29, 37, 62–3, 96, 133–4
Stollmeyer, J. B., 161
Storer, William, 22, 29, 64
Strauss, A. J., 149
Studd, C. T., 46, 78–9, 131
Studd brothers, 78–9
Summers, George, 17, 53–4
Sutcliffe, Herbert, 39, 108–10, 141, 144
Sutcliffe, I. J., 89

. . .

Tarrant, F. A., 38, 107, 135–7
Tattersall, Roy, 110–1
Tavaré, C. J., 172
Taylor, C. H., 84
Taylor, M. A., 105
Taylor, R. W., 159, 172, 185
Tendulkar, S. R., 73, 170
Tennyson, Lord (L. H.), 149
Thesiger, Hon. F. J. N., 80, 133
Thomson, J. R., 104, 147
Thorpe, G. P., 105
Titmus, F. J., 41, 111, 143, 146–7, 162, 165, 168
Tolchard, R. W., 148
Topley, T. D., 166
Tremlett, M. F., 143
Trescothick, M. E., 171
Trott, A. E., 23, 30, 64, 103, 107, 134–5
Trueman, F. S., 111, 120–1, 162, 176
Trumble, Hugh, 94, 96
Trumper, V. T., 97
Tunnicliffe, John, 22, 134
Twining, R. H., 140
Twose, R. G., 182–3
Tyldesley, Ernest, 141, 151
Tyldesley, J. T., 32–3, 139

. . .

Ulyett, George, 15, 20, 62, 93–4, 116, 133
Umpires & umpiring, 82, 97, 122, 162, 165–6, 173
Underwood, D. L., 171

. . .

Valentine, A. L., 103, 161–2
Varey, D. W. & J. G., 88
Vaughan, M. P., 112–3, 167
Vengsarkar, D. B., 73, 169
Verity, Hedley, 100, 110, 171
Vernon, G. F., 132
Voce, William, 162

. . .

Wainwright, Edward, 29, 64, 133
Walker, I. D., 19–20, 45, 55, 58, 92, 131
Walker, R. D., 45, 136
Walker, V. E., 11, 17, 116, 131, 136
Walsh, C. A., 73, 167
Waqar Younis, 172–3
Ward, William, 57–8, 140
Wardle, J. H., 70, 102

Warne, S. K., 105, 187
Warner, Lady, 49
Warner, Sir P. F., 11, 13, 31, 38, 49, 64, 68, 96–8, 119, 134–9, 142–4, 151, 155
Washbrook, Cyril, 121, 177
Wasim Akram, 187
Watmough, C. J., 123
Watson, Alec, 20, 56, 63, 116
Watson, Willie, 102, 111
Webbe, A. J., 15, 19, 27, 62, 67, 76–7, 92, 131, 133
Webbe, H. R., 77, 92, 131
Wellings, E. M., 127, 129
Wells, A. P., 182
Wells, C. M., 31, 81
Wessels, K. C., 107, 177
West, John, 54, 115
West Indies at Lord's, 160–7; World Cup, 185–6
Weston, W. P. C., 181
Wettimuny, Sidath, 173
White, Harry, 110
White, J. C., 35, 157
White, Hon. L. R., 154
Wild (also Wyld), Fred, 20, 26, 53, 56
Willis, R. G. D., 166, 171–2, 185
Willsher, Edgar, 15, 17, 115, 117
Wilson, C. E. M., 62–3, 82
Wilson, E. R., 82
Wisden, John, 9–12
Wisden Trophy, 163
Women's cricket, 123, 184, 186
Woodfull, W. M., 98–100
Woods, S. M. J., 22, 27–30, 80
Woof, W. A., 58, 132
Woolley, F. E., 66, 108
Woolmer, R. A., hat-trick, 104
Wootton, George, 16–17, 53, 61–2, 115
Worrell, Sir F. M. M., 162
Wright, C. W., 21, 63, 134
Wright, D. V. P., 121, 154–5
Wright, P. A., 84
Wright, Walter, 117
Wyatt, R. E. S., 25, 36, 39, 69, 110, 152
Wyld, Fred, see Wild
Wynyard, Capt. E. G., 22, 65, 98

. . .

Yardley, N. W. D., 39, 78, 128, 165, 168
Yardley, William, 26, 75–6, 82, 84–5
Yuvraj Singh, 170–1

Photographic acknowledgments

The editor and designer are grateful to the curator, Adam Chadwick, and the archivist, Glenys Williams, of the MCC Library and Museum at Lord's for their kind assistance in providing many of the photographs and illustrations that appear in this book. Special thanks to Patrick Eagar for supplying photographs, inspiration and Pedro Ximenez Viejo Napoleon. Thanks also to the following libraries for allowing use of their images.

Except where detailed below, all images come from the MCC Collection, or MCC/Bridgeman Art Library.

Patrick Eagar: 13, 52, 71 left, top and below, 72, 73, 103 right, 105, 106, 109, 112, 113, 123, 130, 145, 147, 148, 149, 159, 165, 166, 167, 168 right, 169 centre, 170, 171, 172, 173, 174, 177, 179, 180, 182, 183, 184, 185, 186, 187.

Empics: 6, 40 left, 41, 51, 71 top right, 74 left, 86, 87, 88, 89, 101, 104, 108 left, 110, 111, 120, 121, 128 below, 129, 146, 154, 155 left and right, 163 left and centre, 164, 169 left, 175, 176.

Getty: 46, 50, 54, 99, 135 inset, 163 right.

Roger Mann Collection: 22, 36 left, 61, 160.

National Portrait Gallery: 126.